Veröffentlichungen des Deutschen Historischen Instituts London
Publications of the German Historical Institute London

Veröffentlichungen des Deutschen Historischen Instituts London

Publications of the German Historical Institute London

Herausgegeben von
Christina von Hodenberg

Edited by
Christina von Hodenberg

BAND 95/VOLUME 95

Contested Commoditization

The British South African Second-Hand Military Clothing Trade, *c.* 1870–1910

by

Agnes M. Piekacz

DE GRUYTER
OLDENBOURG

This work was submitted as a doctoral dissertation at Bielefeld University 2022.

ISSN 2192-0257
ISBN 978-3-11-225649-7
ISBN 978-3-11-225650-3 (PDF)
ISBN 978-3-11-225651-0 (EPUB)
DOI https://doi.org/10.1515/9783112256503

Library of Congress Control Number: 2026940868

Bibliographic information published by the Deutsche Nationalbibliothek
The Deutsche Nationalbibliothek lists this publication in the Deutsche Nationalbibliografie; detailed bibliographic data are available on the Internet at https://dnb.dnb.de.

De Gruyter Oldenbourg and Walter de Gruyter GmbH are part of De Gruyter Brill.
www.degruyterbrill.com

Questions about General Product Safety Regulation: productsafety@degruyterbrill.com

Cover illustration: Army clothing repairs at Holloway Road Ordnance and Repair Depot and Stores, 13 Sept. 1943. Source: Private collection.
Image courtesy of piemags/ww2archive / Alamy.

Printing: CPI books GmbH, Leck

MIX
Papier | Fördert gute Waldnutzung
FSC® C083411

Contents

Foreword VII

Introduction 1
The History of the Global Second-Hand Clothing Trade: Research Overview 5
Theoretical-Methodological Approaches: Commodity Chains and Value Contestation 9
Structure 13
Sources 14
Language 17

1 **The British Army and the Production of British Second-Hand Military Clothing** 18
1.1 Second-Hand Military Clothing in the British Army, *c.*1870–1895 21
1.2 'Sandwich-Board Men' and Circuses: British Second-Hand Military Clothing in Street Advertising and Popular Entertainment 30
1.3 The British Army and the Second-Hand Military Clothing Trade, *c.*1880–1895 39
1.4 From the Workrooms to the Docks: Labour, Manufacturing, and Logistics in the British Second-Hand Clothing Sector, 1880s–1920s 47
1.5 Conclusion 58

2 **From Caledonian Road to Emagusheni Trading Store: The Distribution and Consumption of Second-Hand Military Clothing in British South Africa** 61
2.1 Stocking Up with 'Military Bits': Transportation, Communication, Labour, and Customs Duties in Mpondoland, *c.*1880–1895 64
2.2 Contested Consumption? Black African Adoption and Appropriation Second-Hand Military Clothing in British South Africa, *c.*1880–1895 78
2.3 Competing for Black African Consumers: 'Truck Trade' and Second-Hand Military Clothing, *c.*1890–1902 89
2.4 Conclusion 98

3 **Imperial Public Health and the Second-Hand Clothing Trade** 100
3.1 Fomites, Miasmata, and Germs: Second-Hand Clothing and British Sanitary Reform, *c.*1760s–1900s 102
3.2 From Mobile Bodies to Moving Things? Disinfection Practices in Early-Twentieth-Century British South Africa 113

3.3 The 'Historic Case of the Military Blankets' and the Disinfection of Second-Hand Clothing, *c.*1906–1910 123
3.4 Conclusion 131

4 'Tariff Item No. 11': The Classification of a Contested Commodity 134
4.1 Pricing Prestige: British Second-Hand Military Clothing and the Question of Monetary Value, *c.*1899–1903 136
4.2 The South African Customs Union Conventions and the Practices of Classification, 1903–1910 145
4.3 Struggles over Overcoats: Second-Hand Clothing Imports in South Africa, *c.*1910–1945 155
4.4 Conclusion 163

5 Conclusion 166

List of Illustrations 173

Index of Abbreviations 174

Bibliography 175

Index 205

Foreword

This study is a slightly revised version of my doctoral dissertation, defended at Bielefeld University in 2023. Researching and writing the thesis was as challenging as it was illuminating, and at times as frustrating as rewarding. I needed guidance, funding, time and space to think and to err, and distraction—I was privileged, fortunate, and lucky to receive it all. For the academic guidance, supervision, and support I had hoped for, and the freedom I needed, I thank my supervisors, Peter Kramper and Willibald Steinmetz, and I am especially grateful to Thomas Welskopp, who influenced the project in its early conceptual stages; his early passing remains a profound loss.

The German Historical Institute in London (GHIL) and the German Academic Exchange Service (*Deutscher Akademischer Austauschdienst*) funded my research in the UK and South Africa, while a travel grant in connection with my participation in the Winter School 'Global History—Challenges and Opportunities', convened jointly by the Heidelberg Centre of Transcultural Studies, the India Branch Office of the Max Weber Stiftung, and the GHIL provided me with the opportunity to research at the National Archives of India, New Delhi. I am grateful to the reviewers of my applications, who helped transform an idea into a thesis and put me in touch with the many academics and individuals who contributed to this project in different—and entirely positive—ways. At the GHIL, Felix Brahm and Indra Sengupta gave me advice and shared their experiences, and I cherished the time spent with other doctoral fellows as much as I am grateful to my hosts in the UK, South Africa, and India for providing welcoming homes. My last fellowship during my PhD-writing process, awarded by the Leibniz Institute of European History in Mainz (IEG), provided me with an excellent mentor: I would like to thank Bernhard Gißibl for his patience, empathy, generosity, and unfailingly constructive feedback. No less formidable was my temporary PhD family at the IEG. I thank Eva Guldanova, Ian Hathaway, Riley Linebaugh, Stefania Ragaú, Corinna Schattauer, Ewelina Sikora, and Daniela and Matheus Linkevicius de Andrade for listening and sharing, for the laughs and rants, and for the distraction from, as well as in-depth discussions of, project-related details. I am especially grateful to the staff of the archives and museums in the UK, South Africa, and India who—while understaffed and underpaid—guided me through their collections. I deeply appreciated their friendliness, patience, and assistance. While this applies to all institutions at which I researched, I would especially like to thank the staff members at the National Archives of South Africa and the Killie Campbell Africana Library, Durban, who supported my research even under conditions as unfavourable as the load shedding in South Africa in February and March 2019. In addition, thanks to Fiona Keens for patiently helping me to navigate and work through the largely uncatalogued records at the Port and River Archive, Museum

 | HTTPS://DOI.ORG/10.1515/9783112256503-202

of London Docklands, and to Robert Fleming (Templer Study Centre, National Army Museum, London), Rosalie Wiesner (Museum of London), and Hamish Peterson (South African Museum of Military History, Johannesburg) for providing insights into collections beyond the research context of this study.

I thank my dear friends and colleagues who accompanied me on this journey, offering support, distraction, and encouragement, and showing patience and understanding: Maxi-Anna Berg and her family, Christina Brauner, Anna Dönecke, Anne Friedrichs, Anna Grotegut, Jana Hoffmann, Verena Limper, Mathis Lübbert, Torben Möbius, Maja-Lisa Müller, Karin Sandhowe and her family, Dorothee Sigmann, Silke Schwandt, Suzane Suleymani, Dominik Theisel, and Elisabeth Werner. Finally, I am grateful to the GHIL for accepting the thesis for publication in their series, to the editors Markus Mößlang, Marielle Sutherland, and Jozef van der Voort for their thoughtful guidance and careful attention in the publication process, and to Bettina Neuhoff for managing the publication of the book at De Gruyter Brill.

Introduction

Mary A. Barker—a British author of over twenty published books born in Jamaica in 1831—arrived in Pietermaritzburg in 1875. According to her autobiographical account, Barker had followed her husband Frederick Napier Broome, who had received an offer to fill the position of the Colonial Secretary of the Colony of Natal. She stayed in British South Africa for little over one year before she returned to England. In 1877, Barker published her book *Life in South Africa*, a collection of accounts of life in the colony titled 'Letters from South Africa'. In a short passage in one of these letters, allegedly written shortly after her arrival in Pietermaritzburg in November 1875, the author shares the following observations and thoughts:

> It is very curious to see the cast-off clothes of all the armies of Europe finding their way hither. The natives of South Africa prefer an old uniform coat or tunic to any other covering, and the effect of a short scarlet garment when worn with bare legs is irresistibly droll. The apparently inexhaustible supply of old-fashioned English coatees with their worsted epaulettes is just coming to an end, and being succeeded by ragged red tunics, franc-tireurs' brownish-green jackets and much worn Prussian gray coats. Kafir-Land may be looked upon as the old-clothes shop of all the fighting world, for sooner or later every cast-off scrap of soldier's clothing drifts toward it.[1]

As a historical source, Barker's account provides a rich, intriguing, and methodologically challenging text. It is tempting to interpret this passage as a depiction of the mid-1870s socio-economic realities of a conflict- and war-ridden world in which imperial dominance becomes tangible in the importation of European armies' discarded garments into British South Africa. Given Barker's claim that there was a preference among black Africans for European military dress, their bodies clothed in European soldiers' discarded clothing appear to mirror imperial conquest on the African continent and beyond through the changing fashions within, as well as the victories and defeats of, the European armies. However, as Mary L. Pratt points out in her highly influential study *Imperial Eyes: Travel Writing and Transculturation* (first published in 1992), European imperialist travel and exploration writing contributed significantly to European imaginations of colonial settings, and these travel accounts, in many respects, tell us more about the authors and their imagined audiences than the subjects they were writing about.[2] After all, a narrative of changing fashions, fluctuating demand, and consumer

1 Barker, *Life in South Africa*, 28. In addition, see Barker, *Colonial Memories*, pp. ix–xxii and 55–79; Tallie, *Queering Colonial Natal*, 123–5. For remarks on language, see below.

2 Pratt, *Imperial Eyes*. Regarding South Africa, see Dubow, 'How British was the British World?'; Rawlinson-Mills, '"That Far-off Southern Tomb"'.

 | HTTPS://DOI.ORG/10.1515/9783112256503-001

preferences was likely to be perceived as relatable by, and to resonate well with, a British readership whose metropolis had—in terms of clothing and textiles—achieved the status of a global avantgarde by the nineteenth century.[3] These two readings and interpretations of Barker's account—the first more along, the second against the grain—provide different narratives that appear to reveal as much, however, as they tend to obscure and omit.

Since the late 2000s, driven by activist campaigns and investigative reporting, renewed media attention to the international second-hand clothing trade has emerged that underscores the trade's complex economic, environmental, and social dimensions in low-income countries against the background of a rapidly expanding fast-fashion industry and its primary markets in high-income, predominantly Western countries.[4] According to the United Nations Commodity Trade Database (UN Comtrade), in 2024 approximately 4.8 million tonnes of second-hand clothing were exported from predominantly high-income countries (China, the USA, the UK, Germany, the Netherlands, Canada, and Italy were among the top ten exporters) to mainly low-income countries in Central and South America, Africa, and Asia. While the available data has its limitations,[5] it nevertheless captures trends and indicates broad developments in, for example, the detrimental effects of second-hand clothing imports on local textile and clothing production in low-income countries: in 2008, based on his analysis of United Nations (UN) Comtrade data and UN Industrial Development Organization Industrial Statistics for the period 1981–2000, Garth Frazer concluded that second-hand clothing imports were responsible for an annual decline of approximately 39 per cent in the production of clothing in Sub-Saharan African countries.[6] However, proponents and defendants of the international second-hand clothing trade emphasize that second-hand economies not only increase the availability of affordable commodities but also support underprivileged livelihoods and households in low-income countries where high unemployment and poverty rates prevail.[7] Recent examples from Accra, Ghana, underscore the complex contemporary socio-spatial and economic entanglements of the international and global second-hand clothing and 'waste' trade: On 1 January 2025, the biggest fire to date broke out at Kantamanto Market, destroying over 6 per cent of one of the world's largest second-hand clothing sites and over 100 shops, and affecting thousands of traders and households. Incidentally, that same week and shortly after the inauguration of John Ma-

3 For a summary of the situation in London, see Münch, *Cutler Street Market*, 95–8.

4 See the websites *Dead White Man's Clothes* at [https://deadwhitemansclothes.org] and *Stop Waste Colonialism* at [https://stopwastecolonialism.org], both accessed 10 Oct. 2025.

5 See Brooks and Simon, 'Unravelling the Relationship between Used-Clothing Imports and the Decline of African Clothing Industries'; Brooks, 'The International Second-Hand Clothing Trade'.

6 Frazer, 'Used-Clothing Donations and Apparel Production in Africa', particularly 1780–3.

7 See, in summary, Brooks, 'The International Second-Hand Clothing Trade'.

hama as Ghana's president, workers began to return to the Agbogbloshie scrapyard site that had been violently demolished by the previous Ghanian government in July 2021, stripping thousands of the city's urban poor of their source of livelihood.[8] Notably, the terms and concepts 'waste colonialism', 'garbage imperialism', and 'toxic colonialism' are gaining traction in current debates, across activist groups, and in academic research. Occasionally used interchangeably, the concepts refer to the cross-border or trans-boundary disposal of varieties of 'wastes' 'from areas of privilege and affluence to areas with lower economic status and influence', with 'toxic colonialism' referring more specifically to hazardous waste.[9] Initiatives and campaigns led by, for example, the Or Foundation have contributed to an increased awareness of the environmental effects of second-hand clothing imports in low-income countries, where only a small proportion of clothing is reused and the incineration of textile waste, (illegal) landfills, (micro-) rubbish dumps, and a lack of recycling infrastructure and policies cause alarming levels of pollution.[10] Finally, academic research drawing on social (identity) theory emphasizes that the diminishment of local textile and clothing production and the decreasing availability of indigenous fashions (which are integral to cultural heritage) in, for example, Nigeria, lead to a 'loss of social identity' among consumers.[11] Simultaneously, findings from Jordan, for example, underscore the agency of second-hand clothing consumers, arguing that they 'select and adapt consumed commodities to their own desires, knowledge and interests, as they impose their own systems of values and practices on these commodities.'[12] These public, activist, and academic debates reveal two notable tendencies. First, they are marked by a series of contradictions: the global second-hand clothing trade is alternately framed as a sustainable practice that extends commodity 'life cycles', provides affordable goods, and supports livelihoods, or as a mechanism of neo-colonial dependency that undermines local textile and clothing industries and transfers environmental costs to low-income countries. Narratives of resilience and empowerment co-exist with those of exploitation, dispossession, and in-

---

8 See, for example, Akese, Beisel, and Chasant, 'Agbogbloshie'; Johnson, '"Dead White Person's Clothes" Mount Up as Ghana's Kantamanto Market Struggles to Rebuild after Fire'.

9 Liboiron, 'Waste Colonialism'. See also the Or Foundation campaign *Stop Waste Colonialism* aimed at the international second-hand clothing trade at [https://stopwastecolonialism.org], accessed 10 Oct. 2025.

10 See, for example, the latest report on European and Chilean textile waste disposal by the United Nations Economic Commission (UNECE) and the Economic Commission for Latin America and the Caribbean (ECLAC), *Reversing Direction in the Used Clothing Crisis.*

11 Abubakar et al., 'Imperialism and the Loss of Identity in Second Hand Clothes'; Ayorkor Manieson and Ferrero-Regis, 'Castoff from the West, Pearls in Kantamanto?'; Brooks, 'Riches from Rags or Persistent Poverty?'; Norris, 'The Limits of Ethicality in International Markets'.

12 Na'amneh and Al Husban, 'Identity in Old Clothes', 620. See also Isla, 'Investigating Second-Hand Fashion Trade and Consumption in the Philippines'; Milgram, 'Refashioning Commodities'.

equality. Second, although contemporary commentary and academic literature largely acknowledge the trade's deeper historical entanglements with colonial commerce, charitable and missionary networks, and long-standing practices of textile reuse, the debates frequently lack historical depth.

In light of these conceptual inconsistencies and the scarcity of historical research, which constrain the analytical clarity of current discussions and obscure the continuities underlying the contemporary global second-hand clothing trade, it is important to examine the trade in its historical context. Barker's introductory late-nineteenth century observations and allegations and the questions they raise provide an illustrative example of the themes this study explores. Two years after the publication of Barker's book *Life in South Africa*, parts of the afore-cited passage and its narrative were incorporated into newspaper articles. An almost verbatim translation was published in an article in the German newspaper *Berliner Börsenzeitung* on 27 January 1879, stating 'that the British Colony of Natal or Portnatal ... had become a market for the discarded uniforms of all European armies.'[13] During the nineteenth century, British South Africa emerged as a prime destination for exports of British second-hand military clothing, and this study offers the first comprehensive historical account and analysis of the trade in second-hand clothing linking the 'Global North' with the 'Global South'. By reconstructing the full commodity chain and tracing the British second-hand military clothing from its sites of production, through its distribution within a distinct trading network, to its sites of consumption in British South Africa between *c.*1870 and 1910, this study sheds light on the contested processes of commoditization and the corresponding and conflicting negotiations that underpinned it. The period under study is situated between earlier and later phases in which European military dress circulated in (British) South Africa.[14] Colonial government authorities in the Cape Colony, for example, had already critically remarked upon the adoption of British second-hand military dress by black Africans in the 1830s, while in the aftermath of the First World War, South African imports of second-

13 *Berliner Börsenzeitung*, 43 (26 Jan. 1879), 9: 'Noch mehr als andere Schwarze liebt der Kaffer, ein Mitglied der großen Bantu-Negergruppe, die vom Aequator an über das ganze südöstliche Africa verstreut ist, in seiner Kleidung die bunten, schreienden Farben; daher mag es auch kommen, daß die Englische Colonie Natal oder Portnatal, die auf altem Kafferboden liegt, ein Markt für die ausrangirten Uniformen sämmtlicher Europäischer Heere geworden ist. Einen alten Soldatenrock zieht der Kaffer jedem anderen Kleidungsstücke vor und es läßt sich leicht vorstellen, welchen hochkomischen Eindruck die scharlachrothe Englische Uniform hervorbringt, die zu nackten Beinen getragen wird. Abgenützte Preußische Waffenröcke, Französische Frantireur-Blousen, Garibaldihemden, blaue und grüne Husarenattilas, graue Wachtmäntel—das Alles strömt im Kaffernlande zusammen, welches den Altkleiderladen der gesammten kriegführenden Welt zu bilden scheint und von dergleichen Herrlichkeiten nicht genug empfangen kann.'

14 For an excellent discussion of the term and its usage in global history, see Gänger, 'Circulation'.

hand military clothing from the United States, Britain, and other Western European countries increased considerably.[15] In the period between *c.*1870 and 1910, not least in the context and aftermath of the South African War (1899–1902), debates over the 'commodity candidacy' of British second-hand military dress intensified markedly and frequently intersected,[16] ultimately culminating in interventions that shaped both the British South African trade in second-hand military dress and the wider second-hand clothing trade for subsequent decades.

The History of the Global Second-Hand Clothing Trade: Research Overview

Following Sidney Mintz's often-cited monography *Sweetness and Power: The Place of Sugar in Modern History* (1985) and Arjun Appadurai's ground-breaking seminal anthology *The Social Life of Things: Commodities in Cultural Perspective* (1986), interest in cross-border and transcultural commodity 'flows' has grown since the early 2000s, enriching the 'global commodities' research field with an ever-expanding corpus of studies.[17] Simultaneously, despite increased attention to second-hand (clothing) economies in historical research,[18] it is predominantly the social sciences that have taken up the study of the international and global second-hand clothing trade, with the historical contexts that have shaped its emergence and development remaining largely underexplored.[19] This study nevertheless benefits and draws on two research strands that approach the internationalization and globalization of the second-hand clothing trade from different perspectives. Since the 1990s, studies in early modern history—most notably contributions by Beverly Lemire and Laurence Fontaine—have underscored the significance of second-hand clothing for British household economies, in early

15 See NASA WCARS, GH vol. 23/11, no. 54/1837. On developments in the second-hand military clothing trade during the first half of the twentieth century, see chapter 4.3.

16 Appadurai, 'Introduction', 15.

17 As Frank Trentmann proclaimed in 2009: 'Things are back.' Trentmann, 'Materiality in the Future of History', 283. See Mintz, *Sweetness and Power*; Appadurai (ed.), *The Social Life of Things*. For a recent overview of global commodity histories, see Rudolph, 'Das *global commodity*-Narrativ'.

18 See the overview of the growing body of research in Lemire, *Global Trade and the Transformation of Consumer Cultures*, particularly 114–22.

19 For an important exception, see Charpy, 'The Spoils of War', who focuses on second-hand uniforms in the French-Senegalese context at the turn of the twentieth century. With some reference to historical developments, see also the anthropological studies by Tranberg-Hansen, *Salaula* and Norris, *Recycling Indian Clothing*.

modern consumer society, and the transatlantic slave trade.[20] Recent contributions to the research field that provide the most detailed and in-depth nineteenth-century histories of the British second-hand clothing trade include Ole Münch's micro-historical analysis of London's 'Rag Fair' as a social arena and contact zone for actors with different ethnic and religious backgrounds between 1780 and 1850, and Adam Mendelsohn's study on the economic prosperity of Jewish (second-hand) clothing merchants in the United States in the nineteenth century. While these studies differ in their theoretical-methodological approaches and leading research questions, they provide insights into the gradual internationalization and globalization of the British early- and mid-nineteenth-century second-hand clothing trade. The discourse on and the perception of London as the world's marketplace for second-hand clothing during the first half of the nineteenth century was, as Münch points out, more global than the practice: European second-hand clothing reached some parts of the globe and not others as merchants moved along specific trading routes, the gradual expansion of which during the early nineteenth century depended on different interrelated factors. First, as one consequence of the industrial revolution and industrialization, demand for second-hand clothing in Britain and other European countries declined over the nineteenth century as new clothing became more affordable; consequently, while the number of local second-hand clothing dealers in many European cities decreased, they began to tap into overseas markets on a larger scale.[21] Second, the nineteenth-century revolution in transportation and communication —the expansion of steamships routes, railway networks, and telegraph lines—materialized faster in some parts of the globe than others.[22] Third, overseas trading networks developed more readily between business partners with a similar cultural, ethnic, or religious background or family ties. As Mendelsohn argues in reference to Gary B. Magee and Andrew S. Thompson, cooperation between 'relatives, coreligionists, and settlers who had originally come from the same part of the world ... promised a variety of advantages' while doing business with markets abroad.[23] Fourth and finally, British imperialism and the expansion of colonial-

20 See, for example, Fontaine (ed.), *Alternative Exchanges*; Lemire, *Dress, Culture, Commerce*, 32–5; Aplern, 'What Africans Got for Their Slaves'; Levitt, 'Bristol Clothing Trades and Exports in the Georgian Period'.

21 See Münch, *Cutler Street Market*, 100–3; Vries, *The Industrious Revolution*, 140–4; Mendelsohn, *The Rag Race*, 112–33; Lemire, 'The Secondhand Clothing Trade in Europe and Beyond'; Ginsberg, 'Rags to Riches'; Levitt, 'Bristol Clothing Trades and Exports in the Georgian Period', 38–9.

22 Wenzelhuemer, *Connecting the Nineteenth-Century World*; Headrick, *The Tools of Empire*. With regard to trading routes from Ireland, North America, and the East Mediterranean to London during the first half of the nineteenth century, see Münch, *Cutler Street Market*, 103–9; Mendelsohn, *The Rag Race*, 40. For Australia, see ibid. 124.

23 Mendelsohn, *The Rag Race*, 114–16 at 115. See Magee and Thompson, *Empire and Globalisation*, chapters 2 and 4.

ism, Münch and Mendelsohn argue, played a decisive role in the internationalization and globalization of the second-hand clothing trade, as merchants of new and second-hand clothing benefited from the expanding settler colonies and growing export markets of the British Empire,[24] not least due to the efforts of missionaries and mission societies: as anthropologists Jean Comaroff and John L. Comaroff show in their study *On Revelation and Revolution*, evangelist missionaries' attempts to re-dress Tswana in European fashions increasingly depended on second-hand clothing imports and donations.[25]

A second research strand, informed by approaches in anthropology and material culture studies, has focused on the adoption and appropriation of European (second-hand military) clothing in the context of colonial expansion in Africa as symbolic communication. Christraud M. Geary argues that diplomatic gift exchanges between German colonial authorities and the Bamum king, Njoya, included German military regalia and served as precursors to the introduction of European-style military dress in the pre-colonial Kingdom of Bamum (north-west Cameroon). In 1904/05, Njoya established weaving and tailoring workshops in his palace, where Bamum tailors produced German-style military uniforms which were partly designed by the king himself. Moreover, while German reactions to these hybrid dresses ranged between ridicule, admiration, and fear, from the Bamum perspective the clothing signified political alliance with the Germans—an attribute which, according to Geary, helped to secure Njoya's power amidst rival African communities.[26] Robert Ross interprets the adoption of German military regalia by troops in the *Truppenspieler* movement among the Herero in early-twentieth-century Namibia as an assertion of Herero male identity,[27] while in early-twentieth-century Kenya, as Margaret J. Hay shows in her illuminating article, the adoption of European dress including military clothing was viewed by Kenyans as an appropriation of 'symbols of modernity and power from the intruders who had conquered them'.[28] Based on her nuanced and insightful analysis of early-twentieth-century portrait photographs, Sandra Klopper concludes that the wearing of European riding breeches by prosperous black African men attests 'to an increasingly self-assured aspiration to secure access to the social and economic

---

24 According to Mendelsohn, 'by far the largest colonial market for clothing old and new in [*sic*] mid-century was Australia'. Mendelsohn, *The Rag Race*, 114–33 at 116. In addition, see Münch, *Cutler Street Market*, 101–2. For France and French-African colonies, see Perrot, *Fashioning the Bourgeoisie*, 71.

25 See Comaroff and Comaroff, *Of Revelation and Revolution*, 218–73; Comaroff, 'The Empire's Old Clothes'; Ross, *Clothing*, particularly 83–102. Regarding clothing donations in the context of the South African War (1899–1902), see Thompson, 'Publicity, Philanthropy and Commemoration'; Riedi, 'Assisting Mrs Tommy Atkins'.

26 Geary, 'Political Dress'.

27 Ross, *Clothing*, 101–2; Werner, '"Playing Soldiers"'; see also Hendrickson, 'Bodies and Flags'.

28 Hay, 'Changes in Clothing and Struggles over Identity in Colonial Western Kenya', 69.

benefits enjoyed by white settler communities.'[29] Yet, the adoption and appropriation of second-hand military clothing in pre-colonial and colonial Africa was not confined to chiefs, kings, and black elites. As Patrick Harries shows, in one of South Africa's mining centres in Kimberley, (migrant) black African labourers frequently wore articles of second-hand military dress on weekends: 'It was a visible marker of their passage into a new community', Harries argues, as 'their clothing distinguished them from both inexperienced, novice miners and their employers, advertised their wealth and experience, and proclaimed their new status.'[30] Finally, Peter Warwick attributes the illicit wearing of British military dress by black Africans during the South African War to their pursuit of a British *esprit de corps*,[31] while Felix Brahm argues that the prevalence of military objects (firearms and military coats and caps) in diplomatic gift exchanges with East African rulers indicates the latter's affection for European technological-military culture.[32]

These research strands are characterized by two partly interrelated divides. First, the rich and detailed studies of the adoption and appropriation of European (second-hand military) dress in the context of colonial expansion and imperialism on the African continent highlight the potential of micro-historical approaches by shedding light on processes of dressing as a mode of (self-)representation, social distinction, and transgression of social and hierarchical boundaries, and on clothing as a signifier of changing symbolic meanings. These findings, however, remain strangely detached from perspectives that have begun to map out the increasingly international and globalized trade in second-hand clothing during the nineteenth century.[33] Second, while the focus on dressing as symbolic communication uses the adoption and appropriation of these items of clothing as a starting point for highlighting the significance of black Africans as consumers rather than passive recipients of European (second-hand military) dress, transnational and global perspectives on the nineteenth-century second-hand clothing trade are primarily focused on the locales of its production and its domestic markets. The latter tend to reproduce notions long refuted by historians and anthropologists—that 'Africa was a dumping ground for "assorted rubbish"—that early trade goods consisted of cheap liquor, useless trinkets, and defective firearms.'[34] Picking up on late-1970s pioneering studies on African consumerism,

29 Klopper, 'Gentlemen at Leisure', 336.

30 Harries, *Work, Culture, and Identity*, 48–65 at 60. On uniforms and social distinction, see also Callaway, 'Dressing for Dinner in the Bush'; Ruether, 'Heated Debates over Crinolines', 371–3.

31 Warwick, *Black People and the South African War 1899–1902*, 136–41.

32 See Brahm, *Merchandise of Power*, 129–44, particularly 132. See also Brauner, *Kompanien, Könige und caboceers*, 273–393.

33 For similar observations regarding the historiography on British eighteenth-century material culture, see Trentmann, 'Materiality in the Future of History'. On the ongoing topicality of the production–consumption divide, see, for example, Rief, 'Jenseits der Trennung von Produktion und Konsum'.

34 Murillo, *Market Encounters*, 16–17.

historical research has since demonstrated how nineteenth-century African consumer demands influenced global commerce and politics, particularly in the textile and arms trade. Processes of 'domestication', the appropriation of and ascription of meanings to imported European consumer goods highlight Africans' agency and Africa's interconnectedness with the world.[35] Similarly, Felix Brahm shows how local East African contexts and uses shaped the globalization of the arms and weapons trade between 1850 and 1919.[36] Finally, choosing toiletries as a vantage point for African consumption in late-nineteenth- and twentieth-century Zimbabwe, Timothy Burke's study *Lifebuoy Men, Lux Women: Commodification, Consumption, and Cleanliness in Modern Zimbabwe* analyses how uses of these (imported) commodities by Africans on the one hand, and conceptualizations of the same by manufacturers and advertisers on the other changed over the twentieth century.[37] Alongside addressing a gap in historical research, the study foregrounds questions related to commoditization and valuation and engages with commodity and value chain approaches, and thereby aims to contribute to conceptual and methodological discussions that bridge economic and cultural history.[38]

Theoretical-Methodological Approaches: Commodity Chains and Value Contestation

To bridge the consumption–production divide, global historians in particular have over the past decade engaged with commodity chain approaches as narrative and analytical tools to capture, analyse, and narrate economic changes and linkages between producers, manufacturers, and consumers in geographically

35 See Richardson, 'West African Consumption Patterns and Their Influence on the Eighteenth-Century English Slave Trade'; Prestholdt, *Domesticating the World*; Prestholdt, 'Africa and the Global Lives of Things'. See also Hahn, 'Consumption, Identities, and Agency in Africa'.

36 See Brahm, *Merchandise of Power*, particularly 101, for reference to second-hand arms and weapons.

37 See Burke, *Lifebuoy Men, Lux Women*. Since 2010, research on the South African history of consumption has increased, most notably with regard to the twentieth century. See, in summary, Posel, 'Races to Consume'; Iqani and Kenny, 'Editorial'. See also Thomas, 'The Modern Girl and Racial Respectability in 1930s South Africa'; Mager, *Beer, Sociability, and Masculinity in South Africa*; and the contributions on sub-Saharan Africa in Ross, Hinfelaar, and Peša (eds.), *The Objects of Life in Central Africa*. With a focus on twentieth-century consumer magazines, see Laden, '"Making the Paper Speak Well", or, the Pace of Change in Consumer Magazines for Black South Africans'. Regarding the South African history of retail, see, for example, Kenny, 'Servicing a Racial Regime'.

38 See Berghoff and Vogel, 'Wirtschaftsgeschichte als Kulturgeschichte'; Hahn, 'Notizen zur Umwertung der Werte'.

separate spaces.[39] Rather than forming a fixed theoretical framework, chain concepts have multiple origins and have been informed by a wide range of theories; their flexibility and adaptiveness to modification may well account for their popularity. The most influential and often-referenced research strand that has evolved over the past few decades originates from the concept related to world-systems theory developed by Terence H. Hopkins and Immanual Wallerstein.[40] In their 1977 article, Hopkins and Wallerstein—rejecting the idea that markets develop sequentially from national markets to foreign trade and, finally, international markets—proposed to 'take an ultimate consumable item and trace back the sets of inputs that culminated in this item, including prior transformations, the raw materials, the transportation mechanisms, the labour input into each of the material processes, the food inputs into labour.'[41] Picked up and reformulated in the 1990s by development scholars Gary Gereffi and Miguel Korzeniewicz, the aim of the global commodity chain (GCC) framework is to map out and analyse production networks within global industries. GCC proponents suggest analysing four dimensions of commodity chains, namely the input-output structure, territoriality, governance, and institutional context.[42] By the end of the 1990s, the global value chain (GVC) method had emerged out of a critical engagement with the GCC approach and is considered a third chain framework distinct from Hopkins' and Wallerstein's concept (based on world-systems theory) and the GCC approach: influenced by international business literature, the GVC method not only aims to 'establish a shared language among researchers working on global industries' but attempts to explain variations in network relationships between firms and suppliers. One of the central contentions of the GVC approach is the distinction between producer-driven and buyer-driven chains.[43]

Alongside their rising popularity, discussions of the theoretical-methodological implications and consequences of commodity chain approaches in historical analysis and the narratives it produces have revealed shortcomings. Most prominently, GCC and GVC approaches have been criticized for their disregard of, or limited attention to, consumption and the influence of consumers[44]—despite in-

39 Foster, 'Tracking Globalization', particularly 285. For a recent research overview of historical studies drawing on commodity and value chain approaches, see Rudolph, 'Das *global commodity*-Narrativ'. See also Grewe, 'Wie verortet man eine globale Verflechtungsgeschichte?'; Grewe, 'Global Commodities and Commodity Chains'.

40 On related concepts in connection to the new political economy of food and agriculture, particularly the commodity systems approach, see Jackson, Ward, and Russel, 'Mobilising the Commodity Chain Concept in the Politics of Food and Farming', 131; Hamilton, 'Analyzing Commodity Chains'.

41 Hopkins and Wallerstein, 'Patterns of Development of the Modern World-System', 128.

42 For an overview of the genealogy of different chain frameworks, see Bair, 'Global Capitalism and Commodity Chains', 154–61.

43 Ibid. 161–3 at 162. See also Hesse and Neveling, 'Global Value Chains'.

44 See, for example, Marichal, Topik, and Frank, 'Conclusion'.

dications by, for example, GVC proponents that chain analyses should not lose sight of consumer cultures, which 'can subvert the original intention of producers by altering and ascribing meaning to products in ways that designers and marketeers never intended.'[45] Second, Steven C. Topik warns scholars who engage with commodity chain approaches of 'tunnel vision': participants in commodity chains, Topic argues, do not act within closed systems but are involved in broader social networks, production systems, circuits, and markets that influence their actions and practices,[46] 'underscoring the social embeddedness of economic organization'.[47] Third, feminist theorists have drawn attention to the often overlooked geographic and gender(ed) spheres in commodity and value chain analyses.[48] Finally, many scholars have criticized the linearity of chain approaches that imagine and narrate chains as a 'sequential process of value addition—of adding more products and services.' In doing so, Robert J. Foster concludes, the analysis not only distinguishes between but favours exchange (or quantitative, monetary) values over use (or qualitative) values. Thus, the perhaps most substantial problematization of commodity chain frameworks and analyses is centred around one of its greatest virtues, namely its primary focus on value creation, addition, and appropriation.[49] In Jennifer Bair's summary following her GVC analysis of the *Mundo Maya*, most studies in the tradition of chain analysis either do not consider how, by whom, and to what end value is defined, or do so inadequately: 'Ironically then', Bair concludes, 'for a framework that is ostensibly focused on the creation and capture of value, value has been something of a black box within this approach.'[50]

To tackle the issue of 'the multiplicities and ambiguities of social value implicit in the workings of commodity chains and globalization processes', Norman Long and Magdalena Villarreal propose approaching commodity chains from a different angle.[51] Following Arjun Appadurai and Igor Kopytoff's conceptualization of commoditization as process, Long and Villarreal 'examine the moments of value

45 Gereffi, Humphrey, and Sturgeon, 'The Governance of Global Value Chains', 98.

46 Topik, 'Historicizing Commodity Chains', 38. See also Topik, 'Produktbiographien, Warenketten und Kaffeegeschichten'.

47 GCC and GVC proponents have stressed the increasing importance of activities that deal with so-called 'intangibles', such as fashion trends, brands, or design, and pointed out that networks constituting the chain 'are situationally specific, socially constructed, and locally integrated'. Gereffi, Korzeniewicz, and Korzeniewicz, 'Introduction', 2. See also Gereffi et al., 'Introduction', particularly 6.

48 See, for example, the contributions by Jane L. Collins, Wilma A. Dunaway, and Priti Ramamurthy in Dunaway (ed.), *Gendered Commodity Chains*; Bair and Werner, 'Commodity Chains and the Uneven Geographies of Global Capitalism'.

49 Foster, 'Tracking Globalization', 288–9. See Epple, 'Jenseits globaler Warenketten', 276–7; Grewe, 'Global Commodities and Commodity Chains', 225.

50 Bair, 'Constructing Scarcity, Creating Value', 195.

51 Long and Villarreal, 'Small Products, Big Issues', 747.

contestation that take place at critical interfaces wherein normative discourses and social interests are defined and negotiated.'[52] As Koptyoff argues,

> Commodities must be not only produced materially as things, but also culturally marked as being a certain kind of thing. Out of the total range of things available in a society, only some of them are considered appropriate for marking as commodities. Moreover, the same thing may be treated as a commodity at one time and not at another. And finally, the same thing may, at the same time, be seen as a commodity by one person and as something else by another.[53]

Inherent in Kopytoff's description of the volatility of commodities is the notion of frictions arising from conflicting understandings of which things are considered appropriate or legitimate commodities, indicating historically changing processes of valuation and systems of value. Contemporary and historical examples of things partly or largely lacking legitimation as commodities include psychoactive substances, humans, and human organs. Yet the emergence of, for example, black markets not only speaks to the limits of control and regulation over consumer demand but renders them—to borrow Margeret J. Radin's term—'contested commodities.' Contestations of processes of commoditization are historically contingent and may temporarily culminate in interventions that render their production, distribution, or consumption illegal.[54] To crack the black box and to inquire 'into the meaning of value itself',[55] Long and Villarreal propose focusing 'upon processes of value contestation situated in social arenas, wherein the meanings of specific goods, relationships and identities are forged, challenged and reinvented.'[56]

The study reconstructs the commodity chain that increasingly rendered second-hand military clothing 'entangled objects'.[57] At the same time, it foregrounds the nodes and edges of the chain as sites of contestation, where both the legitimacy and 'values' of the commodities were forged, challenged and negotiated, and assessed. In doing so, the study simultaneously disentangles the chain and sheds light on the often-invisible contexts, conditions, and practices of production, transportation, distribution, consumption, and regulation that shaped how and why these garments moved along specific trajectories. Conceptualizing

52 Ibid. 726.

53 Kopytoff, 'The Cultural Biography of Things', 64.

54 Radin, 'Contested Commodities', particularly 81; Radin, *Contested Commodities*. See also the contributions in Schendel and Abraham (eds.), *Illicit Flows and Criminal Things*; Scheper-Hughes, 'Parts Unknown'; and the contributions by Nancy Scheper-Hughes in Scheper-Hughes and Wacquant (eds.), *Commodifying Bodies*; Zelizer, *Morals and Markets*; Welskopp, *Amerikas große Ernüchterung*; Anderson and Carrier, 'Khat in Colonial Kenya'.

55 Bair, 'Constructing Scarcity, Creating Value', 196.

56 Long and Villarreal, 'Small Products, Big Issues', 747.

57 Thomas, *Entangled Objects*.

'value' as historically contingent, relational, and performative and tracing the intersections of correlating value ascriptions illuminates how and by whom the commoditization and the circulation of second-hand military clothing was mediated and shaped.

Structure

The study is structured around four main chapters in roughly chronological order. While all chapters engage with aspects of production, consumption, materiality, and distribution, each main chapter focuses on and renders one of these aspects as a central site of contestation. Chapter one examines the production of British second-hand military clothing as a contested site, initially centred on the bodies of British soldiers. It traces the practices of military clothing reuse within the British army clothing system and through commercial circuits, highlighting how correlating symbolic value ascriptions and assessments of monetary value were negotiated, imposed, and contested. Changes within the British army clothing system gradually monopolized and internationalized the distribution of second-hand military clothing, affecting the domestic second-hand clothing trade and the industry. Chapter two explores consumption in British South Africa as a site of contestation. Offering three distinct perspectives on consumption, the chapter reconstructs the trading network linking African consumers to the workrooms of a London-based second-hand military clothing business. The chapter examines disputes over the adoption and appropriation of these garments in British South Africa, demonstrating how African consumption increasingly shaped the priorities of British manufacturers as well as second-hand clothing exporters. A typhoid outbreak aboard a reformatory school ship near London in 1903 elevated the trade in second-hand military clothing to new levels of public health concern, rendering their materiality a contested domain. Chapter three analyses and reveals the tensions between medical discourse, disinfection, and commercial trade in British South Africa which culminated in the introduction of mandatory disinfection of imported second-hand clothing. Finally, chapter four focuses on the developments after the South African War (1899–1902) which significantly expanded the modes of provision and distribution of British second-hand military clothing in British South Africa and re-intensified disputes over the adoption and appropriation of these garments in the British War Office as well as in the context of the consolidation of the South African Customs Union (SACU). The chapter concludes with an overview of the continued evolution of the British South African second-hand clothing trade in the first half of the twentieth century.

Sources

The study is grounded in an extensive corpus of disparate and dispersed records drawn from archives, collections, and printed sources in South Africa, the UK, and India. The dispersion is both geographical, reflecting the transregional scope of the British South African second-hand military clothing trade, and epistemic. Although the trade constituted a substantial commercial enterprise, it was carried out largely by small-scale businesses, merchants, and traders whose activities have not left comprehensive business records. In addition, traders, shippers, and businesses involved in the international trade in second-hand military clothing—most notably the British War Office—sought to conceal aspects of their participation in it, as it was increasingly subject to regulation and frequently operated at the margins of legality.[58] Finally, while histories of global commodities and trade often rely on statistical records detailing, for example, import and export rates over periods of time, the second-hand clothing trade is characterized by a relative absence of statistical records, incomplete quantitative and quantifiable data, and ambiguous terminology. Colonial trade statistics such as the *Blue Books* did not distinguish between second-hand clothing and new clothing articles, while the British Board of Trade first investigated the second-hand clothing trade, including its export branches, in 1920.[59] As the Cape Colony's Medical Officer of Health (MOH) noted in 1906,

> We are all of us familiar with the variety of old garments worn by the Native, but few of us, I think, have been aware of their origin, and the extent to which the trade in imported second-hand clothing is carried on ... Owing to the fact that in all instances Customs entries of new and second-hand clothing have not been kept distinct, it is difficult to obtain exact statistics on the subject.[60]

Army records such as the yearly published *Army Estimates* provide insights into the profits that the British army expected to realize through sales of second-hand military dress. In addition, the annual *Reports of the Director of Contracts* or *Reports on Army Contracts* indicate auction and contract-based sales of second-hand clothing. However, auction sales were periodically neither recorded nor reviewed, while contract-based sales were mostly listed without additional information or specifications on articles sold, their quantities, or sales profits. After the introduction of duties on imported second-hand clothing in 1906 in the context of the consolidation of the SACU, the South African Customs Statistical Bureau (established in 1891) recorded the origin, quantity, and monetary value of what

58 On this issue in general, see Foster, 'Tracking Globalization', 295. For a call for more methodological reflection in historical commodity and value chain analyses, see Grewe, 'Global Commodities and Commodity Chains', 225.

59 See TNA, LAB 2/668/TBD134/A/8/1920.

60 *Cape of Good Hope: Report of the Medical Officer of Health for the Colony ... 1906*, p. cxxxv.

had been categorized as second-hand clothing to date, namely second-hand coats, vests, and trousers.[61] That same year, after the introduction of mandatory disinfection regulations for second-hand clothing imported into British South Africa, the British *Reports of the Medical Officer of Health* began to record both the quantity of second-hand clothing disinfected as well as the number of disinfection certificates issued.

Exploratory archival research in the National Archives of South Africa (NASA), the UK National Archives (TNA), and the National Archives of India (NAI) produced a body of records that largely comprise colonial government and army administrative sources. Historians' readings and interpretations of the colonial knowledge embodied in this material have been challenged in postcolonial studies in particular.[62] The analysis of these records follows Ann L. Stoler's approach of reading 'along the grain' to expose colonial administrators' and military officials' logics and anxieties regarding the expanding trade in second-hand military clothing and the adoption of these clothing articles by predominantly non-white Africans and civilians.[63] The *Reports of Medical Officers of Health* in British South Africa and the UK offer insights into the implementation of public health measures and issues perceived as pressing by British(South African) medical authorities and practitioners, while the *Annual Reports of the Chief Inspectors of Factories and Workshops*, records held by the Port and River Archive (Museum of London Docklands), and official (colonial) government publications shed light on the British second-hand clothing industry and conflicting perspectives on the domestic and global second-hand military clothing trade.

Colonial, customs, and army administrative records held by the NASA, NAI, and TNA, newspaper articles, advertisements, trade directories, and gazette notices frequently reference businesses, importing and exporting merchants, storekeepers, and traders who engaged in the British South African second-hand military clothing trade. In addition, the Gallagher Family Papers, held by the KCM, provide invaluable records linking producers and consumers in the trade.[64] The

---

61 See *South African Customs Statistical Bureau: British South Africa. First Annual Statement of the Trade and Shipping of the Colonies and Territories Forming the South African Customs Union, 1906*, 5.

62 See Roque and Wagner, 'Introduction', particularly 1–7. For a critical discussion, see Cooper, 'Postcolonial Studies and the Study of History'.

63 See Stoler, *Along the Archival Grain*. See also Ruether, 'Asking Appropriate Questions, Reconsidering Research Agendas'. On different reading strategies, see Roque and Wagner, 'Introduction'.

64 William Beinart's research on European traders and the Mpondo paramountcy is based on these records, which have since been moved from the NASA WCARS repository to the KCM. See Beinart, *The Political Economy of Pondoland 1860–1930*; Beinart, 'Production, Labour Migrancy and the Chieftaincy'; Beinart, 'European Traders and the Mpondo Paramountcy, 1878–1886'. On the potential and limitations of traders' and storekeepers' business records for histories of consumption, see Ross, Hinfelaar, and Peša, 'Introduction', 12.

collection comprises the business records of a trading station in Eastern South Africa, Mpondoland, known in the late nineteenth and twentieth century as Emagusheni Trading Store. While the store had operated as a family and wholesale business for almost ninety years (1883/4–1970), most records (including business and personal correspondence, trading diaries, account and stock books) cover the period 1882–96. During these years, business owner Michael H. O'Donnell and his partners and associates engaged in the trade with the Mpondo population as well as European retailers, wholesale merchants, and storekeepers in Mpondoland and the Colony of Natal.

Finally, while historians of nineteenth- and twentieth-century consumption face similar methodological problems, the relative scarcity of African written sources adds to the challenges for researchers working on South Africa.[65] The study approaches non-white consumption in British South Africa through three genres of sources: first, one of the most important record collections for the study of Eastern South Africa is *The James Stuart Archive of Recorded Oral Evidence Relating to the History of the Zulu and Neighbouring Peoples*, compiled, annotated, and edited by Colin de B. Webb and John B. Wright and published in six volumes between 1976 and 2004. James Stuart, born in Pietermaritzburg in 1868, spent most of his career as a colonial servant in positions related to native administration in Eastern British South Africa. By the late 1890s Stuart had become increasingly concerned about the influence of European culture on African society and concluded that the most effective way to address what he viewed as European-misgoverned African societies was to educate white colonial officials in African customs, history, and institutions. Between the late 1890s and early 1920s, he sought out and interviewed almost two hundred African informants whose testimonies form the core records in the James Stuart Collection held by the KCM.[66] *The James Stuart Archive* is an invaluable source, particularly in the study of pre-colonial Southern Africa. However, informants occasionally remarked on contemporary perceptions of and reactions to colonial rule, Western European dress, and African–European trade. Second, print media including *The British and South African Export Gazette* (first published in 1892) and trade and commission reports provide additional insights into the British perception of African consumption. Finally, European travel accounts include references to, for example, African adoptions and appropriations of European dress including military clothing.

65 See the summary in ibid., particularly 9–12.

66 See Wright, 'Making the James Stuart Archives', particularly 334–7; *The James Stuart Archive of Recorded Oral Evidence*. See also Hamilton, 'Backstory, Biography, and the Life of the James Stuart Archive'.

Language

Direct quotes in this study have not been altered substantially; they contain offensive discriminatory and defamatory language, but the explicitness of the language is essential to the analysis. Unless indicated otherwise in the footnotes, emphases (underlining and italics) are in the original quotes, including quotes from *The James Stuart Archive of Recorded Oral Evidence Relating to the History of the Zulu and Neighbouring Peoples*. I have retained the italicized emphases used by the editors, who applied them to entire passages—to indicate that the testimony was originally recorded in Zulu and translated by the editors—or to individual terms and phrases in Zulu, signalling the challenges of providing an unambiguous translation into English.[67]

Many names of South African towns, suburbs, and streets had already been changed prior to, but primarily after, the end of apartheid in 1994. Since 1998, the renaming and standardization of geographical places are overseen by the South African Geographical Names Council and formally approved by the South African Department for Arts and Culture. The ongoing process of decolonizing place names has resulted in multiple versions of the same locations appearing across academic literature, historical records, and maps. Wherever possible, I therefore provide the most contemporary official designation for geographical places alongside the historical names used.[68] Throughout this study, I use the spellings Mpondoland and Mpondo and contemporary spellings when referring to Mpondoland chiefs, rivers, and names of geographical places.[69] Readers will find that I use the terms 'Cape Colony' or 'Colony of Natal' when situating policies, actors, or practices in historically contingent geographies and politics. When referring to the inhabitants of (British) South Africa, I use the terms 'black Africans', 'Indians', 'coloured', and 'white', as these 'racial boundary markers' are crucial to the analysis of the British South African second-hand military clothing trade and racially politicized consumption.[70] Finally, I use the terms 'British' and 'European' when referring to individuals of British and European descent.

---

67 See Wright, 'Making the James Stuart Archives', 345; Laband, 'African Military History', 35.

68 See Government Notice no. 114 in *Government Gazette: Republic of South Africa,* 668 (23 Feb. 2021). In January 2026, the Sports, Arts and Culture Minister approved 21 geographical name changes. See Libera, 'Goodbye East London and Graaff-Reinet—Big Name Changes Coming to South Africa'.

69 With regard to Mpondoland, I follow Bramwell, 'Loyalties and the Politics of Incorporation in South Africa', p. xi. See also Kepe and Ntsebeza, 'Introduction', 2, n. 2.

70 On the significance of the Black Consciousness Movement for the breaking of these markers see, for example, Desai, 'Indian South Africans and the Black Consciousness Movement under Apartheid', 49.

CHAPTER 1

1 The British Army and the Production of British Second-Hand Military Clothing

FIGURE 1.1
Officer's full-dress tunic, British infantry pattern (*c.*1868).

The National Army Museum (NAM) in London holds an officer's full-dress tunic bearing the facing colours of the British Indian 19th Madras Native Infantry (Fig. 1.1). The red-dyed fabric, gold buttons, and detailed decoration on the facing suggest fine craftsmanship and impressive restoration skills; it is almost inconceivable that the tunic was ever worn. Even without additional information, the observer will probably have no difficulty identifying where the tunic originated from, as the association of certain colours of military clothing with particular nations had been established by the eighteenth century: blue was used by the Prussian army, white by Austria and Russia, and white or blue by France, while scarlet tunics, jackets, and coats were almost unmistakably associated with the British Empire. By the nineteenth century, the colour was worn by many regiments of the British army, some colonial army units, and the Royal Marines.[1] As one anony-

1 See Craik, *Uniforms Exposed*, 33–6.

 | HTTPS://DOI.ORG/10.1515/9783112256503-002

mous Briton stated in a letter to the editors of the military and naval gazette *The Broad Arrow* in March 1877: 'Red with England is an Imperial colour … [a]nd what uniform can compare with the thin red Line of the British Army?'[2] Looking at the tunic's buttons and original facings more closely, however, the observer will make a rather surprising discovery: while the facing colours indicate that the tunic had been manufactured for and was worn by the 19th Madras Native Infantry, the buttons and original facings are in fact those of the 24th Madras Native Infantry. There is, indeed, more to this garment than meets the eye.

The tunic belonged to Major General Montague Cholmeley, who joined the 19th Madras Native Infantry in June 1868. The application of buttons on the tunic from a regiment with whom Cholmeley had not served led NAM staff members to assume that the Major General purchased the clothing article second-hand when he joined the Wallajahbad Infantry in 1865.[3] While the circumstances under which Cholmeley acquired the tunic remain unclear, it exemplifies a widespread practice during the nineteenth century and beyond, namely the reuse of military dress both within and outside the British army's clothing system.

Military clothing contributed substantially to popular militarism in late Victorian Britain. Mass rituals and ceremonies, such as reviews accompanied by martial music, and military bands that frequently performed at private social and non-military public events, were military spectacles that had a deep impact on British society.[4] However, their popularity should not obscure the fact that the British public remained rather suspicious of the army throughout the nineteenth century.[5] Nor was the public appearance of regiments and soldiers dressed in military clothing as glamorous as the military authorities intended. In a letter addressed to the editor of the military gazette *The Broad Arrow* in May 1869, a reader sharply criticized the clothing worn by infantry soldiers during a 'straggling march of a wing of the 98th regiment through London', arguing that

> it need not to be much of a matter to surprise any person if men should fall out and straggle during such a march, if the fashion of their dress and equipment be fairly considered, both of which are in this year … the most uncomfortable, clumsy, and ill-adapted … Although constantly undergoing changes of some sort, each so-called *improvement* leaves the uniform just as bad as before, and changes not the appearance of the British Infantry soldier, who, poor man, invariably turns out in garments that look as if they had been purchased at an old-clothes shop and thrown upon him with a pitchfork.

2 *The Broad Arrow*, 18/458 (7 Apr. 1877), 437.

3 See object description and information by the NAM at [https://collection.nam.ac.uk/detail.php?acc=1974-09-72-1], accessed 2 Oct. 2025; *The New Army List, and Militia List*, 353.

4 See French, *Military Identities*, 234–6; Myerly, *British Military Spectacle*, 139–47. See also Giddins, 'Delusive Seduction'; Russel, '"We Carved Our Way to Glory"'.

5 See, for example, French, *Military Identities*, 233–58.

While the author was particularly concerned with the condition and design of military clothing issued to British infantry that made the soldier 'the most painfully ill-dressed man in the world', his reference to an 'old-clothes shop' was not, in fact, too far-fetched.[6]

Following the army's performance during the Crimean War (1853–6), in response to an intensifying recruitment crisis and rising public criticism, the British army, including its clothing system, underwent considerable reorganization. The Cardwell Reforms—introduced by Secretary of State for War Edward Cardwell between 1868 and 1874—led to the abolition of the commissions purchase system, reduced the period of service to twelve years, ended some disciplinary measures, and introduced administrative reforms that partially changed the organization of the army. The Childers Reforms of 1881, initiated by Hugh C. E. Childers, were a continuation of Cardwell's reforms, which reconfigured the army's infantry regiments.[7] The reorganization of the army clothing system, initiated shortly after the end of the Crimean War, was aimed primarily at improving clothing procurement and supply chains. Key reforms included: first, the abolishment of the system of off-reckonings in favour of public contracts and competition in the procurement of military supplies; second, the centralization of army clothing operations under the War Office, which assumed all responsibility for army clothing; and third, a newly created inspection division was to ensure that all military equipment supplied by government contractors and government clothing factories met material requirements and design standards.[8] In 1870, these developments culminated in the transfer of all clothing operations to the facilities in Pimlico, where the departments for the production, storage, distribution, and inspection merged with the administrative clothing branch of the War Office to form the Army Clothing Department, renamed the Royal Army Clothing Department in 1887.[9] The consolidation and centralization of the army clothing system under the (Royal) Army Clothing Department established the institutional and administrative framework for subsequent modifications of the processes of collecting, sorting, repairing, reusing, and disposing of second-hand military clothing.

Within this context, the commoditization of British second-hand military clothing was shaped by the conditions under which it was produced, reclaimed, and redirected. The late-nineteenth-century army reforms determined how and

6 *The Broad Arrow*, 2/48 (29 May 1869), 676.

7 See Skelley, *The Victorian Army at Home*; Gosling, 'Tommy Atkins, War Office Reform and the Social and Cultural Presence of the Late-Victorian Army in Britain, *c.*1868–1899', 39–51.

8 TNA, WO 377/7, *Instructions for Inspectors*, 6; TNA, WO 377/43, *Stores Inspection Division: A Brief History of the Stores Inspection Division from its Inception in 1855 to 1922. Compiled by Principal Viewer T. J. Haynes.*

9 TNA, WO 33/78; *Report from the Select Committee on Public Departments*, 1873, 183–4, Ev 3916–24.

by whom second-hand military clothing could be retained and reused, provoking disputes over ownership between military authorities and soldiers. Increasingly, the 'afterlives' of British second-hand military clothing—within as well as outside the army clothing system—attracted the attention of the British military authorities, who sought to regulate, control, and contain its circulation. These interventions highlight the correlating value ascriptions to British second-hand military dress, influenced the pathways through which second-hand military clothing entered the British domestic as well as the global market, and reshaped labour and manufacturing practices in the domestic second-hand clothing industry.

1.1 Second-Hand Military Clothing in the British Army, *c.*1870–1895

For every individual joining the army—and regardless of their prospective career path—the changing of clothing at the beginning of basic training can be described as an act of 'initiation'. The surrender of civilian clothing, David French argues, is a symbolic act by which recruits 'shed their civilian identities'; it is thus the first step towards the disciplining of soldiers' minds and bodies and the formation of the 'military identity' constructed and sought after by the British military authorities.[10] Military clothing played a vital role in the construction of martial images and virtues and was essential in communicating a specific set of military values to soldiers.[11] Dressing, as an embodied practice, is situated in specific temporal, spatial, and hierarchal structures and relations. As such, military clothing and related practices in particular have been utilized by army authorities to instil discipline and other specific attributes in soldiers.[12] As Redvers H. Buller—an influential and highly decorated British army officer—stated in 1894:[13]

> Our whole military training is devoted to trying to make a man fond and proud of his uniform ... We train both our officers and men, and with very considerable success, to have a pride in their uniform, and to consider their uniform as a special garment which it is their duty to uphold and honour in every possible way.[14]

During (basic) military training, recruits and soldiers spent a considerable amount of time polishing and cleaning their equipment and uniforms; it was the

---

10 French, *Military Identities*, 64. See also Peoples, 'Embodying the Military'; Roche, *The Culture of Clothing*, 228–9.

11 See Myerly, *British Military Spectacle*, 8–11.

12 See Peoples, 'Embodying the Military', 7–21; Craik, *The Face of Fashion*, 131–2; Roche, *The Culture of Clothing*, 228–9.

13 For an overview of Redvers H. Buller's career at the War Office and in South Africa, see Miller, 'Redvers Buller', and, with special emphasis on Buller in the South African War, Beckett, 'Buller and the Politics of Command'.

14 *Report from the Select Committee on the Uniforms Bill*, 9, Ev 147.

soldiers' responsibility to take care of and repair their clothing, the aim here being to instil discipline through military drill.[15] Used by the military authorities as a means to imbue soldiers with military values, the uniform gradually became a symbol of these qualities: as Jennifer Craik notes, military clothing was 'the visible lexicon of social characteristics, skills, attitudes and habits' valued by the military authorities as well as civil society.[16]

Second-hand military clothing occupied a peculiar position in the British army clothing system. In the 1870s and 1880s, the military authorities distinguished between 'part-worn' and 'worn-out' army clothing. While the term 'part-worn' referred to clothing that had been worn by at least one individual and was subsequently reissued, the term 'worn-out' described clothing that had either been worn by at least one soldier for a predefined period of time and was to be sold or destroyed, or was kept by soldiers upon their discharge.[17] The term 'worn-out' thus referred to clothing that had passed through the British army's internal clothing system, wherein it was possible—in the words of the army's Director of Contracts, Ethan C. Nepean, in 1887—to 'follow the completed article from its cradle to its grave'.[18]

The reuse of part-worn military clothing within the army through reissue to new recruits and soldiers arose from economic necessity. As army officials pointed out in 1877, 'owing to variations, casualties, &c., it is practically impossible that the same clothing should always be worn out by the same man.'[19] It was not uncommon to find a considerable amount of part-worn military clothing circulating within the army, but it was also heavily objected to, particularly by commanding officers: in the context of an internal army investigation of the militia in 1877, a questionnaire broached the issue of soldiers' attitudes towards the issuing of part-worn clothing. In the commanding officers' replies—some of which were significantly more detailed than others—many reported soldiers' disparagement: 'It has often caused great discontent in the regiment', the officer commanding the Cardigan Rifles stated, while in the 1st Cheshire regiment it had continued to be 'a constant subject of difficulty.'[20] 'They are ashamed of themselves, and being laughed at in their old clothes', another commanding officer claimed.[21] Some officers assumed that issuing part-worn clothing to men joining the regiments affected enlistment, as, in their opinion, recruits were 'anxious to turn out clean and

15 See French, *Military Identities*, 67.
16 Craik, *Uniforms Exposed*, 28–30.
17 See *Report of the Committee ... with Respect to the Militia and the Present Brigade Depôt System*, p. xviii.
18 *First Report of the Royal Commission Appointed to Inquire into the Civil Establishments of the Different Offices of State at Home and Abroad*, 49, Ev 1332.
19 Ibid. p. xviii.
20 Ibid. App. II, 403–4. Furthermore, see ibid. App. II, 428, 450–1, and 469.
21 Ibid. App. II, 458. See also ibid. App. II, 436.

smart',[22] 'naturally [took] pride, on enlisting, in having new clothing',[23] and in 'being neatly dressed.'[24] 'Smart dress', as the Mayo South Rifles' commanding officer argued, was 'a great inducement to young men to enroll.'[25]

The commanding officers' interest and, in the words of Director of Clothing Guy D. A. Fleetwood Wilson, 'desire to see the [their] regiment perfect in clothing and equipment' must be considered against the background of the army's continuous struggle to fill its ranks.[26] While the number of recruits increased in the late nineteenth century, so did the regular army's establishment. Regimental officers, David French analyses, were concerned with and complained about the recruits' physical immaturity, low educational standards, and social status: 'The typical Regular Army recruit before 1914', as French puts it, 'was a young, unskilled, and poorly educated urban labourer.' According to French, it was not until the turn of the twentieth century that the military authorities were able to draw the kind of recruits they wanted: people from the 'respectable' working classes.[27]

Officers were particularly troubled by the material condition of reissued military dress, viewing it as detrimental to the efforts to resolve the recruitment crisis and as undermining soldiers' habits of cleanliness and self-presentation. Some of the clothing was supposedly 'in such a disgraceful state that it [was] disgusting to the idea of any respectable man to put it on'. Such clothing was thought to prevent 'good clean soldiers' from 'taking the interest in their appearance and smartness which they would [have taken] if their clothing was new,'[28] and to discourage 'them from any attempt to keep themselves neat and clean.'[29] As part of the 'discipline of appearances', military training was meant to inculcate, among other principles, a habit of cleanliness.[30] In addition to general concerns about hygiene and sanitation within the army, the condition of part-worn clothing evoked images that contradicted the notion of an ideal soldier and the regiment's 'creditable appearance', which could, after all, be seen as a reflection of an officer's—and, by extension, the army's—(in-)competence.[31]

22 Ibid. App. II, 463.
23 Ibid. App. II, 407.
24 Ibid. App. II, 462.
25 Ibid. App. II, 484.
26 BL, Personal and Official Papers of Sir Guy Fleetwood Wilson, Mss Eur F224/17, 3. See *Report of the Committee ... with Respect to the Militia and the Present Brigade Depôt System*, App. II, 426.
27 French, *Military Identities*, 32–6 at 35.
28 *Report of the Committee ... with Respect to the Militia and the Present Brigade Depôt System*, App. II, 403–4. See also ibid. App. II, 473.
29 Ibid. App. II, 477.
30 Roche, *The Culture of Clothing*, 232–4.
31 *Report of the Committee ... with Respect to the Militia and the Present Brigade Depôt System*, App. II, 426.

Following the investigation in 1877, the objections to the internal reuse of military clothing led to minor modifications in the system of clothing issuance in the militia. The military authorities recommended an additional pair of trousers be issued to recruits—the article of clothing which, commanding officers had reported, led to the most complaints when issued part-worn.[32] Despite the criticism expressed by some commanding officers who continued to stress that they thought it 'a great mistake to give recruits part-worn clothing when they join [ed]',[33] the internal system of reuse and issuance of part-worn military clothing remained largely in place at least until the end of the nineteenth century—although not to the same extent in all regiments.[34] Parallel to the discussion of the reuse of part-worn military dress within the British army, a more contentious debate emerged over the internal handling of worn-out military clothing.

When Private D. Difford was examined as a witness before the *Committee Appointed by the Secretary of State of War to Consider the Terms and Conditions of Service in the Army* in November 1891, he had served in the British army for nineteen years. Difford, a labourer from Glastonbury, had joined the 2nd Somerset Militia before enlisting in the army in November 1874 and extending his service in 1886. He apparently stayed out of trouble, was hospitalized only once, and had been to various stations for summer drills. Difford was a lance corporal for a short period of time in 1876 but felt it was too much work for insufficient pay—he thus decided that he 'would rather be a private soldier.'[35] In this capacity, Difford witnessed considerable changes in the army clothing system. In the early 1870s, while some articles of clothing such as great coats and headdresses had already been categorized as property of the public, all regimental clothing remained the property of the soldier when new articles of clothing were issued. Soldiers received, among other items of military equipment, a tunic and a pair of summer trousers every two years, and 'every year a kersey frock, a pair of thick trousers, and two pairs of boots'.[36] After these items of clothing had been worn for a regulated period of time and new articles were issued, soldiers either kept their worn-out clothes or disposed of them to local second-hand clothing dealers, thus supplementing their meagre income.[37] Andrew R. Skelley concluded that between 1856 and 1899, the British army was able to financially compete only with civilian occupations offering the lowest pay. Because of a number of stoppages and de-

32 See ibid. p. xviii.

33 *Report of the Committee … to Consider the Terms and Conditions of Service in the Army*, 354–5, Ev 10795.

34 Colonel W. Green, for example, who was in command of the 75th Regimental District in Aberdeen in 1892, stated that his regimental depot always issued new clothing to recruits. See ibid. 215, Ev 6339–42.

35 See ibid. 458, Ev 13286–325 at Ev 13318.

36 *Report from the Select Committee on Public Departments*, 1873, 195, Ev 4190.

37 See ibid. 195–6, Ev 4190–7.

ductions, the proclaimed minimum army pay of one shilling per day implied by army recruiters was deceptive.[38] In addition, many articles of clothing issued did not last the regulated period of time and had to be replaced by soldiers at their own expense.[39] Nevertheless, soldiers frequently sold worn-out army clothing to second-hand clothes dealers, and the military authorities were well aware of the practice.[40] Private Difford, for example, reported that he used to sell his worn-out military clothing to 'a man named Harris, a Jew, [who] used to come and buy all the battalion clothing.'[41]

From the 1870s onwards, prompted by concerns over the reuse of clothing in non-military contexts, the military authorities introduced a series of acts aimed at second-hand dealers and altered army clothing regulations to restrict the circulation of second-hand military clothing within domestic markets. Initially, their concerns centred around soldiers' conduct. First, in the eyes of the military authorities, the 'making away with necessaries' had become 'a fertile source of courts-martial'.[42] According to the Director of Clothing George D. Ramsay, given the resale value of military clothing in the domestic second-hand clothing trade, allowing soldiers to keep and dispose of articles of clothing served as an inducement to desert.[43] A similar argumentation was used by army officials in retrospect: Viscount Wolseley, for example, recalled in 1888 that military 'authorities were very anxious to prevent the soldier selling his old tunic in the market, because it helped desertion.'[44] Second, the appearance and public visibility of discharged soldiers 'in the worn-out uniform of the service' threatened the image of the soldier that the military authorities were particularly eager to redefine. As Edward P.J. Gosling points out, the military authorities hoped to resolve the recruitment crises following the Crimean War by popularizing the soldier profession and army service in general. While the 'social reimagining of the soldier' that Cardwell 'sought to orchestrate' through reforms and initiatives to raise the status and image of British soldiers did not succeed outright, the reforms nevertheless provided the framework for subsequent—and in part successful—attempts to socially re-

38 See Skelley, *The Victorian Army at Home*, 183–4. See also Myerly, *British Military Spectacle*, 3–8.

39 See Skelley, *The Victorian Army at Home*, 183–4.

40 See, for example, *First Report of the Royal Commission Appointed to Inquire into the Civil Establishments of the Different Offices of State at Home and Abroad*, 117, Ev 3159.

41 *Report of the Committee ... to Consider the Terms and Conditions of Service in the Army*, 458, Ev 13340.

42 *Second Report of the Commissioners Appointed to Inquire into the Constitution and Practice of Courts-Martial in the Army and the Present System of Punishment for Military Offences*, 209, Ev 5241.

43 See *Report of the Committee ... with Respect to the Militia and the Present Brigade Depôt System*, 236, Ev 6597.

44 *Fourth Report from the Select Committee on Army Estimates*, 124, Ev 5968.

habilitate the British soldier in the eyes of the public.[45] In principle, practices of reuse of British second-hand military clothing by discharged soldiers were not perceived by army authorities as particularly problematic. However, discharged soldiers 'going about the country in *old ragged dirty* clothing' contradicted the notion of the soldier and the British army that Cardwell and other military authorities aimed to construct and display.[46]

Unlike in France, for example, where second-hand dealers (*fripier/ière*) and dealers in general (*revendeurs*) had been prohibited to purchase military clothing from soldiers since at least the eighteenth century, the British second-hand clothing trade had remained largely unregulated.[47] The War Department Stores Act 1867 protected stores issued by the War Department as army property marked with 'the Broad Arrow with or without the Letters W. D. or the Letters B. O. ... to denote Her Majesty's Property in Stores' (W ⩚ D or B ⩚ O). Under the provisions of the War Department Stores Act, individuals receiving, possessing, keeping, selling, or delivering 'Stores bearing any such Mark' were to 'be deemed guilty of a Misdemeanour' and liable to imprisonment.[48] Dealers (in second-hand commodities) and pawnbrokers could nevertheless avoid prosecution by proving they had had no 'Knowledge ... that the Stores to which Charges relate[d] bore ... a Mark or Part of a Mark as aforesaid.'[49] Following the introduction of the Public Stores Act in 1875, however, offenders were obligated to disclose the commodities' provenance: in cases in which 'stores [were] found in the possession or keeping of ... a dealer in marine stores or old metals, or a pawnbroker ... then if such person [did] not satisfy the court that he came lawfully by the stores so found, [ought to] be liable ... to a penalty.'[50]

The Public Stores Act laid the grounds for the alteration as well as the introduction of additional army clothing regulations. Shortly after its introduction, Ramsay announced that the military authorities were preparing 'to adopt the

---

45 See Gosling, 'Tommy Atkins, War Office Reform and the Social and Cultural Presence of the Late-Victorian Army in Britain, *c.*1868–1899', 36–51 at 48.

46 *Report of the Committee ... with Respect to the Militia and the Present Brigade Depôt System*, 236, Ev 6597 [emphasis added by the author].

47 While the French norms were, according to Daniel Roche, often ignored by second-hand dealers and not observed scrupulously by law enforcement, they were nevertheless intended to regulate the second-hand clothes trade and its milieu in general. See Roche, *The Culture of Clothing*, 356.

48 *War Department Stores Act 1867*, 2–4. The history of the broad arrow mark and its government use can apparently be traced back to the fifteenth century. In the nineteenth century, either its original form or modified versions can be found in related contexts (such as on prisoners' clothing) in Britain and across the British Empire. See Maynard, *Fashioned from Penury*, 21.

49 *War Department Stores Act 1867*, 2.

50 *Public Stores Act 1875*, 1.

principle … that the clothing should become the property of the public'.[51] On 1 April 1881, a royal warrant and revised clothing regulations, issued under Childers, substantially changed the practice of disposing of worn-out army clothing. Under these new regulations, published shortly afterwards as *Regulations for the Supply of Clothing and Necessaries to the Regular Forces*, most worn-out military clothing was to 'remain the property of the State, and not of the soldier or other person'. Discharged soldiers were allowed to keep '1 frock or jacket, 1 pair of trouwsers, breeches, or trew, 1 pair of ankle-boots of shoes, [and] 1 greatcoat, without cape, worn out', provided these articles had 'been worn at least three months before being taken away'.[52] In addition, the clothing regulations introduced the 'inverted broad arrow' mark (Fig. 1.2). Based on the symbol of the broad arrow and used, for example, to mark horses that were of no further use to the military authorities during and after the First World War and were to be sold by auction,[53] the symbol was applied from 1881 onwards to 'all articles of Clothing handed over to the Contractor, or sold by the Commissariat, or by the Ordnance Store Department, without being torn up'.[54] In comparison, part-worn clothing, when reissued, was to be re-marked by crossing out the original number and date of its first issue and adding the relevant part-worn issue information (Fig. 1.3).[55] Marking second-hand military clothing—whether the items were to be sold or reissued to, for example, new recruits—not only branded the items as used and enabled the identification of a specific category of army products, but also, since these marks were based on the clothes' first issue information and the symbol of the broad arrow, the items remained easily recognizable as (former) government and army property.[56] However, while these symbols indicated that an item of clothing had been used one way or another—which, in practice, did not necessarily mean that it had been worn—the marks did not imply or guarantee specific quality standards. As the director of the Army Contracts Department pointed out in 1888, regarding the quality of the second-hand clothing that contractors tendered for, 'there will be some good part-worn clothing in every year, but other garments again are little better than rags.'[57]

---

51 *Report of the Committee … with Respect to the Militia and the Present Brigade Depôt System*, 236, Ev 6597.

52 'Army Circulars, 1881. Clause 88. Issue of a Royal Warrant and Revised Regulations for the Provision of Clothing and Necessaries for the Regular Forces', in *Army Circulars 1881*, 10–3, at 11.

53 See, for example, Winton, *Theirs Not to Reason Why*, 297; MacDonald, *Supplying the British Army in the First World War*.

54 *Regulations for the Supply of Clothing and Necessaries to the Regular Forces*, 1881, 72.

55 See ibid. 72–3 and *Regulations for the Clothing of the Army*, App. VIII, 173.

56 See chapter 1.1.

57 *Army: Return to an Address of the Honourable The House of Commons, dated 10 July 1889;—for, Copies 'of Departmental Minutes Relative to the Army Contracts Department'*, 4.

FIGURE 1.2
Pattern for inverted broad arrow (1881).

First issues.	Part-worn issues.	
1418	~~1472~~	121
41 Reg.	43 B. D.	
4.79	~~4.79.~~	
	12.79.	

FIGURE 1.3
Pattern for marks on first issued and part-worn reissued military clothing (1881).

The changes to the system of disposing of worn-out military clothing met with strong resistance from soldiers and commanding officers. Prior to the introduction of the revised clothing regulations, the latter already predicted that refusing soldiers their 'old clothing when it [had] served the proper period' would not only have an unfavourable effect on recruitment:[58] Major B. Thornhill, for example, argued that his men would be 'very angry if they [did] not get' their old clothes.[59] Indeed, during the following decades, the 'worn-out clothing question' remained central to soldiers' complaints about army service.[60] A lieutenant colonel stated that 'Men who had served seven years in the reserve considered that they were entitled to a suit of clothing ... The Director of Clothing, however, decided that unless the clothing [had] been in wear seven years the men [were] not entitled to it, with which decision they [were] not satisfied.'[61] Ten years later, Lieutenant General Charles C. Fraser explained that 'a soldier rather considers it a hardship that he should be compelled to return his worn-out clothing into store ... He has paid for mending it, and he considers that it is his.'[62] To Fraser and other military personnel, the lack of direct compensation for clothing that the soldier was expected to maintain and care for constituted an unjust consequence of the new clothing regulations. The military authorities expected soldiers to be responsible for the upkeep and repair items of clothing not only as part of the formation of a specific military identity but also because prolonging the 'life span' of items of military clothing through these labour inputs was, in many cases, necessary to ensure that the clothing lasted the prescribed amount of time and

58 *Report of the Committee ... with Respect to the Militia and the Present Brigade Depôt System*, App. II, 400. See also ibid. App. II, 402 and 488.
59 Ibid. 195, Ev 5565.
60 *Army and Navy Gazette: Journal of the Reserve and Auxiliary Forces*, 15/1262 (1885), 5.
61 *Report of a Committee ... on Army Re-Organization*, App. XLVII, 596.
62 *Fourth Report from the Select Committee on Army Estimates*, 7, Ev 5212.

did not have to be replaced at the soldiers' expense. As well as this matter of uncompensated labour—which was much discussed at the time—soldiers' individual ascriptions of value to their articles of clothing were noted by, but ultimately remained intangible to, army authorities. Thornhill, for example, claimed that it was 'not the value of the thing' in the sense of 'sufficient pay or good pay' that led to discontent among soldiers, 'but [that] it [was] less than what [soldiers] used to have.'[63] Moreover, as another colonel argued, soldiers 'attach a value' to their clothing, 'and of course the old soldier tells the young one.'[64] In 1892, when there were 'very few men in the regiment ... who [had] served under the old Clothing Regulations', the change in the latter in 1881 was said to have 'been handed down by tradition as a sore point among the men.'[65] Finally, Ramsay's choice of words in this context is particularly instructive: on the one hand, the Director of Clothing defended the revised clothing regulations that reduced the number of items of clothing at soldiers' disposal 'as a matter of policy; because the proceeds of the sales of old clothes [would] enable [the Army Clothing Department] to make improvements in the material at present supplied.' In his opinion, soldiers would eventually be compensated 'by getting better clothing';[66] on the other hand, Ramsay admitted that the returning of old clothing to the regiments after it had been worn for a prescribed period of time was considered by soldiers 'a very great grievance ... moreover', he stressed, 'not a money grievance exactly, [but] a sentimental grievance, and a sentimental grievance is one that is always very difficult to redress.'[67]

The controversy over worn-out military clothing extended beyond military circles and reached a wider audience, featuring in newspapers, gazettes, and debates within the British parliament. In 1884, the editors of *The London Evening Standard* published a letter in which 'An Army Officer' called attention to the 'system of disposing of old clothing, and the hardship it entail[ed] on all ranks.' The anonymous author criticized 'the amount of extra work, courts martial, discontent, and heartburnings' in consequence of the clothing regulations introduced in 1881.[68] The letter received attention from other individuals, who referred to the officer's complaints in subsequent issues of the newspaper: 'A Victim' was convinced that the points raised by the officer would 'be fully endorsed by every one connected with the Army', while 'An Infantry Officer' pointed out the injustices imposed on

---

63 *Report of the Committee ... with Respect to the Militia and the Present Brigade Depôt System*, 195, Ev 5567–8.

64 Ibid. 36, Ev 770.

65 *Report of the Committee ... to Consider the Terms and Conditions of Service in the Army*, 174, Ev 4861.

66 *Report of the Committee ... with Respect to the Militia and the Present Brigade Depôt System*, 236, Ev 6598–601.

67 Ibid. 424, Ev 12467.

68 *The London Evening Standard*, 18610 (8 Mar. 1884), 3.

discharged soldiers.[69] 'The Worn-Out Clothing Question', as the *Army and Navy Gazette* titled yet another reader's letter,[70] gained increased public attention and led MP George Sclater-Booth to critically address the army clothing disposal system in parliament in July 1885.[71] Yet, opinions were deeply divided on the subject. Sclater-Booth did not find supporters, and officers' concerns and soldiers' complaints remained largely ignored. As an anonymous reader cynically put it: 'The question was thoroughly argued and ventilated ... the danger and dissatisfaction were fully pointed out; but no, reason would not be listened to, commanding officers' experienced opinions must be thrown aside.'[72]

Still, over the following ten years, a number of small changes were introduced in the army clothing disposal system, allowing, for example, soldiers to sell their worn-out clothing inter-regimentally to one another, and increasing the amount of clothing soldiers were permitted to keep upon discharge.[73] Frequent moving of goalposts in the question of to whom the worn-out military clothing belonged and at which point, delays in the communication of new orders, and variation across regiments in terms of the timetable for clothing issue led to confusion, miscommunication, and false assumptions among commanding officers and other military authorities. Viscount Wolseley, for example, who was strongly in favour of soldiers being allowed to keep their worn-out clothing, admitted he had not been aware that in 1887 the tunic remained government property after it had been worn for the prescribed period of time.[74]

1.2 'Sandwich-Board Men' and Circuses: British Second-Hand Military Clothing in Street Advertising and Popular Entertainment

In 1906, an unusual publicity stunt caught the attention of London's law enforcement as well as German and British politicians. Metropolitan Police officers reported in May 1906 'that a number of men dressed in a kind of imitation German Military costume were seen ... carrying boards advertising a novel entitled "The Invasion of 1908."' An officer at the Vine Street police station noted that 'Mr Thomas Smith ... an advertising agent, ha[d] employed them for this purpose.' Police officers and superintendents eventually concluded that because the incident involved clothing resembling German, not British military dress, they had no

69 *The London Evening Standard*, 18612 (11 Mar. 1884), 6.
70 *Army and Navy Gazette: Journal of the Reserve and Auxiliary Forces*, 15/1262 (1885), 5.
71 Hansard, House of Commons, 27 July 1885, vol. 300, cc. 111–9.
72 *Army and Navy Gazette: Journal of the Reserve and Auxiliary Forces*, 15/1262 (1885), 5.
73 *Report ... on the Uniforms Bill*, 10, Ev 170.
74 See *Fourth Report from the Select Committee on Army Estimates*, 124, Ev 5960–7.

reason or legal power to interfere. Thus, although the issue was considered worth reporting, it seemed resolved.[75]

In the meantime, however, this street advertisement for Walter Wood's novel *The Enemy in Our Midst: The Story of a Raid on England* (first published in 1905) had prompted a certain Herbert E. A. Furst to write to the editors of *The Times*, who published his letter under the title 'A Legitimate Complaint' on 14 May 1906:

> I have just noticed a row of sandwich-men walking the streets of the West-end dressed as German soldiers. On their boards they display the following words: —"An Enemy in our Midst" ... Allow me ... to express my utmost disgust with the unscrupulous manner in which some people are allowed to wheedle halfpennies out of their country-men's pockets. Neither the French in the days of the Boer war and Fashoda nor the Germans down to this date have, in my opinion, ever committed so gross a breach of international courtesy and common fairness than the employer of these sandwich-men. In my eyes, and in those of every right-minded person, English or German, this method of making money can only be regarded as a scandal, ultimately reflecting on the whole British nation.[76]

Furthermore, shortly before the publication of Furst's letter, Wilhelm von Stumm —a diplomat at the German embassy in London—'complained that a number of "sandwich-men" [had] been in evidence on the streets of London displaying advertisements' for the book, 'dressed in Prussian helmets and military uniforms bearing an unmistakable resemblance to that worn by the German Army.' According to Stumm, the practice was 'offensive and derogatory to the honour of the German Army.'[77] Expecting a 'visit to London of certain German municipal authorities', members of the British Parliament subsequently asked the Secretary of State 'to take steps to restrain an exhibition of this character', arguing that it would 'likely ... be resented by the officers and men of the German Army, as a similar use of the British uniform would be resented by [their] own Army.' Ultimately, 'this abuse of the national uniform',[78] considered 'foolish and offensive' by the British Home Secretary Herbert J. Gladstone,[79] led British politicians to put a stop to the book promotion. After being informed about this action, Stumm stated gratefully that he would 'not fail to bring [it] to the knowledge of [his] imperial government.'[80]

This small and seemingly unimportant incident led to political interventions and calls for explorations of legal manoeuvres. In several letters, different officials involved in what some of them construed as an impending diplomatic conflict

---

75 TNA, MEPO 2/974.

76 *The Times*, 38019 (14 May 1906), 10.

77 TNA, FO 371/78/16143, fol. 9.

78 Hansard, House of Commons, 14 May 1906, vol. 157, cc. 187–8.

79 TNA, FO 371/78/16143, fol. 5.

80 Ibid. fol. 19.

unsuccessfully referred to the Uniforms Act (introduced in 1894), which prohibited the unauthorized adoption and appropriation of British army or navy clothing by civilians. Imitating British military dress and adopting and appropriating it in non-military contexts was a widespread practice throughout the nineteenth century, when military imagery had come to influence a wide range of genres such as popular entertainment, art, literature, theatrical productions, and fashion, as well as notions of gender, children's toys, and costume.[81] The latter did not go unnoticed by the military authorities. In 1893, Assistant Director of Naval Intelligence Henry D. Barry pointed out that imitation uniforms had become 'the most popular dress in England for most boys between five and 10'—and that, in his opinion, this kind of 'imitation [was] the sincerest form of flattery in many respects.'[82] Overall, however, the military authorities did not agree that the British army and navy benefited from the reuse or imitation of military dress, or the appropriation of second-hand military clothing in non- or semi-military contexts. By the early 1890s, street advertising and circuses emerged as two realms in which the reuse of (semi-)military clothing appeared to threaten the image of the British soldier and the army by contesting or falsely appropriating the values represented by their uniforms.

Nineteenth-century publications, reports, illustrations, and paintings document the widespread practice of reusing, appropriating, or imitating British military clothing for street advertising. By the mid nineteenth century, advertising agents had noticed that the visibility and appearance of their employees affected consumers and consumption practices. Sandwich-board men and their clothing became a focal point in several articles, illustrations, and books. In the introduction to his publication *Advertise: How? When? Where?* (1863), William Smith explained that the term 'sandwich man' derived from the association of men wearing advertising boards with the food item: '"Sandwich"—a term which, originally applied in jest, the man or boy in the middle representing the meat, between the two slices of bread, is now used technically to describe boards slung in front and behind the bearer, and carried through the streets.'[83] Smith's book suggested employment conditions, outfits, and board designs to merchants and advertising agents, and while he did not explicitly recommend the employment of former soldiers, the reuse of military dress, or imitations thereof, contemporary paintings, illustrations, and reports suggest that sandwich-board men dressed in (British)

81 See Myerly, *British Military Spectacle*, 139–47; Peoples, 'Embodying the Military'; Martin and Koda (eds.), *Swords into Ploughshares*. On the relation of military dress and gender, see Craik, *Uniforms Exposed*, and Craik, 'The Cultural Politics of the Uniform'. Craik draws attention to the appropriation of military dress in transgressive and subversive contexts such as pornography, crossdressing, subcultures, etc. See ibid. 129, and Langkjær, '"Then How Do You Explain Sgt. Pompous and the Fancy Pants Club Band?"'

82 *Report ... on the Uniforms Bill*, 17, Ev 277–8.

83 Smith, *Advertise*, 12. See Foutch, 'Moving Pictures', particularly 749–53.

military clothing were a common sight in the nineteenth century and that they featured as subjects in socialist realist Victorian art. Exhibited at the Royal Academy in 1881 and currently part of a private collection, Eyre Crowe's oil painting *Sandwiches* (1881), for example, depicts a group of sandwich-board men on a break in Trafalgar Square and shows at least one figure wearing what looks like a military headdress, with another, presumably military helmet lying on the stairs next to him.[84] In addition, two illustrations by C. Paul Renouard published in the weekly newspaper *The Graphic* in 1894 suggest that advertising agents preferred to hire applicants who dressed in (imitation) British military clothing. Ellery F. Foutch interprets these images in terms of the rising importance of visibility and an acceptable appearance in the work of sandwich-board men towards the second half of the nineteenth century. Renouard's illustrations depict successful and unsuccessful candidates for the position of a sandwich-board man. The applicants' posture, dress, and overall appearance differ considerably (Figs. 1.4 and 1.5). Moreover, at least three of the figures in *Recruiting the Sandwich Men: Accepted* are depicted wearing clothing resembling military uniform. The neatly dressed prospective employer appears to be facing one of these men, whose posture—upright and, alone among the applicants, looking straight ahead—and clothing evoke images of military drill (Fig. 1.4). The second illustration—*Recruiting the Sandwich Men: Rejected*—shows the unsuccessful applicants in the foreground, none of whom are in military dress, while at least the figure bringing up the rear of the line of accepted applicants walking down the alley in the background is wearing what looks like a military headdress and uniform (Fig. 1.5).[85]

84 See Treuherz (ed.), *Hard Times*, 105.

85 See Foutch, 'Moving Pictures', 752–5. See also Richards, *The Commodity Culture of Victorian England*, 45–6; Day, *The Demographic Imagination and the Nineteenth-Century City*, 107–47; Cronin, *Advertising Myths*, 35–6; Church, 'Advertising Consumer Goods in Nineteenth-Century Britain'.

FIGURE 1.4
C. Paul Renouard, *Recruiting the Sandwich Men: Accepted* (1894).

FIGURE 1.5
C. Paul Renouard, *Recruiting the Sandwich Men: Rejected* (1894).

Advertising practices were contested and regulated throughout the entire nineteenth century, but criticism increased significantly towards the end of the century. While British legislation only marginally restricted advertising in general, several laws aimed at sandwich-board men specifically were introduced from the mid nineteenth century onwards and restricted the men's movements on the streets, among other things.[86] The National Society for Controlling the Abuses of Public Advertising (SCAPA), founded in 1893, influenced the passing of several bills that further regulated street advertising practices. However, SCAPA and other campaigners did not target advertising for its 'manipulative powers. Rather, the criticism was aesthetic in nature, lamenting the proliferation of advertisements and their consequent aesthetic pollution of public ... spaces.'[87] The expansion of legal restrictions on street advertising was accompanied by increased criticism of the clothing worn by sandwich-board men, who were frequently accused of wearing military, naval, or police uniforms inappropriately when advertising consumer products.[88] William Davis, Superintendent of the Executive Branch of the Police Commissioner's Office, noted in 1893 that he 'constantly' witnessed the wearing of uniforms by unauthorized persons, 'generally sandwich men ... sent out, no doubt, by some advertising theatrical lessee or manager.'[89] Like members of SCAPA, however, Davis, some MPs, and the British military authorities were less concerned with the spread of misinformation about consumer products or the impact of street advertising methods on consumer culture in general. Rather, they saw the reuse or imitation of British military dress in street advertising as a threat to the image of the army. While MP Robert Hanbury argued in more general terms that the armed forces were being 'disgraced by the use of worn-out uniforms by sandwich men and others',[90] military officials voiced fears of more specific negative effects, particularly in relation to recruitment: 'When a young fellow from Essex went to Trafalgar Square where recruiting sergeants congregated ... and there saw a procession of men clothed in parts of military uniforms and carrying advertisements of somebody's soap or somebody's pills', a major stated in 1894, 'one was not so desirous of wearing the uniform himself.'[91]

This disapproval among military officials arose from perceptions that sandwich-board men held a low socio-economic status. 'The system of advertising by means of boards, which the men themselves carry on their backs,' Adolphe Smith wrote in the late nineteenth century,

86 Including, for example, the London Hackney Carriage Act (1853) and the Metropolitan Streets Act (1867, reinforced in 1893). See Foutch, 'Moving Pictures', 749–51 and n. 55.

87 Cronin, *Advertising Myths*, 35.

88 See ibid.

89 *Report ... on the Uniforms Bill*, 19, Ev 311.

90 Hansard, House of Commons, 19 Feb. 1891, vol. 350, c. 1097.

91 Hansard, House of Commons, 9 May 1894, vol. 24, c. 708.

> has proved the most useful, as this is the work which any one can perform, and therefore boardmen ... are often recruited among the most hopeless of our poor ... The boardmen are often men who have fallen in the world, some have even once enjoyed the title of 'gentleman,' boast of an excellent education, but have been reduced to their present pitch of degradation through what they fashionably term dipsomania![92]

Representatives of the British army and navy such as Redvers H. Buller and Henry D. Barry agreed that a sandwich-board man in military uniform did not 'tend to raise the service whose dress he imitate[d].'[93] The negative image of advertising workers—at one point, Buller described sandwich-board men as 'dilapidated people'—was reproduced by MPs and witnesses interviewed in connection with the planned introduction of the Uniforms Act in 1894 and remained uncontested throughout the proceedings of the select committee.[94]

However, street advertising was not the only context in which British military officials and politicians feared that the army's image was threatened by the reuse or imitation of military clothing. The equestrian military drama, or hippodrama, emerged during the first half of the nineteenth century to become one of the most popular theatrical spectacles. These entertainments combined equestrian acts with narratives of the nation's military victories, thus contributing, Brenda Assael argues, to public memory and processes of 'national mythmaking'.[95] Moreover, re-enactments of, and performances relating to, battle scenes in circuses and theatres frequently involved either the reuse of original British military dress or imitations of army or navy uniforms. One of the most famous and successful late-nineteenth-century circus entrepreneurs in London was George Sanger, proprietor of the popular Sanger Circus. Sanger's rise to fame began in the second half of the century: while running several travelling exhibitions between *c.*1860 and 1880, Sanger and his brother gradually established and expanded their entertainment business. In 1871, they purchased Astley's Amphitheatre in London. During the following decade, the brothers organized exhibitions and erected further circus buildings before breaking up their partnership in 1884. George Sanger retained Astley's Amphitheatre until it was closed in 1893.[96] According to his autobiography, he continued to travel with his circuses across the country, and among the most prominent features of his entertainments 'were big military spectacles, in which were reproduced as faithfully as possible dramatic incidents of real war-

---

92 Thompson and Smith, *Street Life in London*, 22–3 at 22.

93 *Report ... on the Uniforms Bill*, 16, Ev 269.

94 Ibid. 6, Ev 92.

95 Assael, *The Circus and Victorian Society*, 61. See also Baston, '"New" Hippodrama, or "Old" Circus?', particularly 21–7. On the equestrian drama from an animal studies perspective, see, for example, Mattfeld, '"I See Them Galloping!"'.

96 See Assael, 'Sanger, George [*known as* Lord George Sanger]: (1825?–1911)'.

fare.'[97] These shows—some of which apparently involved over 300 human and animal performers—included battle scenes from the Anglo-Zulu and South African War.[98]

When Sanger was called as a witness before the Select Committee on the Uniforms Bill in 1893, he testified that he dressed his performers—including British ex-servicemen, mostly 'old soldiers'—in uniforms 'of all nations.' Sanger further explained that he recruited soldiers in garrison towns to appear in his shows, some of whom performed regularly.[99] The employment of soldiers and the use of military dress in theatrical productions was not unusual; yet as early as the first half of the nineteenth century, some units forbade their soldiers from performing on stage in original uniform, possibly fearing, as Scott H. Myerly suggests, that the British army might be ridiculed.[100] By the end of the nineteenth century, however, these performances were highly popular among civilians and soldiers alike. According to Sanger, a large portion of the audience consisted of soldiers who did not object to the performances—'quite the reverse', Sanger stated, giving an example of 'a young fellow who was so affected when he saw [a] scene that he fainted away.'[101] Yet the costumes in these theatrical productions, which partly accounted for their popularity, were increasingly objected to by the military authorities, for whom the reuse or imitation of military dress posed a threat to the image of the British soldier and the army. While examining witnesses, members of the Select Committee on the Uniforms Bill voiced concerns about performers dressed as 'pseudo-soldiers ... doing ridiculous or base actions' such as 'picking pockets or ... running from the enemy'.[102]

However, the potential ridicule of soldiers and the British army in theatrical productions and re-enactments only partly accounted for the military authorities' heavy objections to the reuse (or imitation) of British military dress in such performances. Redvers H. Buller, who recalled having seen 'occasions when the original uniform [had] been worn on stage, or, at all events, an exact imitation', repeatedly and firmly stated his disapproval of the use of British military dress in these contexts.[103] His objections appear more comprehensible when considered alongside his argument against the reuse or imitation of British military dress by non-military bands: 'Why', Buller asked rhetorically,

97 Sanger, *Seventy Years as a Showman*, 245–6.

98 See, for example, the programme for George Sanger's 'Royal Circus', *c.*1900, NFCA, University of Sheffield at [https://cdm15847.contentdm.oclc.org/digital/collection/p15847coll3/id/79328/rec/1], accessed 24 Nov. 2025.

99 *Report ... on the Uniforms Bill*, 22–4, Ev 392–424, at 22–3, Ev 392–98.

100 See Myerly, *British Military Spectacle*, 144.

101 *Report ... on the Uniforms Bill*, 24, Ev 437. On the popularity of circuses, see Assael, *The Circus and Victorian Society*.

102 *Report ... on the Uniforms Bill*, 24, Ev 439–40.

103 Ibid. 5, Ev 80. See also ibid. 5, Ev 81 and 7, Ev 108.

> does a man wear a uniform? He must have some reason for putting on an imitation uniform. He believes he will gain something by it ... I would think if a country band copied our uniform it would be because they wanted to be taken by the country bumpkins for the band whose dress they copied ... I believe they only put on that uniform because they believe it will increase in some way the value of their band.[104]

Buller further specified that he objected not to 'their wearing *a* uniform but to wearing *the* uniform of a particular corps.'[105] In Buller's opinion, by 'assuming the appearance of any particular corps of the Army' through the wearing of military dress, civilians were unjustly appropriating values that the army endeavoured to convey to its soldiers.[106]

When the Uniforms Act was eventually passed in March 1894, it restricted the unauthorized wearing of naval and military uniforms 'for any person not serving in Her Majesty's Naval or Military Forces'.[107] Aimed at prohibiting the adoption and appropriation of military dress by civilians, the legislation appears to have had the desired effect on advertising practices in the decades that followed.[108] However, as the introductory example of reused German military dress indicates, it did not prohibit the appropriation and adoption of foreign military and other uniforms for advertising purposes—an omission that was initially considered an advantage in light of the continuous civilian demand for second-hand military dress. During the sittings of the Select Committee on the Uniforms Bill in 1893, sandwich-board men were apparently 'parading' in several locations of the city 'wearing the Dutch uniform'. According to one committee member, 'cast-off uniforms of Dutch soldiers [were] put on the market without any restrictions [and found] their way to the Strand and to those other places in London.' Representatives of the British army such as Redvers A. Buller seemed pleased to hear about the apparently unrestricted imports of Dutch second-hand military uniforms to Britain, as this would, in his opinion, 'relieve the request for [British] uniforms.'[109]

The legislation also failed to end the domestic circulation of British second-hand military uniforms and articles of clothing in all non-military or semi-military contexts. Military dress continued to be reused in public entertainment despite the restrictions of the Uniforms Act. The Royal Agricultural Hall in Islington, for instance, hosted two events in 1896 and 1899—a 'World's Fair' and an exhibition by the Salvation Army—that were reported, by Metropolitan Police officers and civilians, to have involved the illicit wearing or misuse of British military and

104 Ibid. 86, Ev 56. See also ibid. 4–6, Ev 96.
105 Ibid. 4, Ev 56.
106 Ibid. 5, Ev 71.
107 *Uniforms Act 1894*, 1–2.
108 See Stearn, '"To Rid the Army of a Scandal"', particularly 230.
109 *Report ... on the Uniforms Bill*, 8, Ev 126–30.

semi-military uniforms. At the 'World's Fair' exhibition, one performance reportedly included two mounted men dressed in clothing resembling the official uniforms of the British Household Cavalry. Furthermore, at two stalls in the hall gallery, visitors could win an orange or a cigar for successfully knocking back dummy figures—dressed in 'an old red army tunic ... a soldier's tunic, and ... [a] policeman's tunic'—with a ball. According to police reports, most attendees enjoyed the performances and readily participated in the entertainments; however, at least one visitor was 'surprised and disgusted to see Her Majesty's Uniform, held up to ridicule'.[110] Opinions on the adoption and appropriation of British military dress in civilian contexts continued to be divided. Perceived by some (particularly the military authorities) as a contestation of the values that military dress had come to symbolize, the exertion of control over consumer demand had clear limits not only domestically but also—due to the internationalization of the trade in British second-hand military dress—most notably, abroad.[111]

1.3 The British Army and the Second-Hand Military Clothing Trade, *c.*1880–1895

In a short reference in his autobiography *Letters to Somebody*, published in 1922, Guy D. A. Fleetwood Wilson described the five years he held the position as Director of Clothing in the Royal Army Clothing Department between 1893 and 1899 as very positive, referring in particular to his 'relations with the hundreds of men of the Inspection and store branches and the women of the factory' as 'more than cordial' and 'affectionate'.[112] Writing to his soon-to-be predecessor George D. Ramsay, Fleetwood Wilson expressed appreciation of Ramsay's 'kindness ... in the various pour parlers which have taken place in regard to the Directorship.' He assumed that as the prospective Director of Clothing he had 'a difficult task before' him that would 'require all the help and advice which [Ramsay] alone [could] give.'[113] When Fleetwood Wilson joined the department in 1893, some questions relating to the disposal of soldiers' and officers' worn-out clothing were —for neither the first nor last time—left unanswered. 'Almost since I first went to the War Office,' Fleetwood Wilson stated in 1893, the issue of British second-hand military uniforms had 'been more or less prominently before the Department, and ... before me since I have been Director of Clothing ... It has frequently

110 TNA, MEPO 2/351.

111 On the domestic consumption of British second-hand military clothing during the twentieth century, see Ugolini, 'The Illicit Consumption of Military Uniforms in Britain, 1914–1918'; Langkjær, '"Then How Do You Explain Sgt. Pompous and the Fancy Pants Club Band?"' See also chapter 2.

112 Fleetwood Wilson, *Letters to Somebody*, 73.

113 BL, Ramsay Papers, Add MS 46450, fols. 237–41.

cropped up in the course of ordinary official work ... and ... it certainly has appeared to me to be distinctly a serious grievance.'[114]

Reducing the amount of worn-out items of military clothing that soldiers were allowed to dispose of—however much both commanding officers and soldiers disliked and objected to this—and restricting their resale were merely two facets of the issue Fleetwood Wilson was referring to. Prompted by the reuse of British army dress outside military contexts, which the authorities saw as a contestation of the symbolic values of British army clothing (and, by extension, the British army and its soldiers), the internal changes to the clothing system and the introduction of restrictive legislation were meant to prohibit and discourage the reuse of British military dress. In consequence, the British army was faced with the accumulation of vast amounts of worn-out clothing. Storage capacities were limited, and conditions unfavourable to the long-term storage of textile goods. In 1887, a lieutenant general described how he had been to the 'large stores ... and seen this clothing stacked out in a terrible state'[115]—an observation that is echoed in reports relating to the general condition of Woolwich Ordnance Stores and Stores Accounts, investigated in 1888 and found to be 'in a most unsatisfactory state,' particularly the 'returned stores section at the Dockyard ... both as regards storekeeping ... [and] accounting.' The storerooms were apparently 'so constructed that it [was] almost impossible for a storeholder or foreman to look after the condition of the stores properly.'[116] The Financial Secretary of the War Department confirmed the lack of facilities 'where used clothing [could] be stored. To construct them and to appoint the necessary storekeepers', he further stated, 'would involve heavy expense.'[117] Finally, limited storage affected the Army Contracts Department's sales practices in the so-called 'condemned store', which held damaged, rejected, and replaced military equipment. In 1882, Director of the Army Contracts Department Ethan C. Nepean, who organized and supervised sales of army stores, had drawn attention to the limited storage capacity of the condemned store that was 'constantly being filled up with old bedding, serge cuttings', which needed 'to be got rid of quickly as the place would overflow.' Finally, limited storage space was given as the main reason for 'the necessity for Monthly

114 *Report ... on the Uniforms Bill*, 9–10, Ev 162–4.

115 *Fourth Report and Special Report ... on Army and Navy Estimates*, 7, Ev 5212.

116 TNA WO 33/2870, *Report of a War Office Departmental Committee in 1888 on the Woolwich Ordnance Stores and Store Accounts* (H & S, 1797), 5–8.

117 Hansard, House of Commons, 26 Apr. 1888, vol. 325, c. 586. Many Ordnance Store stations (in, for example, Dover, Chester, Montpellier Hill, Tynemouth, and Haulbowline) reported in 1886 that their storehouses were 'crowded' and 'insufficient'. TNA WO 33/2870, *Report of a War Office Departmental Committee in 1888 on the Woolwich Ordnance Stores and Store Accounts* (H & S, 1797), App. X, 54–5.

sales at which the same articles are put time after time and ... sold whether the Market [was] overstocked or not.'[118]

In its role as the sole producer, and by restricting the resale of large amounts of second-hand military clothing, the British army had monopolized the wholesale trade. In this unique position, army officials significantly influenced the distribution of British second-hand military clothing from the early 1880s onwards by gradually replacing auction sales with sales by tender. Local auction houses had been selling stores on behalf of the British government and the Army Contracts Department since at least the early 1870s. The firm of *Messrs. Fuller and Horsey*, for example, frequently sold 'old stores at various dockyards, obsolete stores and old machinery ... old furniture, old china, glass, and such articles'[119] as well as 'some police ... and hospital clothing'.[120] In addition, obsolete and unserviceable army stores, including worn-out military clothing, were put up for auction by representatives of the Army Contracts Department at Woolwich and Pimlico on a regular basis. The employment of local auctioneers by the Army Contracts Department speaks to the need for prerequisite knowledge of local second-hand clothing markets and commodities: auctioneering, army authorities argued, required considerable, highly specialized knowledge of second-hand commodity markets, experience, a certain standing within the community, and (since the auctioneer could potentially increase his salary with the commission he earned by sales) trustworthiness.[121] The difficulty of finding a suitable auctioneer for sales of worn-out military clothing became evident when the department's 'auctioneer Mr. Spillman who had been employed for many years and who advised the Commissary General' in auction sales, passed away in 1878. His successor, it turned out in 1882, was 'not the best man that could be found' for the job. While he was considered 'a very respectable young man', his performance led the Director of Contracts to assume that the auctioneer 'had never held an auction sale'. Army officials subsequently complained that unlike the Admiralty and the India Office they had failed to 'employ a high class competent auctioneer', 'a good ... London man well acquainted with markets.' The unpopular auctioneer's contract was eventually terminated in 1882 and an 'efficient auctioneer' appointed shortly afterwards, whose advice would, the Director of Contracts stated confidently, 'be useful in finding markets and conducting auction sales.'[122]

While the appointed auctioneer played a major part in the favourable outcomes in sales of second-hand military clothing, the military authorities' percep-

118 TNA, WO 32/7039.

119 *Report from the Select Committee on Public Departments*, 1873, 139, Ev 3005.

120 Ibid. 140, Ev 3029. Messrs. Fuller and Horsey continued to auction for the Admiralty at least until the early 1900s. See TNA, WO 32/7039; TNA WO 32/9118.

121 See TNA, WO 32/7039.

122 TNA, WO 33/42, *Report of the Director of Army Contracts for the Year Ended 31st December 1883* ([A13] – 15WO), 21.

tion was that the auction sales were rigged, and were failing to deliver the anticipated profits. Nepean accused participants of practices of 'combination' (better known as the 'ring') and 'knockout' at the 'Condemned Store' where the sales took place.[123] These practices are particularly well documented for sales of damaged goods by the East India Company in eighteenth- and nineteenth-century British antique and curiosity markets: a 'combination' or 'ring' involved a group of dealers who agreed not to bid against one another prior to an auction sale. Commodities were thus purchased by one dealer without competition and could be re-auctioned in the so-called 'knockout', a private auction held by dealers after the public auction sale had been concluded. The price difference between the private and public auctions was afterwards distributed among the dealers. Although these auction practices were not illegal during the eighteenth and nineteenth centuries, public criticism was increasing considerably by the 1860s.[124]

According to Nepean, auction sales of 'condemned' army stores were attended predominantly by Jewish second-hand dealers who bought 'Old Clothes [and] other Pimlico Stores from [him] ... and as the Jews' combination and knock out [was] well known there [was] little inducement for an outsider to go there to bid.' Nepean further noted that he thought it 'well to make the Jews hunger for articles which they [had] bought ... at low prices for years. Such as Bluff and never sell too many of the same things at once.'[125] Jewish dealers dominated London's second-hand clothing wholesale and retail trade throughout the nineteenth century, and were apparently perceived by the military authorities as an organized community. Similar accusations had been common throughout the century (and beyond); however, as Ole Münch points out, these cartel-like practices were less organized and stable than contemporaries assumed. While ethnic solidarity was frequently sought out by dealers who participated in auction sales, the auction was itself a site of contestation that did not necessarily lead to agreement between the participants.[126] Nepean's observations are thus rather a reflection of the conspiracy-minded antisemitic sentiments that dominated the contemporary discourse on Jewish second-hand clothing dealers.[127] At the same time, however, the Director of Contracts was very clear about the Army Contracts Department's dependency on its business relations with Jewish second-hand clothing dealers:

---

123 TNA, WO 32/7039. In 1874, army personnel had already complained that 'a combination frequently exists among the buyers' at auction sales in Woolwich; see *Report from the Select Committee on Public Departments*, 1874, Rep., p. v.

124 See Westgarth, *The Emergence of the Antique and Curiosity Dealer in Britain, 1815–c.1850*, 140–1; Westgarth, 'The Auction Ring'. Regarding eighteenth- and early-nineteenth-century auction sales of second-hand clothing and damaged goods, see also Münch, *Cutler Street Market*, 111–14; Yogev, *Diamonds and Coral*, 74–6.

125 TNA, WO 32/7039.

126 See Münch, *Cutler Street Market*, 111–14.

127 See, for example, Mendelsohn, *The Rag Race*, 117–18.

'This trade is really in the hands of the Jews, and they alone can make a profit out of it, or can combine to hold stock in bad times.'[128]

Still, these disputed auction practices ultimately led the Army Contracts Department to gradually withdraw worn-out military clothing from auction sales and instead sell it by system of tender. Selling by tender was thought of as 'a method of selling by auction' but differed distinctively: in many cases, it seems, calls for tenders were not advertised publicly but were sent to selected firms only, who then submitted their offers individually.[129] Since at least the early 1870s, and increasingly after the changes in the clothing regulations in 1881, the Army Contracts Department appointed government contractors who had tendered for and —after securing the contract—bought worn-out military clothing in bulk at fixed prices one to three years in advance. Nepean recognized that this change in sales practices would not suppress the practice of 'combination', since agreements between dealers prior to their offers were still possible and likely. However, in his opinion, while Jewish dealers could allegedly 'combine by tender as well as by auction', the system of tendering at least enabled 'outsiders to make offers without the fear of a knock out.'[130] Sales by tender enabled the Director of Contracts to select potential buyers, compare offers, and withdraw when expectations were not met. In addition, they did not require an auctioneer, thus sparing the army the costs of the auctioneer's salary and commission. Overall, army officials hoped to increase the profits by undermining the dealer-dominated determination and stabilization of pricing that characterized auction sales at that time.[131]

While sales by tender did not fully replace auction sales of worn-out military clothing, the former were increasingly favoured and used by the Army Contracts Department from the early 1880s. Based on records that offer quantitative data on sales of worn-out military clothing in the 1880s and 1890s, it remains questionable whether sales by tender were indeed more profitable. In 1884, the amount realized through the sale of clothing had doubled in comparison with previous years from about £ 30,183 in 1882 to £ 61,778.[132] However, this increase appears not to have been a direct result of more profitable sales in general. On the contrary: as Nepean noted in the *Report of the Director of Army Contracts* in 1884, 'the contract ... that [had] caused the greatest amount of trouble, [was] that for the sale of old clothes and boots at home and abroad ... The market still continues a bad

128 TNA, WO 33/42, *Report of the Director of Army Contracts for the Year Ended 31st December 1883* (1884, [A13] – 15wo), 13–14.

129 *Second Report from the Committee of Public Accounts*, 34–5, Ev 624.

130 TNA, WO 32/7039.

131 See, for example, ibid. and Westgarth, who draws on Charles W. Smith's observation that in 'dealer-dominated auctions, collective judgements are the most important factors determining value.' Smith, *Auctions*, 166–79 at 166; Westgarth, *The Emergence of the Antique and Curiosity Dealer in Britain, 1815–c.1850*, 139–40 at 139.

132 See *Army Appropriation Account, 1881–82*, 182; *Army Appropriation Account, 1883–84*, 11.

one'.[133] Rather, the sudden increase, it seems, was related to the changes in the clothing regulations and accounting methods: until the early 1880s, the *Army Estimates* and the *Army Appropriation Accounts* listed expected and realized profits of clothing sales based on the so-called 'exchequer' (extra) receipts, which did not include auction sales.[134] According to the Director of Artillery and Contracts, up to the early 1880s auction sales had been 'practically uncontrolled', 'never reviewed at all', and had remained undocumented by the Army Contracts Department.[135] Profits realized through auction sales appear to have been included in the Army Estimates between 1882 and 1894. From the mid 1890s, the sales by tender in the *Reports of the Director of Army Contracts* were once again listed 'as distinct from the usual auction sales'.[136] These changes might explain why the amounts realized through the sale of clothing increased from a yearly average of £ 25,000 (1873–82) to £ 55,000 (1883–94), and decreased again to an average of £ 25,000 per year (1895–9).[137]

Apart from the disputable profitability, contemporaries such as commanding officers appear to have nevertheless favoured the tender-based contractor system: when the system of disposal of worn-out military clothing was once again addressed in 1892 in the context of a broader internal review of the terms and conditions of army service, some commanding officers voiced their support, arguing that 'in making a large contract a higher price [could] be obtained than by calling two or three Jews into a barrack yard and selling the clothing to them.'[138] At the

133 TNA, WO 33/42, *Report of the Director of Army Contracts for the Year Ended 31st December 1883* (1884, [A13] – 15wo), 9.

134 See, for example, the 'Statement of Sums Passed to the Credit of Her Majesty's Exchequer in the Books of the War Office, Vote 3: Proceeds of Old Clothing, Great-coats, Cuttings, Stoppages for Prison Necessaries, &c. and Votes 12 & 13: Proceeds of Old Stores', in *Army Estimates of Effective and Non-Effective Services, for 1870–1*, 128; TNA, WO 32/7039. The estimates were reviewed and compared with sales in the *Army Appropriation Accounts*, where significant deviations were commented on. See, for example, the 'Statement showing the Difference between the Amounts Estimated and those realised on account of the Exchequer Extra Receipts during the Year Ended 31st March 1882', in *Army Appropriation Account, 1881–82*, 184–5, where a deficit was explained with the comment that the 'amount realised for Old Clothing was less than was anticipated.' Ibid. 185. Regarding quantitative and quantifiable data on second-hand (army) clothing in the late nineteenth and early twentieth century in general, see the introduction.

135 TNA, WO 32/7039.

136 TNA, WO 395/1, *Report of the Director of Army Contracts for the Year Ended 31st December 1894* (1895, [B134] – 323wo), 26.

137 See, for example, *Army Estimates of Effective and Non-Effective Services, for 1873–74*, 120; *Army Estimates of Effective and Non-Effective Services, for 1881–82*, 136; *Army Estimates of Effective and Non-Effective Services, for 1882–83*, 132; *Army Estimates of Effective and Non-Effective Services, for 1895–96*, 52.

138 *Report of the Committee … to Consider the Terms and Conditions of Service in the Army*, 424, Ev 12471.

same time, sales by tender and to contractors increased the Army Contracts Department's expenditure on evaluation and on communication with (potential) contractors. Records suggest that between 1880 and the mid 1890s the Army Contracts Department was keen to reduce the number of contractors tendering for used textile goods in general by, for example, combining contracts for old boots and old clothing in order to reduce the amount of correspondence with contractors and other departments:[139] 'Over and above', Nepean stated in 1890, by reducing the number of contractors to a minimum 'the money saving there is a saving of clerical labour'.[140]

The Army Contracts Department's increased preference for selling second-hand military clothing by tender did not go unchallenged. According to MP Robert W. Hanbury, the system of tendering employed by the Director of Contracts—and particularly sales of large quantities of worn-out military dress—curbed free competition, gradually excluded small second-hand clothing dealers, and encouraged speculation.[141] In his accusations against the Army Contracts Department in 1889, Hanbury touched upon a wide range of topics related to the system for disposing of worn-out military clothing, including the quality of the clothing sold, army contractors, and competition. He read out several letters to MPs in parliament, in which his 'constituents' had reported that the quality of the second-hand uniforms they had bought on different occasions suggested that the articles of clothing were 'nearly new' or 'had never been used at all'. In Hanbury's view, the quality of the clothing did not correspond with the low prices they were sold for by the officials of the Army Contracts Department: 'These things', Hanbury claimed, 'are being sold for a mere song.'[142] Hanbury's criticism of what he considered 'speculative sales' on the part of the Army Contracts Department was certainly not unjustified:[143] the accumulated worn-out military clothing tendered for by potential contractors was characterized by a high degree of quality uncertainty, and the contracts specified neither the exact quantity nor the quality the contractors could expect. Contractors were obliged to collect worn-out clothing regardless of its material condition: 'It must be clearly understood', a contract dated July 1900 specified, 'that the articles, whether incomplete, damaged by moth, age, active service, or other causes, or should they be in an exceptionally bad condition, must be taken as they lie. Claims for allowances or compensation on these grounds will not be recognized.'[144]

---

139 See TNA, WO 33/38, *Report of the Director of Army Contracts for the Year Ended 31st December 1881* (1882 – H & S – [85]27wo), 13.

140 TNA, WO 395/1, *Report of the Director of Army Contracts for the Years Ended 31st December 1889 and 1890* ([B483] – 675wo), 18.

141 See Hansard, House of Commons, 21 June 1889, vol. 337, cc. 455–64.

142 Ibid. cc. 455–64 at cc. 459–60.

143 Hansard, House of Commons, 20 Mar. 1888, vol. 323, cc. 1785–6 at c. 1785.

144 TNA, WO 32/9118.

Following Hanbury's criticism of the Army Contracts Department, Nepean used 'the opportunity in 1889 and 1890 of testing the value of Mr. Hanbury's views to the mode of disposing of old stores and worn-out military clothing.' The Director of Contracts issued tenders for the purchase of condemned army clothing and announced that firms could 'offer for the whole, for one description of garment only, or for a portion only of a lot.' Small buyers were thus given the opportunity to participate but remained unsuccessful: 'The smaller firms did not offer such good terms as the others for the small lots. It is of course our business', Nepean explained, 'to make the best terms we possibly can for the public, and not to consider small buyers.'[145] In addition to favouring dealers who were able to tender for large quantities, the number of potential contractors was reduced by the restrictions that second-hand military clothing could only be sold abroad on specific markets: according to the Director of Contracts, since at least the early 1880s, government contractors were not allowed to sell British second-hand military clothing 'in the United Kingdom, British North America, Egypt, and Ceylon'.[146] While the circumstances under which British army officials had decided upon these restrictions remain unclear, it is as noteworthy that army contractors frequently ignored them, particularly those connected with sales on British domestic markets: in 1893, for example, circus proprietor George Sanger stated that he received all second-hand uniforms he dressed his performers in locally from the army contractor for second-hand clothing.[147]

The restrictions imposed by the military authorities on the distribution of British second-hand military clothing appear to have effectively excluded the majority of domestic second-hand clothing dealers from participation in the trade. Firms and dealers with established transnational trading networks and connections to specific overseas markets were instead favoured by officials within the Army Contracts Department. Consequently, between 1880 and the early twentieth century, the appointment of contractors to undertake the resale of British second-hand military clothing was marked by a notable degree of continuity. During this period, two firms, namely Samuel Moses & Sons, Ltd. and Mallett, Porter & Dowd, Ltd., obtained contracts regularly and in many cases alternately: in 1890, the former entered into the contract for the purchase of second-hand army boots but partially lost the contract for second-hand military clothing to the latter.[148] The firms competed for the same contracts again in 1893, when 'the best offers were offered by Messrs. Moses & Sons, who retained the home contract … and

145 TNA, WO 395/1, *Report of the Director of Army Contracts for the Years Ended 31st December 1889 and 1890* ([B483] – 675wo), 18.

146 *Army: Return to an Address of the Honourable The House of Commons, dated 10 July 1889;—for, Copies 'of Departmental Minutes Relative to the Army Contracts Department*', 4.

147 See *Report … on the Uniforms Bill*, 10, Ev 170.

148 TNA, WO 395/1, *Report of the Director of Army Contracts for the Years Ended 31st December 1889 and 1890* ([B483] – 675wo), 18.

secured the foreign contract previously held by Messrs. Mallett, Porter & Dowd, at the latter firm's price.'[149] Between July 1905 and June 1906, Mallett, Porter & Dowd, Ltd. advertised their appointment as 'Contractors to His Majesty's Government for the Purchase of Condemned Army Clothing' in trade journals such as *The British and South African Export Gazette*, offering 'every description of second-hand Civilian, Railway, Volunteer, Police, and Army Clothing' (Fig. 1.6). Finally, both firms continued to engage in the second-hand clothing trade well into the twentieth century; Mallett, Porter & Dowd, Ltd.'s history and involvement in the global trade in second-hand clothing and trade in second-hand military dress can be traced through to the 1960s.[150]

FIGURE 1.6 Advertisement by Mallett, Porter & Dowd, Ltd. (1905–6).

1.4 From the Workrooms to the Docks: Labour, Manufacturing, and Logistics in the British Second-Hand Clothing Sector, 1880s–1920s

Based on an interview with Norman Potts, the manager of a factory in Hirwaun—a village in South Wales near Aberdare—a newspaper article published in the *Western Mail* in 1956 reported a 'big demand for postmen's striped trousers and policemen's overcoats among natives in West Africa.' Inside the aforementioned factory, eighty women 'cleaned, dyed, and repaired' 'part-worn Government and

149 TNA, WO 395/1, *Report of the Director of Army Contracts for the Year Ended 31st December 1893* ([B26] – 41wo), 16.

150 See the investigation of the second-hand clothing trade by the Board of Trade in 1920, which lists Samuel Moses, Ltd. and Mallett, Porter & Dowd, Ltd. among the businesses that exported second-hand clothing to South Africa and India. TNA, LAB 2/668/TBD134/A/8/1920, *Second-Hand Clothing Summary Report,* Part A, 4th edn., 17–18.

civilian clothing': '"It is an amazing business," said Mr. Potts. Each week it turns out 5,000 garments—policemen's raincoats, Army gas caps, bus company uniforms—... looking like new ... "We have been in business for more than a century—and are doing very well"'. According to the anonymous author, the factory was 'the only Welsh branch of an old-established London firm Mallett, Porter and Dowd (exports), Ltd.' While the article claimed that by 1956 the firm had been dealing with second-hand clothing for an entire century, most traces of the firm's activities date from the early 1870s, when Mallett, Porter & Dowd, Ltd. relocated to their newly constructed warehouse at 465 Caledonian Road in Islington, London.[151] Shortly afterwards, the business owners and their company were listed in trade directories as contractors 'for army, naval and civil cloth cuttings [and] wholesale mungo merchants.'[152] Between 1877 and 1912, they were referred to as 'horse hair manufacturers',[153] as 'general merchants',[154] and as 'shippers & government contractors & band outfitters (shippers & warehousemen supplied with every description of army, police, railway & civilian clothing), dealers in woollen & cotton cuttings, rag & general merchants'.[155]

The varying commercial descriptions in the directories illustrate the diverse branches in the reuse of textile remnants that the firm engaged in—often simultaneously—over multiple decades: until 1901, Robert Porter and an associate led a 'business as Mattress and Bedding Manufacturers at Holcombe Mills ... under the ... firm of Mallett, Porter and Dowd' in Nailsworth, an area in Gloucestershire known for its woollen cloth industry, textile and water mills, and the manufacture of flock and shoddy as mattress fillings from (woollen) rags.[156] As band outfitters and shortly after the introduction of the Uniforms Act in 1894, Mallett, Porter & Dowd, Ltd. advertised 'uniforms in accordance with Act of Parliament', 'new and second-hand, at lowest possible prices'. An advertisement in the journal *The Kinematograph and Lantern Weekly*, published in 1912, suggests that the firm continued to supply new and second-hand uniforms in the performative arts.[157] Finally, as frequent army contractors, the firm's directors and managers regularly obtained British second-hand military clothing. The scale and variety of the firm's operations were reflected in the composition of its workforce. Records suggest that between 1879 and 1920, Mallett, Porter & Dowd, Ltd. employed (wool) cut-

151 *Western Mail*, 26978 (30 Jan. 1956), 33.

152 *The Islington Directory for 1874*, 570.

153 *The Islington Directory for 1883*, 761.

154 *The Islington Directory for 1894*, 762.

155 *The Post Office London Directory for 1912*, 1072.

156 *The London Gazette* (15 Jan. 1901), 341. See Mills, 'The Origins, Development, Decline and Reuse of Cloth Mills of the Stroud Valleys of Gloucestershire'. On the emergence of the shoddy industry during the nineteenth century, see, for example, Shell, *Shoddy*, 19–60.

157 *Wright and Round's Brass Band News*, 181 (1 Oct. 1896), [n. p.]; *The Kinematograph and Lantern Weekly*, 11/281 (12 Sept. 1912), 1435.

ters, sorters, and packers at its different establishments, including the Holcombe Mills in Nailsworth.[158] Notably, the facilities in Islington appear to have contained workrooms predominantly for the processing of second-hand clothing. According to a short newspaper article on the outbreak of a fire on the firm's premises in Caledonian Road in 1904, Mallett, Porter & Dowd, Ltd. employed approximately 200 workers, who sorted through, altered, and repaired items of second-hand clothing, including British and foreign military dress.[159]

The emergent second-hand clothing sector in late-nineteenth-century Britain both overlapped with and diverged from other textile-related industries, occupying a liminal position within the broader textile and clothing economy, and distinct even from similar branches that relied on textile remnants such as (woollen) rags for the manufacture of shoddy, mungo, or paper. Labour conditions in the workrooms of businesses engaged in the second-hand clothing trade closely resemble those of the contemporaneously much discussed and criticized 'sweated labour',[160] yet in certain aspects appear to have been more adverse. In the *First Report from the Select Committee on the Sweating System*, which was based on a commission sparked by independent inquiries into the British clothing industry conducted by *The Lancet* in 1876 and 1886–7, Morris Stephany—Secretary of the Jewish Board of Guardians—testified that while he had not witnessed many cases in which insufficient living wages were paid in the textile trades, 'there are some persons who … are employed in what is termed the second-hand clothing, and that work is paid very badly. They make up from second-hand garments; they are remade; the Government stores are bought up, and the clothing is remade. In that part of the trade the wages are very low indeed.' Stephany argued that wages and labour costs in the second-hand clothing sector were particularly low 'because the things [were] sold much cheaper' and the work required was 'less

158 The demand for tailors' woollen and cotton cuttings for the mills in Nailsworth was occasionally advertised in the newspaper *The Tailor & Cutter*. See, for example, *The Tailor & Cutter*, 19/908 (28 Feb. 1884), 20; *The Tailor & Cutter*, 32/1580 (14 Jan. 1897), 23. According to another newspaper article, a young man was prosecuted in February 1879 for 'stealing from the warehouse of his employers, Messrs. Mallett, Porter, and Dowd … 23 lbs. of pieces of woollen cuttings, value 15s. It appears that the prisoner had been in the employ of the prosecutors for some years … For some time past small quantities of woollen cuttings had been missed … On Police-constable John Panther … going to the prisoner's house he found under the bed about 30 lbs. of cuttings.' *Islington Gazette*, 2002 (28 Feb. 1879), 3. Regarding the employment of sorters and packers in the second-hand clothing trade, see also TNA, LAB 2/668/TBD134/A/8/1920.

159 See *Daily Mirror*, 336 (30 Nov. 1904), 4.

160 For an overview on the literature on 'sweated labour' in homes, workshops, and in factories, see Blackburn, '"Between the Devil of Cheap Labour Competition and the Deep Sea of Family Poverty?"'; Blackburn, *A Fair Day's Wage for a Fair Day's Work?*. For a historical analysis with a focus on health and safety risks and reference to contemporary textile industries, see Gregson and Quinlan, 'Subcontracting and Low Pay Kill'.

skilled' than in the tailoring and garment-making industries.[161] The large-scale investigations of the British 'sweating system' between *c.*1880 and the mid 1890s confirmed the initial findings of the inquiries by *The Lancet*, underscoring the abject poverty of employed workers, the low wages, and the unsanitary and partially dangerous working conditions. These findings continued to be echoed well into the twentieth century in the *Annual Reports of the Chief Inspector of Factories and Workshops*, which offer unique insights into the second-hand clothing and rag workrooms.

Businesses that engaged in industries based on textile remnants—woollen and cotton rags, textile cuttings and clippings—and second-hand clothing employed an above-average number of female workers from the poorest class.[162] In particular, an inspector noted in 1907 that the

> number of mothers of illegitimate children who work in these rag sorting workshops ha[d] been noted as remarkable ... The explanation undoubtedly is, that in the lowest class of such workshops the work is casual, 'hands' are taken on daily and paid a day's wage, no questions are asked, and no character is required.[163]

Business owners of rag-sorting and second-hand clothing workrooms seldom kept or disclosed employee records, and some of them knowingly contravened the provisions of the Factories and Workshop Act 1891, which prohibited, for example, the employment of women within four weeks after childbirth.[164] However, inspectors claimed that workers themselves occasionally tried to evade the regulation by changing employers shortly after childbirth or through false statements about their infants' age. Some inspectors argued that for women who were, at the same time, in highly precarious living circumstances—unmarried pregnant women, women in abusive marriages, or whose husbands were out of work—rag-sorting workshops were one of the few opportunities to earn a livelihood.[165] As Stephany noted, wages in the sector devoted to the processing and reuse of textile remnants and second-hand clothing were considerably lower than in other textile industries: on average, female rag-sorters earned between 7s. and 10s. per week in the 1890s—approximately half as much as female employees in, for example, steam laundries.[166] In addition, irregular employment and working hours were

---

161 *First Report from the Select Committee on the Sweating System*, 20–1, Ev 225–32.

162 See *The Employment of Women*, 295.

163 *Annual Report of the Chief Inspector of Factories and Workshops for the Year 1907*, 186.

164 See ibid. and *Factories and Workshop Act 1891*, 18.

165 See, for example, *Annual Report of the Chief Inspector of Factories and Workshops for the Year 1905*, 321; *Annual Report of the Chief Inspector of Factories and Workshops for the Year 1907*, 186; *Annual Report of the Chief Inspector of Factories and Workshops for the Year 1911*, 158.

166 Wages differed depending on the sector and tended to be lower in urban centres: in paper mills, female rag-sorters and -pickers earned up to 2s./day, while the average wage for rag-sorters in the shoddy and flock manufacture in the west of England was 7s. 6d./week. Female

common in rag and second-hand clothing workrooms, and the sector experienced seasonal fluctuations such as were common in, for example, the fur trade. Employees regularly worked overtime and on rest days during busy seasons, while rag-sorters, for example, simultaneously complained about periods of 'occasional slack time' during which they were laid off.[167] Finally, a factory inspector reported in 1911 that in a 'large firm of second-hand clothing [in East London] repairers were detected in the employment of Christian workers on Saturdays and Jewish workers on Sundays.'[168]

Unsanitary and hazardous working conditions in the manufacture of paper from rags, for example, had already attracted the attention of the British medical authorities in the 1860s, but criticism rose considerably towards the end of the nineteenth century, when the potentially health-threatening properties of rags and second-hand clothing were discussed in the broader contexts of disease origin, spread, and transmission.[169] While Stephany confined his remarks on workers' health in the second-hand clothing sector to male workers operating pressers, arguing that they got 'into a bad state', the adverse health effects of sorting through textile remnants and second-hand clothing were a recurring theme in the *Annual Reports of the Chief Inspector of Factories and Workshops*. As inspectors frequently stressed, workroom and working conditions in those sectors of the textile industry that specialized in the processing of textile remnants and second-hand clothing were highly dependent on the materials' condition: tailors' textile cuttings and clippings, and rags or second-hand clothing that had been washed or disinfected prior to the sorting process produced less dust and left the air largely unpolluted.[170] In most cases, however, workers sorted through and repaired textiles that had not been cleaned or disinfected. When, for example, May E. Abraham 'visited a number of places where the three processes of sorting, picking, and carbonising [of rags] was carried on' in 1892, she reported that she 'found in most of them the atmosphere foul and loaded with dust': 'In one place ... the atmosphere was particularly offensive in a top room where French rags were being sorted. Immediately after my visit I was attacked by "shoddy fever", a complaint from which new hands suffer.' As pointed out by Abrahams, complaints by workers in rag-sorting factories in the 1890s centred around the dust and smell of for-

---

sorters in steam laundries received 12–18s./week. See *The Employment of Women*, 18, 143, and 295.

167 Ibid. 296. In addition, see *Annual Report of the Chief Inspector of Factories and Workshops for the Year 1911*, 18.

168 Ibid.

169 See, for example, *Illustrated Times*, 9/600 (15 Sept. 1866), 174. See also Shell, *Shoddy*, 109–58. On medical and public health discussions about second-hand clothing and rags from the 1860s onwards, see chapter 3.

170 See, for example, *Annual Report of the Chief Inspector of Factories and Workshops for the Year 1906*, 14.

eign rags in particular, which 'arrived in a filthy condition having been packed closely together, sometimes for over twelve months.'[171] Further reports on working conditions in wool-sorting and similar trades confirmed Abraham's observations, arguing that in addition to the possible transmission of diseases such as smallpox—outbreaks of which had been observed among rag-sorters—workers were particularly 'liable to intermittent attacks of "shoddy fever" or "flock fever", evidently due to the inhalation of dust', with symptoms resembling those of influenza.[172]

Dust-laden air, combustible textile materials, overcrowding, and poor ventilation not only affected workers' health but increased the risk of fire substantially; these same conditions, contemporary accounts illustrate, partly account for the temperature extremes in the workrooms. In 1904, several newspaper articles reported that the facilities at Caledonian Road had been severely damaged by an outbreak of fire. Firemen found the three-story building 'well alight' when they arrived at the scene: the warehouse roof had burned down entirely.[173] Over the following decades, at least two more fires damaged the warehouse and other buildings owned by Mallett, Porter & Dowd, Ltd. where employees prepared 'old Army khaki tunics and uniforms for export to Africa and other British Colonies.'[174] Due to the fire risk and high insurance rates, businesses were reluctant to heat workrooms; inspectors frequently noted that even during winter months workrooms remained cold.[175] Simultaneously, compared to other industries—particularly non-textile enterprises—accident rates remained low in second-hand clothing workrooms, and the instances reported were highly exceptional in character: in 1904, a worker employed in a South Wales factory was severely injured when a cartridge in the pocket of a coat she was sorting through exploded.[176]

171 *The Employment of Women*, 100.

172 *Report of the Departmental Committee Appointed to Inquire into the Conditions of Work in Wool-Sorting and Other Kindred Trades*, 22–7.

173 *Daily News*, 18315 (30 Nov. 1904), 12. See also *Daily Mirror*, 336 (30 Nov. 1904), 4.

174 *East London Observer*, 3425 (27 Aug. 1927), 3. See also *Dundee Evening Telegraph* (13 Sept. 1934), 1.

175 In 1904, some paper mill owners in west London argued they could not 'heat the rag sorting rooms, for fear of fire.' *Annual Report of the Chief Inspector of Factories and Workshops for the Year 1904*, 10. See also *Annual Report of the Chief Inspector for Factories and Workshops for the Year 1905*, 296; *Annual Report of the Chief Inspector for Factories and Workshops for the Year 1906*, 200; *Annual Report of the Chief Inspector for Factories and Workshops for the Year 1907*, 89.

176 See *Annual Report of the Chief Inspector of Factories and Workshops for the Year 1904*, 65. See also, for example, the table of 'Accidents in Different Branches of Manufacture', in *Annual Report of the Chief Inspector of Factories and Workshops for the Year 1900*, 5. Accident rates were higher in factories and workrooms where certain steps in the preparation of woollen or cotton rags for the manufacture of paper and shoddy had been mechanized. Rag-cutting, -grinding, and -carbonizing, for example, had in some factories already been replaced by

Overall, the conditions in these workrooms barely improved in the early twentieth century. While some inspectors reported that the ventilation of workrooms in flock-making factories and paper mills and 'the proper use of screens' in rag-sorting workrooms had 'greatly improved' working conditions,[177] lack of ventilation and low temperatures remained the main source of workers' complaints. An inspector noted in 1909 that she had

> found [the] matter of ventilation ... a particularly hard one with which to deal ... In one Jewish workroom, where second-hand clothes were being repaired and renovated, I found 13 men and women working with every aperture closed, the gas having been lit till midday to heat the room, which, combined with the smell arising from the old clothes stacked in every available space, rendered the atmosphere almost unbreathable.[178]

Wages increased overall but remained low for sorters: in the context of the investigation of the second-hand clothing industry by the Board of Trade in 1920, a representative of Mallett, Porter & Dowd, Ltd. stated that female sorters employed by the firm earned half as much as male (un-)packers and porters (30–33s. vs. 60–80s. per week). In general, however, inspectors noted that 'information as to wages [had] been found to be most difficult to obtain', and while firms claimed to be paying better wages than fixed by The Bespoke Tailoring Trade Board, they did not provide access to books and figures.[179]

Although the working conditions in the second-hand clothing workrooms closely resembled those found in the rag-sorting branch of the trades in textile remnants, the second-hand clothing sector nonetheless occupied a distinct position within the industry, characterized mainly by its limited mechanization. The second-hand clothing sector shared the first preparatory step with other branches whose businesses engaged in the reuse of textile remnants, requiring workers to sort through textiles according to quality, colour, fabric, and other characteristics. The author of a handbook titled *The Art of Paper-Making* argued in 1890 that 'in sorting rags, a good deal of judgement and skill [was] required to avoid mixing the better qualities with those of an inferior class'.[180] Similarly, the bulk of second-hand military dress received through army contracts by Mallett, Porter &

---

machines that were 'fed' with textile remnants by a worker, a process that occasionally led to burn injuries. *Annual Report of the Chief Inspector of Factories and Workshops for the Year 1911*, 180. See also the number of accidents involving rag grinding and -cutting machines in *Annual Report of the Chief Inspector for Factories and Workshops for the Year 1900*, 255–6.

177 *Annual Report of the Chief Inspector of Factories and Workshops for the Year 1909*, 7. See *Annual Report of the Chief Inspector of Factories and Workshops for the Year 1906*, 14–15; *Annual Report of the Chief Inspector of Factories and Workshops for the Year 1907*, 10, 89, 116, and 202.

178 *Annual Report of the Chief Inspector of Factories and Workshops for the Year 1909*, 130–1.

179 TNA, LAB 2/668/TBD134/A/8/1920.

180 Watt, *The Art of Paper-Making*, 19.

Dowd, Ltd. was characterized by its quality uncertainty, and skills were required in order to judge which of the articles of clothing should be repaired, altered, and resold. During the nineteenth century, however, most subsequent manual processing steps in the manufacture of paper from rags were gradually mechanized. Rag-dusting machines (so-called 'dusters' or 'shakers'), which removed dirt and dust (Fig. 1.7) appear to have been operated in some businesses in the 1890s and were considered particularly effective and beneficial to workers' health, potentially decreasing the amount of dust in the workrooms' atmosphere.[181] In addition to the recommendation of 'suitable means, mechanical or otherwise ... for minimising the production of dust', a report on the working conditions in the woolsorting trades advised all rags to be washed or 'shaken' prior to preparatory processes of sorting, tearing, or grinding.[182] In practice, however, rag-dusting machines do not appear to have been used regularly, and if they were, it was predominantly after the first sorting process, rendering their potential benefit to workers' health ineffective but increasing the volume of processed materials.[183] Processing steps such as rag-cutting, -grinding, and -carbonizing (used to, for example, decompose organic matter in woollen rags), however, were replaced by machinery. For example, in addition to a drying stove and looms, the facilities of Mallett, Porter & Dowd, Ltd. at the Holcombe Mills in Nailsworth, where (woollen) rags were processed for mattress fillings, were equipped with a carbonizer and tearing machines (used to tear up woollen rags).[184] In the case of the workrooms in Caledonian Road and other facilities, there are no indications that machinery was implemented. Just as the preparatory step of sorting through sec-

181 'The cylinder of this machine, which is conical in form, to enable the rags to travel from one end to the other, whence they are ejected, revolves, as also does a second cylinder of a skeleton form, but in opposite direction. Each cylinder is fitted with knives, or spikes—those of the outer cylinder projecting towards the centre; the knives of the centre cylinder being attached to its exterior surface: when the machine is in motion the two sets of blades pass each other so that when the rags come between them the action is that of scissors. When the rags are ejected at the end of the cylinder, they pass into another cylinder of wire, through which the dust falls and leaves them in a fairly clean condition'. Watt, *The Art of Paper-Making*, 26–7. See also Magee, *Productivity and Performance in the Paper Industry*, 183.

182 *Report of the Departmental Committee Appointed to Inquire into the Conditions of Work in Wool-Sorting and Other Kindred Trades*, 22–7.

183 *Annual Report of the Chief Inspector of Factories and Workshops for the Year 1904*, 15. See also *The Employment of Women*, 100 and, in addition, the summary of the court case Paterson v. Hunt: 'Only an exceedingly small proportion of the respondent's rags are passed through the "shaker"; which is not ordinarily at work, but is used only intermittently and at considerable intervals. The last occasion before the hearing when it was used was two months back.' *Annual Report of the Chief Inspector of Factories and Workshops for the Year 1909*, 221–2.

184 Regarding the equipment at the Holcombe Mills, see the notice of the auction sale of the premises in the newspaper *Gloucestershire Echo*, 28 (5 Dec. 1900), 2. On mechanization in the manufacture of paper, mungo, and shoddy, see Magee, *Productivity and Performance in the Paper Industry*, 184–94.

ond-hand clothing was—and still is—manual labour, so were minor alterations and repairs of second-hand military clothing, which were not only necessary but became mandatory towards the end of the nineteenth century.

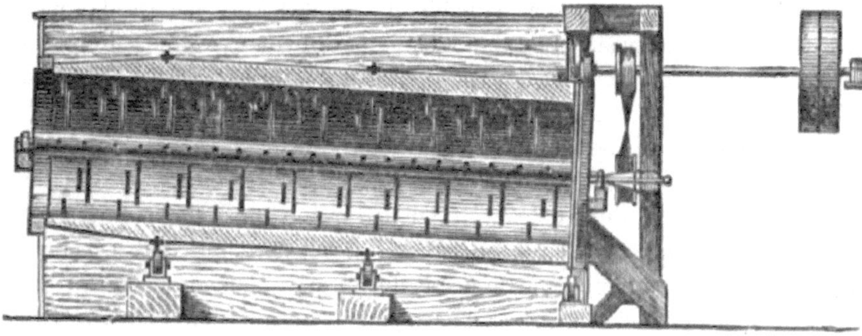

FIGURE 1.7 Rag-dusting machine manufactured by Bryan Donkin and Co., London (1890).

The revisions to the army's clothing regulations from the 1880s onwards regulated aspects of production by rendering the repair and alteration of British second-hand military clothing essential. Following the enactment of the Uniforms Bill and new clothing regulations in 1894, two changes had an immediate impact on the manufacturing process in the second-hand clothing branch responsible for processing military clothing: first, prior to returning military clothing articles categorized as public clothing to the regimental stores, soldiers were allowed to remove badges, buttons, and other insignia from jackets, tunics, coats, frocks, and trousers. Second, contractors were mandated to alter second-hand military clothing in such a manner that they would not 'be recognised as having been used as uniform of the regular army.'[185] At the same time, the ambiguous phrasing of the contract conditions was perceived as intentional: distinctive facings, buttons, badges, and other insignia rendered British military dress recognizable, and it was this recognizability that accounted for the continuous demand for military dress among civilian consumers. In the words of the collector of customs of the Colony of Natal: 'The War Office knows perfectly well ... that the retention on the uniforms of the buttons and insignia enhances the value, that they are not converted into rags and that consequently they are exported.'[186]

Repairing and altering British second-hand military dress in line with these regulations constituted one of the subsequent steps in the manufacturing process in the second-hand clothing sector. In the workrooms of Mallett, Porter & Dowd,

185 See *Report ... on the Uniforms Bill*, App. 4, 35. This condition was still in place in 1910; see NASA SAB, GG vol. 1509, no. 49/1911. See also *Regulations for the Supply of Clothing and Necessaries to the Regular Forces*, 1894, 3–11.

186 NASA SAB, GG vol. 1509, no. 49/1911.

Ltd., however, the specifications for the alteration of British second-hand military dress were frequently not followed (with articles of clothing resold with their original insignia), or were circumvented by having employees sew mixed insignia from the military dress of different British and foreign regiments onto British and foreign military clothing. In 1906, a merchant named H. Möschke based in Pietersburg, Colony of Transvaal (Polokwane, Limpopo Province), who according to an advertisement specialized in commodities for the European–African trade (so-called 'kaffir truck', Fig. 1.8), imported nine bales of clothing valued at £107. The bales originated from the warehouse of Mallett, Porter & Dowd, Ltd. and contained 1,700 items of clothing, including '100 Military Overcoats scarlet lined'. When some of the clothing bales were opened by customs officers in Maputo, a number of the items were found to have been 'recognisable as British but the large proportion, however, being unmistakably foreign. Many of the latter had the original buttons cut off and British line regiment buttons sewn on with two or three threads. The original threads were plainly visible.' According to the inspector who examined the clothing, Möschke explained 'that naturally most of the buttons on secondhand clothing would probably be missing, & that when these goods get relined they are generally rebuttoned'.[187]

FIGURE 1.8 Advertisement by H. Möschke, Polokwane, Limpopo Province (1895/6).

Prior to the introduction of regulations on disinfecting second-hand clothing in 1907, once the items had been sorted, altered, and repaired they were either stored until ordered or immediately prepared for shipment. Second-hand clothing intended for shipment to, for example, British South Africa was packed in 'cases

187 NASA TAB, DCU vol. 75, no. 638/1906.

lined with oil paper' or pressed into bales.[188] The mechanization of bale pressing expanded in the textile industries towards the end of the nineteenth century, however, manual pressing was still prevalent in the second-hand clothing sector, where pressers used 'a heavy iron which [was] hot, and ... worked across a damp rag'.[189] Bound with iron wire, each manually or hydraulically pressed bale consisted of 50–100 articles of clothing,[190] while boots and other footwear were packaged in cases. By the early twentieth century, Mallett, Porter & Dowd, Ltd. were employing pressers at their facilities in Islington, and the business appears to have partly subcontracted the packing of second-hand clothing intended for export. According to an investigation of the second-hand clothing trade, including its export branches, by the Board of Trade in 1920, the London-based firm John Stevenson & Sons, Ltd. specialized in packing textile commodities in general and second-hand clothes in particular, pressing clothing bales hydraulically and delivering them to the docks for shipment.[191] In the 1920s, South African customs authorities noted that only three exporters of second-hand clothing were carrying out their own packing, and recognized John Stevenson & Sons, Ltd. as one of four 'approved export packers' in the second-hand clothing trade.[192] In addition, records indicate that the shipping firm W. Bolus & Sons, Ltd. (identified in the 1920 Board of Trade investigation as 'shippers of all classes of commodities to and from South Africa'), the packing business of John Stevenson & Sons, Ltd., and the workrooms of Mallett, Porter & Dowd, Ltd. remained financially and operationally linked throughout the early twentieth century.[193] Finally, once second-hand clothing had been sorted and pressed into bales, invoiced, and accompanied by a growing number of certificates from 1903 onwards, it left the premises of Mallett, Porter & Dowd, Ltd. and the packing subcontractor and was sent to Lon-

188 See *Cape of Good Hope: Report of the Medical Officer of Health for the Colony ... for the Two Calendar Years 1904 and 1905*, pp. cxxxv–cxxxvii at p. cxxxvi. On the introduction of mandatory disinfection in the British South African second-hand clothing trade, see chapter 3.3.

189 *First Report from the Select Committee of the House of Lords on the Sweating System*, 21, Ev 235.

190 See NASA TAB, DCU vol. 82, no. 1139/1906; NASA TAB, DCU vol. 75, no. 638/1906; NASA TAB, DCU vol. 96, no. 284/1907.

191 According to the report by the Board of Trade, the firm of J. Stevenson & Sons, Ltd. employed packers, 'carmen' (drivers of horse-drawn vehicles), labourers, and clerks. See TNA, LAB 2/668/TBD134/A/8/1920.

192 NASA SAB, DEA vol. 204, no. A10/16X.

193 See the liquidator's statements of accounts of W. Bolus & Sons Ltd. in 1921/22 for references to Mallett, Porter & Dowd, Ltd., Samuel Moses & Sons, Ltd., and John Stevenson & Sons, Ltd., TNA, BT 34/3100. W. Bolus & Sons, Ltd. functioned as shippers of second-hand clothing, and the Board of Trade investigators also found that they were buying 'considerable quantities of second-hand clothing which they sell to dealers in South Africa, and so become dealers in second-hand clothing ... The second-hand clothing is not handled in any way by the firms' staff, as it is either bought ready packed from wholesale dealers, or collected, fumigated, and packed by sub-contract and delivered at the docks.' See TNA, LAB 2/668/TBD134/A/8/1920. See also *The British and South African Export Gazette*, 6/65 (3 Dec. 1897), 388.

don's docks for shipment, where charges for the collection of goods, the conveyance of docks, wharfage, and portage increased during the early twentieth century. Notably, however, costs for handling second-hand military clothing, and especially second-hand civilian clothing, were considerably lower than for ready-made clothing, especially for shipments exceeding twenty tonnes.[194]

1.5 Conclusion

Within, as well as outside, the British army clothing system and its regiments, reuse of military clothing remained contested throughout the second half of the nineteenth century, highlighting the correlating and competing ascriptions of value to military dress. Objections to the issuance of part-worn military clothing to, for example, militia recruits, and the criticism voiced by commanding officers regarding the collection of worn-out clothing from soldiers shed light on the values that military authorities endeavoured to instil in their soldiers. Individual ascriptions of value to military dress by soldiers did not only originate from the maintenance and care they were expected to afford to their clothing. Perceived by military officials to have found expression in intangible emotions, these ascriptions contributed to the incommensurability of second-hand military clothing. Military items of clothing resembled each other materially because of designs, distinguishable badges, buttons, and other insignia. However, wear and tear and the soldiers' differing approaches to repairing and maintaining the clothing left individual traces. Charged with a set of partly correlating meanings, the British army and its soldiers produced highly recognizable yet unique and distinctive articles of second-hand clothing.

The fact that the reuse of military dress outside the army clothing system was perceived as a contestation by the military authorities highlights the significance they ascribed to military clothing as a marker of distinction. Reuse of second-hand military clothing in street advertising was perceived as a threat to the image of the soldier that the British army was keen to uphold. While fears of ridicule voiced by British army officials in the context of theatrical production speak to the fragility of this image, the introduction of the Uniforms Act in 1894 and subsequent restrictions levied on civilian reuse and commercial trade exemplify the military authorities' efforts to exert control over the 'afterlives' of military dress.

However, contrary to the assumption that increased regulation would end the circulation of British second-hand military clothing in the domestic market, sales

194 See the annotated export rates in 2 vols. in Museum of London Docklands, Port and River Archive, 21.7.4., Box 14, and the tables of rates, charges, and regulations for the London and India Docks Company and by the Port of London Authority (partly issued to the docks only) in ibid. 9.2.6.

and purchases involving soldiers did not cease in the following decades.[195] The regular reuse of British military dress in non-military contexts highlights, not least, the limits of control over consumer demand.

Overall, the commoditization of second-hand military clothing and the internationalization of the trade thereof seem to have been a rather unintended consequence of the monopolization of its production and wholesale by the British army. By reclaiming soldiers' worn-out clothing and restricting resales to regiments as sites of second-hand military clothing exchange, military officials were faced with an extensive accumulation of worn-out military clothing that filled the army's warehouses beyond capacity. Due to the limited storage available, auction was the most prevalent method of sale, yet overhasty sales and supposedly cartel-like auction practices led to an increase in sales by tender to select army contractors. In addition, by the time British second-hand military clothing reached the workrooms of the emerging second-hand clothing industry, most exhibited a variety of material qualities and traces of wear. In contrast to the manufacture of paper, shoddy, or mungo, in which mechanization gradually replaced workers and influenced labour productivity, the second-hand clothing trade continued to rely primarily on manual labour.[196] Preparatory processes such as sorting, relining, and rebuttoning in particular remained in the hands of low-paid, predominantly female workers. Finally, while sorting was intended to reduce quality uncertainty in garments obtained through army contracts, it did not eliminate it. When importers in British South Africa tendered for colonial government department contracts in Pietermaritzburg in 1897, some offers included sample coats which, according to one offer, 'fairly represent[ed] the bulk' but 'did not guarantee that all coats would be the same as the sample sent.'[197]

Crucially, the commoditization of British second-hand military clothing unfolded as a contested process at its site of production from the mid 1870s onwards, shaped by institutional and regulatory practices, labour, and material conditions. By the end of the nineteenth century, the British military clothing 'disposal chain' had been increasingly formalized and regulated, setting boundaries within which value assessments were both recognized and contested. Labour practices were central to how clothing was deemed suitable for reuse and additional manufacturing processes. The wear, upkeep, and repairs carried out by soldiers produced traces and shaped the material condition of each garment, influencing how it was subsequently perceived and processed. Labour practices in the second-hand clothing industry further affected which garments could continue in circulation. The material characteristics of the clothing reinforced vari-

195 See, for example, *First Report ... to Inquire into the Civil Establishments of the Different Offices of State at Home and Abroad*, 117, Ev 3165; Ugolini, 'The Illicit Consumption of Military Uniforms in Britain, 1914–1918'.

196 See Magee, *Productivity and Performance in the Paper Industry*, 189–94.

197 NASA NAB, PWD vol. 2/37, no. PWD 3767/1897.

ability; despite standardized designs, each article remained distinctive. These intertwined processes demonstrate that the value of military clothing was not fixed at its point of issuance but actively renegotiated and contested across multiple stages, highlighting the social and material production of commodities.

CHAPTER 2

2 From Caledonian Road to Emagusheni Trading Store: The Distribution and Consumption of Second-Hand Military Clothing in British South Africa

FIGURE 2.1 Sign next to the main road for Emagusheni Trading Store (1970), photograph by Lance James.

In November 1970, *The Kokstad Advertiser and East Griqualand Gazette* featured a front-page article drawing attention to the forthcoming closure of a local trading post known as Emagusheni (Trading) Store (Fig. 2.1). Located next to the main road connecting the cities of Kokstad and Flagstaff in the Eastern Cape, South Africa and in close proximity to KwaZulu-Natal, Emagusheni Trading Store had, over the past few decades, become what the anonymous author described as 'the centre of activity for the area'. By 1970, buses carrying workers from the surrounding mines and sugar plantations were calling daily at the trading store, vendors

 | HTTPS://DOI.ORG/10.1515/9783112256503-003

were selling commodities at stalls on the property, and a doctor was treating patients once a week in a room inside the building provided to him by the storekeeping Gallagher family. We learn that Emagusheni Trading Store functioned as a Postal Agency, a Railway Agency, and an office for 'officials of the Bantu Affairs', where old age and disability pensions were paid out every six weeks. After almost ninety years of trading, in November 1970 storeowner Brian Gallagher took 'stock at Emagusheni for the last time during this month.' The article's author noted that he could not 'help but feel a sense of loss in the knowledge that by [the Gallagher family's] departure a link with the past [was] being broken.'[1]

Almost a century earlier, Michael H. O'Donnell, born in Ireland in 1853, arrived in Southern Africa.[2] In 1883/84, O'Donnell took over Emagusheni Trading Store and entered into a close business relationship with William and Josiah P. Bouverie, two English brothers who had established one of the leading wholesale businesses in Eastern Mpondoland by the early 1880s. William Bouverie ran a trading station at Mtamvuna Drift along one of the main waggon routes between Mpondoland and the Colony of Natal, while his brother Josiah P. Bouverie worked closely with O'Donnell at Emagusheni Trading Store.[3] During the 1880s and 1890s, O'Donnell and Josiah P. Bouverie entered into and upheld business relations with many local storekeepers and merchants in the proximity of Emagusheni Trading Store, including the import and export merchant John F. Rethman and his Ihluku Store in Alfred County, Enhlenzie Store in Emfundisweni (eMmfundisweni), and the firm of Strachan & Co., a business established in Umzimkhulu in *c.*1858 and comprised, as of 1906, of a bakery, hotel, blacksmith, and general store.[4]

As for many traders in the area, the trade in cattle and hides with the Mpondo population and leaders formed the core business activities at Emagusheni Trading Store. Trade in Eastern Mpondoland began to flourish and expand from the 1860s onwards, when the Mpondo started to trade cattle with Europeans on a larger scale and their demand for manufactured commodities such as beads, blankets, firearms, metal products, and agricultural implements increased. While cattle and hides formed the key export goods from Mpondoland, blankets were one of the major import commodities during the second half of the nineteenth century.[5] During the 1880s and 1890s, Emagusheni Trading Store operated largely as a wholesale business, and its proprietors and business partners engaged in what came to be widely known as 'kaffir truck', 'kaffir trade', or 'truck trade'—discriminatory terms used by contemporaries to describe a group of commodities for a

1 KCM 95/11/80, *The Kokstad Advertiser and East Griqualand Gazette,* 89/45 (12 Nov. 1970), 1.

2 See *The Natal Who's Who*, 150.

3 See Beinart, 'European Traders and the Mpondo Paramountcy, 1878–1886', 474–5; Beinart, 'Production, Labour Migrancy and the Chieftaincy', 64–5.

4 Regarding Strachan & Co. (and Donald Strachan's involvement in colonial politics), see *Twentieth Century Impressions of Natal,* 646–8.

5 See Beinart, *The Political Economy of Pondoland 1860–1930*, 22–30.

specific group of consumers, predominantly black Africans. As Timothy Burke shows, for late-nineteenth-century colonial Zimbabwe, truck traders and stores —'even when explicitly racist in the physical separation of goods for white and black shoppers under the same roof'—made a wide range of imported commodities available to local consumers.[6]

Second-hand military clothing was a significant component in the commodities offered by importing merchants, wholesale businesses, and storekeepers who catered for black African consumer demand during the late nineteenth and early twentieth century, as exemplified in contemporary travel writing: Charles H. Du Val noted in his travel account *With a Show Through Southern Africa, and Personal Reminiscences of the Transvaal War* (1882) that due to 'evidently large business with natives' in Verulam (a small town approximately thirty kilometres north of Durban, KwaZulu-Natal), it was

> not surprising that the storekeepers [kept] an attractive stock calculated to rivet the attention ... of the dusky brother. As a consequence, wrist wraps, highly-coloured handkerchiefs, blankets ... strings of beads, belts, bags, bangles, second-hand uniforms from that of a gay hussar to the more plebeian foot-soldier, jostle each other in captivating confusion in the windows and shelves of the stores devoted to what is called the 'Kaffir trade'.[7]

Storekeepers and trading posts like Emagusheni Trading Store linked black African consumers to the locales of production—including the workrooms of Mallett, Porter & Dowd, Ltd.—and global trading networks. At the same time, regional conditions and developments significantly shaped the second-hand military clothing trade. Mpondoland, one of the last independent kingdoms until its annexation in 1894, William Bramwell argues, featured as 'something of an anomaly on the landscape' of late-nineteenth-century Southern Africa, and trading conditions were influenced by the tense relationship between the predominantly white trading community, rivalry between Mpondo leaders, and British colonial authorities.[8]

The consumption and appropriation of European-style dress, including British second-hand military clothing, as indicated in Du Val's account, was contested and racially politicized throughout the late nineteenth and early twentieth centuries. While I use the term 'consumption', following Deborah Posel, loosely to subsume the practices of acquisition or the adoption of goods, their uses, and display, I apply the term 'appropriation' when referring to specific incorporations of European-style clothing articles: as Hans-Peter Hahn argues in connection with object uses in transcultural contexts, the term 'appropriation' emphasizes the cre-

6 Burke, *Lifebuoy Men, Lux Women*, 61–90 at 69. See also Harries, *Work, Culture, and Identity*, 101–3; Comaroff and Comaroff, *Of Revelation and Revolution*, 249–52.

7 Du Val, *With a Show Through Southern Africa*, 220.

8 Bramwell, 'Loyalties and the Politics of Incorporation in South Africa', 98.

ative and self-conscious practices of object use, transformation, and incorporation (through to the formation of new traditions).[9] Accounts by European travellers and Africans demonstrate how black African dressing styles were perceived and interpreted, highlighting the conflicting meanings ascribed to the adoption and appropriation of second-hand military garments. Colonial officials increasingly expressed unease about the adoption and appropriation of military clothing by black Africans, raising broader questions about the intersection of dress, consumption, and imperial authority. At the same time, the commercial trade's perceptions of growing competition for black African markets from the 1890s onwards reveals ongoing tensions surrounding market control and consumer influence.

2.1 Stocking Up with 'Military Bits':[10] Transportation, Communication, Labour, and Customs Duties in Mpondoland, *c.*1880–1895

On 19 January 1906, a director of Mallett, Porter & Dowd, Ltd. signed the shipping invoice for an order numbered 1591 that he had received from the importing merchants Randles, Bros. & Hudson in Durban. 1,700 pieces of clothing—sorted, broadly categorized, grouped, and pressed into bales—were about to leave London on the steamship 'Umzoti'. The bales had been numbered, weighed, and measured, each containing (as per the descriptions noted on the invoice) between 50 and 200 pairs of trousers, cycling breeches, vests, blue military overcoats, and volunteer tunics. The shipment reached the port of Maputo during the first week of March 1906, from where it continued its journey via railway, eventually reaching the stores of H. Möschke in Pietersburg, Colony of Transvaal (Polokwane, Limpopo Province) and Machadadorp (eNtokozweni, Mpumalanga Province) in April. While Möschke's frustration over the delayed arrival of the goods at their final destination—caused by a dispute with Maputo customs authorities over the misdescription of some of the bales' contents—is noteworthy, it had apparently been an uneventful journey overall.[11]

By the early twentieth century, the importing firm of Randles, Bros. & Hudson had expanded significantly: after the establishment of offices in Manchester and Pietermaritzburg prior to 1872, additional offices and stores were opened in London and Durban in the mid 1890s, and in Johannesburg and Utrecht (Colony of

9 See Hahn, *Materielle Kultur*, 99–107; Hahn, 'Cultural Appropriation'. See also Prestholdt, *Domesticating the World.*

10 KCM 95/11/8, letter from Hamilton McNicholas to Josiah P. Bouverie, 12 Jan. 1884.

11 NASA TAB, DCU vol. 75, no. 638/1906. On disputes over imported second-hand clothing between customs officials, authorities, importers, and storekeepers, see chapter 4.2.

Natal/KwaZulu-Natal) in the early 1900s.[12] The business owners were not only well known as importers for traders in Eastern South Africa, but also for granting credit on reasonable terms to Indian traders in the middle of a period that was characterized largely by anti-Indian sentiment among British storekeepers, traders, and merchants.[13] In addition, according to a list compiled by the collector of customs for the Colony of Natal in 1905, Randles, Bros. & Hudson were among the four largest importers of British second-hand military uniform in Durban.[14] Throughout the 1880s and 1890s, the firm not only imported considerable amounts of this type of clothing for further distribution through merchants, traders, and storekeepers in the Colony of Natal, the South African Republic/ Transvaal Colony, and Cape Colony, but also tendered for colonial government contracts: when the Pietermaritzburg audit office called for tenders for the supply of '150 New Military Coats and 300 Second-hand Military Great Coats' in December 1897, it received offers from six firms, including an offer by Randles, Bros. & Hudson to provide 300 second-hand military overcoats.[15] Moreover, the business formed a link between Mallett, Porter & Dowd, Ltd. and Emagusheni Trading Store in Mpondoland. According to the Gallagher Family Paper records, Michael H. O'Donnell and his business associate Josiah P. Bouverie began to trade with Randles, Bros. & Hudson on a larger scale in 1886. Key imports through the latter included foods (flour, coffee, mealies, oats, tobacco, and brandy) and other commodities partly intended for the 'truck trade' (such as beads, handkerchiefs, blankets, and so-called 'Kaffir pots') as well as a wide range of textile goods and articles of clothing such as different types of shirts, jackets, and trousers.[16] By the early 1890s, Randles, Bros. & Hudson provided the majority of imported commodities purchased and distributed in Mpondoland by the business owners of Emagusheni Trading Store. Finally, these imports regularly included articles of military and police clothing, such as police and soldiers' overcoats, army sandals, and military pouches.[17]

The vast number of handwritten letters and receipts, account and stock books that form the core of the Gallagher Family Papers is indicative of the main mode

12 See *Twentieth Century Impressions of Natal*, 456 and 627; KCM 95/11/67, receipt by Randles, Bros. & Hudson (now in Durban), 14 Mar. 1895; *The British and South African Export Gazette*, 4/48 (3 July 1896), 742.

13 See, for example, 'Randles Bros. & Hudson v. The Standard Bank & Others', in *Natal Law Reports*, 253–4; Hiralal, 'The Economic Role of the Indian Commercial Class in Colonial Natal', 141–2. On the British perception of Indian traders as competitors in the trade, see chapter 2.3.

14 See NASA SAB, GG vol. 1509, no. 49/11.

15 See NASA NAB, PWD vol. 2/37, no. 8595/1897.

16 KCM 95/11/22, letter addressed to Michael H. O'Donnell, 27 Sept. 1886. See also KCM 95/11/23.

17 See receipts for goods received by Emagusheni Trading Store from Randles, Bros. & Hudson. KCM 96/11/23, 10 Nov. 1886; KCM 96/11/34, 14 Sept. 1887; KCM 95/11/52, 8 July 1889; KCM 95/11/59, 27 Jan. 1890; KCM 95/11/60, 7 Mar. 1890.

of communication and flow of information, as their contents illustrate key characteristics of inland transportation, labour migrancy, and customs policies in late-nineteenth-century Eastern South Africa. The impact of the revolution in transportation and communication during the nineteenth century on the development of global trade led to an overall decrease in the cost of international transportation.[18] Shipping freights in the British South African trade nevertheless fluctuated between the 1880s and the early twentieth century, and while the correspondence between, for example, Randles, Bros. & Hudson and Emagusheni Trading Store does not indicate that trade relations and conditions were significantly affected, fluctuations in costs and shipping times frequently led to adaptations of schedules, renegotiation of delivery times, and reorganization of inland transportation.[19] Irregular shipping intervals were perceived as a nuisance by traders, while freight rates had only a minor impact on the South African transportation cost structure: 'for the most part', Vivian Solomon points out, 'the cost of inland transportation, for journeys involving a few hundred miles, was far greater than the corresponding cost of sea carriage over some 6,000 miles.'[20]

On New Year's Eve 1883, William Bouverie left his trading station at Mtamvuna Drift with six head of cattle. Upon his departure, he informed his brother and O'Donnell at Emagusheni Trading Store about his future whereabouts. His letter was accompanied by a waggon 'loaded with alsorts of stuff' that Bouverie wanted unpacked and inventoried at Emagusheni Trading Store. Among 'a lot of odds and ends', the waggon carried tobacco, sacks, a carbine manufactured by the Birmingham gun and rifle makers Westley Richards, and an 'old black bag and ... a sack' containing 'a lot of old shirts ... two old military coats and two Emdaga Blankets striped.'[21] Apart from illustrating that throughout the 1880s and 1890s, O'Donnell and his associates acquired imported goods through an extensive local trading network comprised of storekeepers, traders, importers, and auction houses in Mpondoland and the Colony of Natal, the letter points to the mode of transportation widely used by the business associates at Emagusheni Trading Store, Mtamvuna Drift, and other traders, storekeepers, and merchants in the area: in contrast to most other African countries, animal-drawn waggons (despite their shortcomings) dominated inland transportation in Southern Africa for most

18 See Magee and Thompson, *Empire and Globalisation*, 67; O'Rourke and Williamson, *Globalization and History*, 33–6.

19 See KCM 96/11/22, letter from Randles, Bros. & Hudson to Michael H. O'Donnell, 6 Jan. 1886; KCM 96/11/22, letter from Randles Bros. & Hudson to Michael H. O'Donnell, 4 Nov. 1886.

20 Solomon, 'Early Commonwealth Action against Shipping Conferences', 308–17 at 310. On shipping conferences in South Africa, see also Solomon, *The South African Shipping Question, 1886–1914*.

21 KCM 95/11/7, letter from William Bouverie to Josiah P. Bouverie and Michael H. O'Donnell, 31 Dec. 1883.

of the nineteenth century.[22] Due to the limited expansion of railway lines into Mpondoland and East Griqualand, animal-draught waggons remained the most important mode of transportation and covered most of the trading routes in these regions until the late 1890s. Second-hand military clothing and other commodities purchased from importers such as Randles, Bros. & Hudson, from other traders in the area, or at marketplaces in, for example, Pietermaritzburg, thus travelled towards and through the Colony of Natal and Mpondoland packed in sacks, bales, cases, or trusses, and loaded onto waggons drawn by oxen, mules, and, to a lesser extent, donkeys. Traders in Mpondoland used a variety of different waggons, such as sledges, Clark's and buck waggons, on different routes depending on the requirements given the partly rough terrain, while the stature, build, and training of draught-animals in turn had to meet the requirements of different waggon types. In 1889, Josiah P. Bouverie informed O'Donnell that sixteen of the eighteen young oxen that were on the way to Emagusheni Trading Store had been 'worked regularly ... in Small waggon[s] & Clarkes' only, either as 'front [or] after oxen',[23] while a trading partner explained his delayed arrival at the store with the unavailability of a waggon suitable for 'very thin' oxen.[24]

Waggon routes frequently used by O'Donnell, Josiah P. Bouverie, and other drivers led to William Bouverie's store at Mtamvuna Drift and further north to Harding, Umzimkhulu, and Durban, as well as to the coastal town Port St. Johns, south of Emagusheni Trading Store.[25] On some of the trading routes, waggons had to be dismantled or at least unloaded to cross difficult or rough terrain.[26] Other trading routes were suitable for specific waggons only, and the route from Eastern South Africa's interior to the east coast proved particularly challenging: while organizing and planning transportation of goods ordered by a customer near Port St. Johns in September 1892, Josiah P. Bouverie remarked that 'a buck wagon would be too much ... unless the material would stand pulling down & building up again'.[27] Rough terrain not only limited the choice of waggons and animals but also increased the cost of waggon maintenance and repairs; the latter were frequently carried out in, for example, Pietermaritzburg and Harding.[28] In addition, seasonal heavy rains in the region slowed transportation and increased the risk of damage to waggons and goods, even if the latter had been covered

22 Pierie, 'Slaughter by Steam'. See also Sunderland, 'General Introduction', pp. ix–lxiv.

23 KCM 95/11/45, letter from Josiah P. Bouverie to Michael O'Donnell, 6 Oct. 1889.

24 KCM 95/11/45, letter addressed to Michael H. O'Donnell, 9 Sept. 1889.

25 See the map of trading stations and waggon routes in Mpondoland in the 1880s in Beinart, 'Production, Labour Migrancy and the Chieftaincy', 45–6.

26 See KCM 95/11/40, letter from general merchants Hill & Holwell to Michael H. O'Donnell, 24 July 1888.

27 KCM 95/11/63, letter from Josiah P. Bouverie to Michael H. O'Donnell, 16 Sept. 1892.

28 See KCM 95/11/17, letter by Josiah P. Bouverie, 26 Mar. 1886; KCM 95/11/32, receipt for waggon repairs in Pietermaritzburg, July 1887; KCM 95/11/20, receipt for waggon repairs in Richmond, Aug. 1886.

properly: 'We have had a heavy rain', a trading partner explained to O'Donnell in May 1887, adding that 'though the goods have been covered I fully expect you will find some of the Bales damaged when you unpack'.[29]

Once trained, due to their strength and resilience, Mpondo oxen were valued as the most suitable draught-animals. In addition, oxen could survive solely on pasturage, so costs for oxen husbandry were comparably low.[30] However, transportation by animal-drawn waggons was slow, and oversights on the part of business partners in providing goods for Emagusheni Trading Store slowed returns on trade and threatened the reputation of storekeepers and traders. White woollen cotton blankets that had been forgotten by the staff of Randles, Bros. & Hudson had forgotten to load onto a waggon from Pietermaritzburg to Emagusheni Trading Store in April 1887 led to a delivery delay of almost one month and several apologetic letters by Josiah P. Bouverie to the customer, who was repeatedly—and apparently successfully—put off until the blankets finally arrived at Emagusheni Trading Store.[31] Despite these and similar occasional setbacks as well as keen competition between wholesale businesses in Mpondoland and Natal, merchants, storekeepers, and traders appeared to have coped with the challenges of animal-draught transportation mainly through cooperation. The widely dispersed trading network in Mpondoland that had grown from the 1860s onwards along the main waggon routes allowed for breaks and offered food and lodging for animals and drivers on transport rides. On particularly difficult waggon routes where the terrain required different animals and waggons, loads were occasionally shifted between sellers' and buyers' waggons at some point along the route.[32]

Throughout the 1880s and 1890s, trade in Mpondoland, including inland transportation, was affected by political unrest, outbreaks of cattle disease, locust plagues, and droughts. In September 1889, in a letter addressed to traders in Mpondoland, John F. Rethman noted that given the recent increase in property damage and theft, 'life & property [in Mpondoland] seem[ed] to be hanging on a mere thread': 'I think the time has at last arrived for all of us to take some course to prevent any further looking or smelling out of Traders in Pondoland.'[33] Theft of goods on transport routes was not unheard of. Regarding missing coats on a waggon from Harding to Emagusheni Trading Store in 1886, for example, the seller noted that 'they were all there when knocked down as [we] counted them as they

29 See KCM 95/11/25, letter addressed to Michael H. O'Donnell, 20 May 1887.

30 See Beinart, *The Political Economy of Pondoland 1860–1930*, 23.

31 It remains unclear whether Randles, Bros. & Hudson delivered the blankets at the later date or Emagusheni Trading Store acquired them elsewhere. See KCM 95/11/25, letters by Josiah P. Bouverie, 12 Apr. 1887, 4 May 1887, 5 May 1887, and 9 May 1887.

32 See Beinart, *The Political Economy of Pondoland 1860–1930*, 23; KCM 95/11/63, letter from Josiah P. Bouverie to Michael H. O'Donnell, 16 Sept. 1892; KCM 95/11/56, invoice by The Ruthville Estate, 10 Jan. 1890.

33 KCM 95/11/45, letter by John F. Rethman, 5 Sept. 1889.

were put up, they must have been jumped, there has been a lot of it going on.'[34] Towards the end of the 1880s, when the rivalry between Mpondo paramount Sigcau (Mqikela's elected successor) and Mhlangaso—formerly Mqikela's leading councillor at the Great Place—intensified, damages to traders' property and theft in the region increased.[35] Rivalry and political unrest between Mpondo leaders posed a threat to the thriving trade in cattle, hides, and European commodities with the Mpondo, and as William Beinart shows, European traders in Mpondoland intervened in Mpondo politics particularly between 1878 and 1886, a period marked by growing tensions between Cape colonial authorities and the Mpondo paramountcy.[36] As some records suggest, gifts to Mpondos in potentially influential positions may have supported Europeans' efforts to build relationships with the Mpondo, and these occasionally included second-hand military clothing: Hamilton MacNicholas, for instance, asked Josiah P. Bouverie in early 1884 to send to 'Uhmlangaso's Brother one of those Military Bits', and added: 'I have promised him a Bit some time ago and have not been able to get him one. He is the best of the family, so do not disappoint him if you have one.'[37] Finally, an attempt to smooth negotiations between Sigcau and Mhlangaso in November 1889 on the premises of Emagusheni Trading Store, Josiah P. Bouverie claimed, had cost him £8, including expenses for board, lodging, and gifts.[38] During the same period, outbreaks of cattle disease such as redwater, East Coast Fever, and so-called 'lungsickness' (contagious bovine pleuropneumonia, CBPP) were partly contained but affected transportation, trading relations, and profits: three of six oxen purchased by a customer from O'Donnell died or were suffering from CBPP in July 1899. In a letter addressed to O'Donnell, the customer argued that, as guaranteed by the storeowners, he held the business owners 'responsible for all loss uncovered' and asked O'Donnell 'to take back the remainder of the cattle'.[39]

34 KCM 95/11/18, letter from Horace C. Downes to Michael H. O'Donnell, 2 Dec. 1886.

35 On the growing tensions between Sigcau and Mhlangaso, see Bramwell, 'Loyalties and the Politics of Incorporation in South Africa', 171–3 and 200–1. Sigcau himself apparently participated in the looting of stores during this period. See Beinart, 'Production, Labour Migrancy and the Chieftaincy', 108–13.

36 As Beinart concludes, the intervention into Mpondo politics 'serves to illustrate that some traders were prepared to act independently of the colonial powers in order to protect their interests.' Beinart, 'European Traders and the Mpondo Paramountcy, 1878–1886', 486.

37 KCM 95/11/8, letter from Hamilton MacNicholas to Josiah P. Bouverie, 12 Jan. 1884. On political relations between European traders, Mpondo leaders, and British colonial authorities, see, for example, Reid, 'The Aborigines' Protection Society as an Anticolonial Network; Beinart, 'European Traders and the Mpondo Paramountcy, 1878–1886'.

38 KCM 95/11/45, letter by Josiah P. Bouverie, 29 Nov. 1889. See also ibid., letter by Josiah P. Bouverie, 26 Nov. 1889.

39 KCM 95/11/46, letter addressed to Michael H. O'Donnell, 29 July 1889. For additional examples of customers' claims for refunds, see ibid., letter addressed to Randles, Bros. & Hudson, 20 July 1889. On purchases of lung-sick cattle by O'Donnell see KCM 95/11/17, letter by Michael H. O'Donnell, 1 Jan. 1886.

Droughts and locust plagues between 1894 and 1896 were followed by the rinderpest, which reached the region in 1896, decimated cattle herds, disrupted transportation, and drove up costs for waggon carriage. Despite preventive measures such as the closing of borders and the temporary isolation of herds, most cattle died in the second half of 1897. According to William Beinart, the cattle population in Mpondoland only reached pre-rinderpest levels again by the end of the century.[40]

The trading network in Mpondoland thus to some extent benefited from the extension of the Natal Government Railways (NGR) lines towards Mpondoland.[41] Business owners and traders in Mpondoland had pushed for the construction of a railway line from Port St. Johns to the interior. While these plans were never realized, since a new harbour with railway connections posed a threat to the commercial interests in the established colonial ports,[42] the NGR completed the extension of one branch of the Durban-Pietermaritzburg line along the coast to Isipingo, approximately nineteen kilometres south of Durban, shortly before the rinderpest outbreak. The newly established railway stations in Isipingo and Richmond Road (near Pietermaritzburg)—the latter would eventually connect Richmond to the Durban–Pietermaritzburg line—were frequented by the importing merchants Randles, Bros. & Hudson to transport commodities from the port in Durban to Emagusheni Trading Store.[43] Railway transportation alleviated the consequences of the oxen shortage during and in the immediate aftermath of the rinderpest outbreak, increased transportation speed, and reduced the risk of damages to commodities. However, the joint expenditure on railway and waggon carriage increased transportation costs for storekeepers and traders in Mpondoland, where inland transportation by animal-draught waggons had been comparably inexpensive.[44] Notably, the railway expansions threatened the livelihoods of independent transport riders, many of whom were African entrepreneurs.[45]

Similar to the limited expansion of railway lines, which never reached the Mpondoland interior, the development of telegraph lines in this region was constrained. Global telegraphy was introduced in sub-Saharan Africa after 1879, with

40 See Beinart, *The Political Economy of Pondoland 1860–1930*, 47–51. On the outbreak of East Coast Fever in 1911, see ibid. 70–84.

41 See Pierie, 'Slaughter by Steam'; Mbem, 'Rethinking Railway Histories of the Transvaal', 37–9.

42 Beinart, 'Production, Labour Migrancy and the Chieftaincy', 136.

43 See various receipts for railway carriage to Isipingo and Richmond Road station by Randles, Bros. & Hudson in KCM 95/11/68 and KCM 95/11/69.

44 On the impact of railway construction on transport systems in Lesotho, see Keegan, 'Trade, Accumulation and Impoverishment'. See also Pierie, 'Slaughter by Steam'; Mlambo, 'From Dirt Tracks to Modern Highways'; Sunderland, 'General Introduction'.

45 See ibid. and, for example, Solomon Mabaso's observation in 1900: '[H]ere in Natal many natives who had purchased waggons and to some extent depended on transport were deprived of that means of earning a livelihood owing to the coming of the railway.' *The James Stuart Archive of Recorded Oral Evidence*, 252.

cable lines laid by private companies between Aden, Yemen, along the African east coast through Mombasa, Dar es Salam, Maputo Bay, Durban, and Cape Town, thus connecting Southern Africa to Europe, Asia, and—following extensions of cable lines along the West African coast in 1890—South America.[46] South African inland long-distance communication, too, became increasingly wired.[47] Mpondoland, however, remained largely untouched by extensions of the inland telegraph system until, presumably, the late 1880s or early 1890s, although Cape and Natal colonial government authorities had already expressed interest in wiring the region in the 1870s.[48] However, when Cape colonial authorities sought to lay telegraph lines between the Colony of Natal and Cape Colony through parts of Mpondoland in 1877, Mpondo paramount Mqikela refused to allow their construction, fearing that colonial authorities would afterwards claim the land surrounding the telegraph posts and cable lines. Consequently, Cape colonial authorities carried the telegraph line through East Griqualand, thus connecting Pietermaritzburg with Umzimkhulu, Kokstad, Mount Frere, and Mthatha.[49]

Hence, for most of the nineteenth century, communication and the flow of information in Mpondoland remained attached to the movement of peoples and goods.[50] At least temporarily, Emagusheni Trading Store employed a 'Postboy',[51] but most letters and receipts appear to have accompanied deliveries—as in the introductory example of William Bouvarie's letter—or were passed along by transport drivers. Although traders and merchants were keen to share information on delays promptly with their customers, communication about, for example, the whereabouts of transports in general or missing or out-of-stock goods frequently reached addressees only when the waggons and transport riders in

---

46 See Wenzelhuemer, *Connecting the Nineteenth-Century World*, 113–15; Winseck and Pike, *Communication and Empire*, 92–112.

47 While the history of submarine telegraphy continues to be a flourishing research field, the history of communications in Africa remains an underexplored area. See Giuntini, 'ITU, Submarine Cables and African Colonies, 1850s–1900s', particularly 37–43.

48 According to a sketch map depicting South African telegraph and railway lines, by the late nineteenth century parts of Mpondoland had been connected to the Pietermaritzburg–Mthatha telegraph line (for example, Mthatha to Port St. Johns via Libode and Kokstad to Flagstaff via eMaxesibeni). See *Sketch Map of South African Telegraphs* (1896), ibali Digital Collections UCT at [https://ibali.uct.ac.za/s/jacobson-africana/item/98424#lg=1&slide=0], accessed 24 Nov. 2023.

49 See 'Memorandum of Mr. Under-Secretary H. E. R. Bright, being a Précis of Papers on Pondo Affairs, Presented to Parliament during Session of 1880', in *Cape of Good Hope: Return of Papers on Pondo Affairs*, 1–14, particularly 1–2. See also Beinart, 'Production, Labour Migrancy and the Chieftaincy', 79; Bramwell, 'Loyalties and the Politics of Incorporation in South Africa', 98.

50 On the dematerialization of information flows through telecommunication, see, for example, Wenzelhuemer, *Connecting the Nineteenth-Century World*, 1–29.

51 KCM 95/11/6, fol. 340.

question arrived.[52] In addition, while storekeepers in Mpondoland obtained general information on developments in the colonies through other sources such as print media, a considerable amount of news relating to Mpondoland politics in particular—however (in-)accurate—circulated through personal and business networks, including information and rumours on armed conflicts.[53] Finally, while trading partners frequently negotiated terms at personal meetings, correspondence was often used for haggling over commodity prices and complaining about product quality.[54] At least from the 1880s onwards, following the extension of telegraphic communication systems through East Griqualand, telegrams were occasionally passed between O'Donnell, Josiah P. Bouverie, and trading partners.[55] This did not, however, dematerialize communication, nor did it necessarily accelerate the flow of information in Mpondoland: since the business associates did not own a telegraph, telegrams were carried between telegraph stations in Kokstad or Umzimkhulu and Emagusheni Trading Store by messengers. Hence, throughout the nineteenth and early twentieth century, due to the limited extension of railway and telegraph systems in Mpondoland, transportation and communication in the region depended significantly on the provision of labourers.

The comparably late advent of labour migrancy in Mpondoland did not translate into what the trading network in Mpondoland needed: the steady availability of a black, predominantly male African labour force. The wealth in cattle—'the crux of Mpondo economic independence', William Beinart argues—provided the Mpondo with sufficient income to purchase commodities and made labour migration into mining, or from Mpondoland to other urban centres, largely unnecessary for the greater part of the nineteenth century. According to Beinart, labour migration among the Mpondo increased slightly in the 1890s after locust plagues and droughts had hampered cultivation, and once again significantly after the

52 See, for example, KCM 95/11/17, letter by Josiah P. Bouverie, 15 Mar. 1886; KCM 95/11/27, letter to Michael H. O'Donnell, 8 Sept. 1887.

53 O'Donnell, for example, subscribed to the *Natal Witness* and other newspapers through the printers and publishers P. Davies & Sons in Pietermaritzburg. See KCM 95/11/41, letter to Michael H. O'Donnell, 22 Mar. 1888. See KCM 95/11/54, letter to Michael H. O'Donnell, 6 Mar. 1890, on the subscription by Josiah P. Bouverie to the *The Graphic*. Regarding political unrest, armed conflicts, and rumours of wars, see, for example, KCM 95/11/18, letters by Josiah P. [?] Bouverie, 11 Aug. 1886, 12 Aug. 1886, and 30 Oct. 1886; KCM 95/11/26, letter from Hamilton MacNicholas to Josiah P. Bouverie, 21 Aug. 1887; KCM 95/11/63, letter from William Bouverie to Michael H. O'Donnell, 4 Jan. 1892.

54 Regarding a complaint about the quality of tobacco and the negotiation of prices for suits, see, for example, KCM 95/11/27, letter addressed to Michael H. O'Donnell, 12 Sept. 1887, and letter addressed to Josiah P. Bouverie, 23 Sept. 1887.

55 See, for example, KCM 95/11/25, letter by Josiah P. Bouvarie, 9 May 1887, stating that Michael H. O'Donnell had informed him about the delayed delivery of blankets via telegram. See also KCM 95/11/22, letter from Randles, Bros. & Hudson to Michael H. O'Donnell, 20 Dec. 1886; KCM 95/11/56, receipt by the Forwarding Agency, Richmond Road Station, 1 Feb. 1890.

outbreak of rinderpest in the late nineteenth century.[56] The account books for Emagusheni Trading Store, which contain, inter alia, labourers' accounts, give insight into periods of employment and in many cases indicate whether workers were discharged or dismissed, had 'disappeared', or 'left'. The bulk of the records covers the period 1887–9, and the entries rarely indicate the employee's specific occupation—the aforementioned 'Postboy' who delivered mail to Emagusheni Trading Store between August and November 1887 at 15s./month is one of few exceptions.[57] Given the high employee turnover at Emagusheni Trading Store during this short period—most labourers appear to have only been employed for two to four months, some of whom were re-employed—the records do not allow for an in-depth analysis of the development of black African wage labour in late-nineteenth-century Mpondoland.[58] However, by offering a snapshot of employment rates and wages at Emagusheni Trading Store, the records are nevertheless instructive. Most labourers employed by O'Donnell and his associates for transport rides, cattle drives, deliveries of mail and portable amounts of commodities, or housekeeping were probably drawn from the surrounding areas and consisted of black Africans, many of whom were Mpondo men.[59] While O'Donnell and his associates ran their own waggons, they too appear to have depended on independent transport riders, an occupation that became particularly popular among black African entrepreneurs during the nineteenth century.[60] In addition to the use of independent riders, at least two transport riders who owned waggons were on the payroll of Emagusheni Trading Store almost continuously between 1886 and 1889, and their wages were significantly higher than for other employees: labourers listed in the accounts (or named in letters) as 'Adam Russo driver' and 'Jim Driver' were paid 30–40s./month for their services, while for most labourers wages varied between 1–8s./month. Furthermore, wages were apparently paid after deductions for absences without leave or sick days and for commodities purchased by employees when they were dismissed or had left.[61]

---

56 Beinart, *The Political Economy of Pondoland 1860–1930*, 54–63 at 55.

57 KCM 95/11/6, fol. 340.

58 KCM 95/11/5 and KCM 95/11/6, Emagusheni Trading Store account books in 2 vols.

59 See Beinart, 'Production, Labour Migrancy and the Chieftaincy', 134–5. See KCM 95/11/47, letter to Michael H. O'Donnell, 14 Aug. 1889; KCM 95/11/44, letter to Josiah P. Bouverie, 8 Aug. 1889.

60 See, for example, Müller, 'Black and Coloured Entrepreneurship in Historical Perspective'. On specialist transport riders in Mpondoland, see Beinart, 'Production, Labour Migrancy and the Chieftaincy', 52. On the hire of specialist transport riders by Michael H. O'Donnell, see KCM 95/11/21, letter from Strachan & Co. to Michael H. O'Donnell, 14 Dec. 1886; KCM 95/11/55, letter to Josiah P. Bouverie, 15 Oct. 1890. Regarding waggon licenses issued to the latter in 1887, see KCM 95/11/30.

61 See KCM 95/11/5, KCM 95/11/6, and, more specifically, KCM 95/11/5, fols. 148–9 (for 'Jim Driver'), and KCM 95/11/13, letter from Tyrell & Co. to Michael H. O'Donnell, 14 Nov. 1885 (for 'Adam Russo driver').

With a few exceptions, discussions or negotiations of wage labour are absent from the Gallagher Family Paper records. It is nevertheless noteworthy, first, that labour shortage—particularly regarding transport riders and messengers—did occasionally increase costs for transportation and communication: 'Considering the trouble of finding messengers & the correspondence caused by it', a representative of Strachan & Co. informed O'Donnell in 1886, 'we feel bound ... to charge a small commission.'[62] Second, as some correspondence indicates, delays in the delivery of goods or cattle, too, occasionally derived from the unavailability of labourers: a cattle drive of untrained mules, for example, failed in July 1888 because it required an above-average number of drivers, which the author was currently 'very short of'.[63] Messenger fees and wages for independent transport riders varied depending on the distance covered, and while auctioneers competed for the cattle frequently sold via auction by O'Donnell, lower costs for cattle drives and communication in connection with auction sales in Harding (instead of Pietermaritzburg) could prove a persuasive argument in securing sales.[64] Thus, and third, labour shortage and costs potentially influenced the distribution of commodities in the region, particularly during the period of rivalry between Mhlangaso and Sigcau, tensions between colonial authorities and the Mpondo population, and the colonial public health measures which restricted the movement of goods and people. When unrest in the region intensified from the late 1880s onwards, O'Donnell struggled to find independent transport riders who would move goods through Mpondoland: a trading partner who had apparently 'seen various owners' of waggons for O'Donnell in 1890 stated that 'in the present state of Pondoland', transport riders were 'afraid to go there & prefer[red] loading at Kokstad'.[65] Quarantine regulations imposed by colonial authorities on Mpondoland during a smallpox epidemic in 1887 were perceived as particularly harmful by traders who engaged in the cross-border trade in the Colony of Natal. Mpondoland traders were prohibited to receive goods or send goods across the border, restrictions which, according to a representative of Randles, Bros. & Hudson, inflicted 'great hardship' on the local trading network.[66] Moreover, the colonial authorities' racialized conceptualization of disease origin and spread translated into public health measures that were predominantly aimed at black Africans, thus

62 KCM 95/11/21, letter from Strachan & Co. to Michael H. O'Donnell, 22 Apr. 1886. On commission charges on cattle drives by Strachan & Co., see KCM 95/11/21, letter from Strachan & Co to Michael H. O'Donnell, 12 May 1886.

63 KCM 95/11/40, letter to Michael H. O'Donnell, 23 July 1888. See also Josiah P. Bouvarie's search for 'any boys who can drive pigs', KCM 95/11/18, letter by Josiah P. Bouverie, 30 Oct. 1888.

64 KCM 95/11/18, letter from Horace C. Downes to Michael H. O'Donnell, 2 Dec. 1886. See also KCM 95/11/21, letter from Strachan & Co. to Michael H. O'Donnell, 14 Dec. 1886.

65 KCM 95/11/53, letter to Michael H. O'Donnell, 6 Oct. 1890.

66 KCM 95/11/30, letters by Randles, Bros. & Hudson and the colonial secretary of Natal dated 4, 5, and 8 Mar. 1887.

targeting the population that formed the core of the labour force in the translocal trade.[67] During the aforementioned smallpox epidemic, O'Donnell and Josiah P. Bouvarie continued to send black African labourers across the border, but their disregard for quarantine regulations was not always well received by trading partners, who feared that the discovery of a Mpondo on their premises might lead to extensions of quarantine regulations beyond Mpondoland: 'I don't thank you for sending a Pondo boy to sleep at my place', a trading partner in Harding wrote to O'Donnell in June 1887, and added: 'Had the police known of his being here they would have put him in the Lazaretto & perhaps my place in quarantine.'[68] Since the Gallagher Family Paper records do not cover the crucial period at the turn of the twentieth century when labour migrancy began in Mpondoland, it remains unclear how these developments affected O'Donnell and his business.[69] However, incomplete balance sheets and accounts suggest that between 1904 and 1911—after cattle herds had been rebuilt in the region and before the outbreak of East Coast Fever—O'Donnell continued to hold and trade cattle, hides, and other commodities in Mpondoland.[70]

Finally, the 1880s were marked by the establishment of customs houses along the major waggon routes between Emagusheni Trading Store and the Colony of Natal, the aim of which was to protect and secure the commercial interests of Cape merchants. Throughout the second half of the nineteenth century, inland customs duties had been utilized by the colonial administrations of the Cape Colony, the Colony of Natal, and the Boer Republics (South African Republic/Transvaal and the Orange Free State) to stimulate trade. From 1867 onwards, for example, the Colony of Natal levied duties below those of the Cape Colony in order to secure more traffic and increase income from customs duties, which formed the main source of the colonial administration's revenue.[71] Competition between Cape and Natal merchants for markets in Mpondoland and East Griqualand grew significantly from the early 1880s onwards, once the Cape Colony had successfully established railway links to the interior and the Cape colonial government's attempt to undermine Natal merchants' influence through the imposition of customs duties had shown some success in East Griqualand.[72]

---

67 See chapter 3.2.

68 KCM 95/11/25, letter by Horace C. Downes to Michael H. O'Donnell, 22 June 1887. See also Du Bois, 'Smallpox and Vaccination in Colonial Natal, 1850–1894'.

69 See Beinart, *The Political Economy of Pondoland 1860–1930*, 55–69.

70 On cattle losses in Mpondoland during the East Coast Fever endemic, see Beinart, *The Political Economy of Pondoland 1860–1930*, 70–84. See also KCM 95/11/71.

71 See Colesky, 'A Comparative Study on Customs Tariff Classification', 35–6.

72 See Beinart, 'Production, Labour Migrancy and the Chieftaincy', 67.

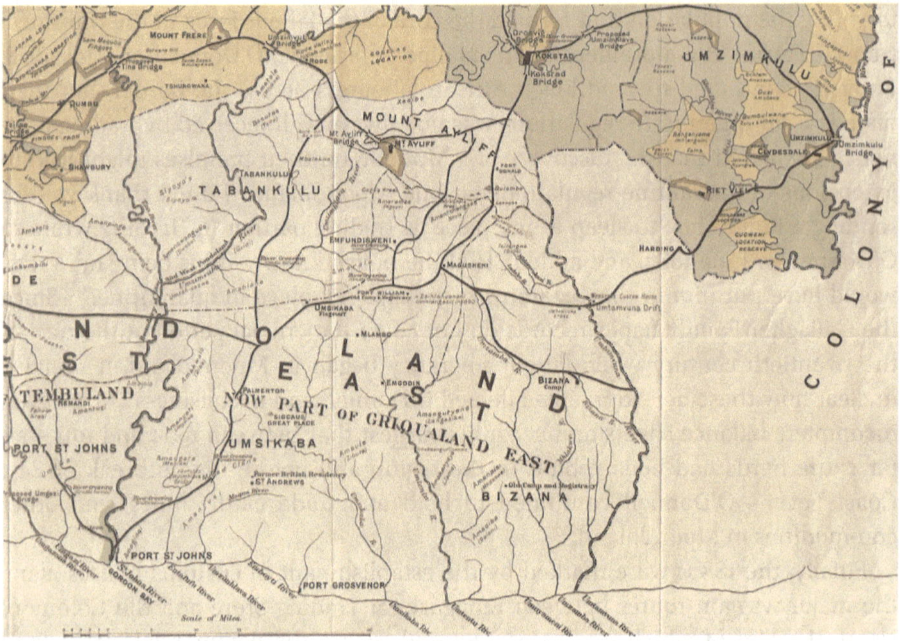

FIGURE 2.2 Detail of J. Fleming, *Sketch Map Shewing Districts and Principal Trading Routes in the Territories of Transkei, Tembuland, Griqualand East and Pondoland* (1899).

The customs houses established in Umzimkhulu between East Griqualand and Natal in 1885 and shortly afterwards at Mtamvuna Drift between Mpondoland and Natal were perceived by traders in these areas as a significant nuisance, mainly because they slowed trade and increased paperwork. In June 1890, for example, the customs border officer at Mtamvuna Drift assured Josiah P. Bouverie that while 'it was quite impossible to examine waggons during the night time', he would otherwise 'not throw any obstacle in the way of any Waggon's progress, so long as [he was] acquainted with the nature of the content of the packages carried on such' a waggon.[73] While the customs border houses offered lodging and a (limited amount of) storage possibilities for goods, inspections of waggon loads that were not accompanied by, for example, invoices listing the contents of bales, trusses, cases, and packages were limited to border crossings during the daytime.[74] Moreover, the main and fastest waggon and transport route from, for example, Pietermaritzburg to Emagusheni Trading Store now involved two border crossings and customs houses. For commodities subject to customs duties, such

73 KCM 95/11/53, letter from customs border officer, Mtamvuna Drift, to Josiah P. Bouverie, 11 June 1890.

74 On storage possibilities at the customs border house at Mtamvuna Drift, see KCM 95/11/25, letter to Michael H. O'Donnell, 20 May 1887.

as blankets or rugs, Natal customs authorities thus charged twice: 'In this Colony', Robert I. Finnemore explained to O'Donnell in 1890 regarding the transportation of rugs, 'import duty is charged every time the goods are imported … I am wholly unable to make a refund of duty on the ground that the same goods had been once before in Natal'.[75] O'Donnell and Josiah P. Bouverie were keen to redirect transports but had few alternatives, not least because of the limited number of roads, bridges, and raft or ferry services that enabled waggons to cross rivers (Fig. 2.2).[76] While custom duties and bonds were indeed low, they still increased the cost of inland transportation, as did Pass Laws that required Mpondo transport riders, cattle drivers, and messengers to take out passes from a colonial government official for s.1 per pass when crossing borders.[77]

It remains unclear when and under what circumstances O'Donnell broke off his trading relations with the business owners of Randles, Bros. & Hudson, as indicated in his will in 1915,[78] and while it is uncertain whether Emagusheni Trading Store continued to distribute second-hand military clothing in the region and beyond from the mid 1890s onwards, it appears likely. According to William Beinart, Emagusheni Trading Store continued to hold one of the most important positions in the local trade of Eastern Mpondoland, with the store 'stocked from top to bottom with goods for the Native trade'.[79] The Gallagher Family Paper records indicate that '15 prs Mens Army Rejects' were among the last commodities that O'Donnell and his associates acquired through the firm of Randles, Bros. & Hudson, who continued to import British and foreign second-hand military clothing into British South Africa from the firm of Mallett, Porter & Dowd, Ltd. in London until at least the mid 1900s, and from the United States until the 1920s.[80] On the one hand, European traders relied heavily on African labour, and trading activities were not only shaped by recurring plagues and cattle diseases but also by fluctuations in access to, and the availability of, workforce. The persistence of the

75 KCM 95/11/53, letter by Robert I. Finnemore to Michael H. O'Donnell, 14 Nov. 1890.

76 On ferrying fees at Umzimkhulu Drift, see KCM 95/11/56, receipt issued to Michael H. O'Donnell, 6 Jan. 1890. For cradle services, pontoons, and (proposed) bridges in the region, see Fig. 2.2.

77 See KCM 95/11/44, letter by customs border officer, Mtamvuna Drift, to Josiah P. Bouverie, 8 Aug. 1889. See also KCM 95/11/47, letter to Michael H. O'Donnell, 14 Aug. 1889, and KCM 95/11/45, letter to Michael H. O'Donnell, 21 Nov. 1889: 'I have the honor to call your attention to the pass regulations … which require that every Native entering or leaving the Colony shall take out a pass on which a fee of one shilling, for each person is chargeable. These passes may be had either at this office or from Mr Hughes, Umtamvuna, and my police have instructions to arrest all Natives who fail to comply with the law'.

78 KCM 95/11/73. For additional biographical information on Michael H. O'Donnell and the Gallagher family, see the Gallagher family history compiled by Jen Simpson at the Killie Cambell Africana Library (KCAL), KCM 95/11/1.

79 Cit. in Beinart, 'Production, Labour Migrancy and the Chieftaincy', 66.

80 See NASA TAB, DCU vol. 75, no. 638/1906; NASA SAB, DEA vol. 204, no. A10/16X.

trading network demonstrates, on the other hand, how the predominantly European merchant class in Mpondoland maintained continuity by navigating competing colonial commercial structures and political tensions through interference in colonial and Mpondo politics and sustained cooperation among traders. According to Gallagher Family Papers records, trade at Emagusheni Trading Store never ceased but remained notably stable: even at the height of political tensions in the late 1880s, commodities continued to reach customers. While '3 Military Over Coats to sell at 15[s.]' (among other textile goods) were delivered to Enhlenzie Store in eMfundisweni in January 1888, presumably via waggon,[81] a blanket, 'one of those old military "jas"-es ... and a flask of gin' were delivered to a customer by a carrier.[82] Finally, purchases by returning customers in particular suggest that second-hand military clothing distributed in the area and by Emagusheni Trading Store indeed reached predominantly black African consumers.[83]

2.2 Contested Consumption? Black African Adoption and Appropriation Second-Hand Military Clothing in British South Africa, *c.*1880–1895

> *There used to be a folk tale which said that there were white people living, and that they would one day come. The old women of former times ... would say, 'There are white people who wear clothes. They will one day come to this country.' Our forefathers would ask, 'Where will they come from?' The answer was, 'They are on the other side of the sea.' Our people would query this, saying 'How could they cross the sea?' But indeed there came white people who wore clothes.*

Recalling this story during an interview with James Stuart on 31 May 1916, Lugubu kaMangaliso—noting that he '*no longer remember*[ed] *these stories well*'—added that it '*was only a tale, but when* [his ancestors] *talked about it they would say, "It came true."*'[84] As kaMangaliso reminds us, European dress—and the knowledge thereof—reached the African continent well before the era of increased colonial

81 KCM 95/11/41, receipt for goods received by Enhlenzie Store from Emagusheni Trading Store, 26 Jan. 1888.

82 KCM 95/11/7, letter from Henry N. Gaika to Michael H. O'Donnell, 24 Apr. 1883. The term 'jas' could either be an abbreviation for jacket or, as I suggest, Dutch or Afrikaans (*jas*, pl. *jasse*) for coat or overcoat. See Donaldson, *A Grammar of Afrikaans*, 75–6.

83 Waggon loads for Enhlenzie Store, for instance, regularly included commodities intended for the African trade, such as handkerchiefs and blankets. See, for example, KCM 95/11/20, receipt for goods purchased by Enhlenzie Store from Emagushenie Trading Store, June 1886; KCM 95/11/31, receipts for goods received by Enhlenzie Store from Emagusheni Trading Store, 25 Apr. 1887 and 24 May 1887.

84 Testimony by Lugubu kaMangaliso, 31 May 1916, *The James Stuart Archive of Recorded Oral Evidence*, 291.

expansion during the nineteenth century in the context of, for example, the transatlantic slave trade, commodity trade encounters, and diplomatic gift exchanges.[85] In nineteenth-century Southern Africa, adoption of European dress by Africans was catalysed by missionaries' attempts to clothe black Africans in European fashion and thereby imbue specific values and effect changes in African habits—attempts that, Jean and John Comaroff show in the case of the Tswana, did not produce the intended outcomes. The 'most immediate and visible response' by the majority of Tswana who appropriated European dress, the anthropologists argue, was 'a synthetic, syncretic style which, to European eyes, appeared absurd.'[86] These increasing disputes over clothing between missionaries and Africans, Kirsten Rüther argues in the context of nineteenth-century Lutheran mission stations in the Colony of Transvaal, 'reflected the growing complexity of social and economic tensions in the industrial era'.[87] While these findings are partly mirrored in contemporary accounts, observations, and restrictive colonial clothing regulations, attitudes towards and opinions on African adoption and appropriation of European fashions in general and military clothing in particular diverged throughout the late nineteenth and early twentieth centuries.

Between October 1900 and January 1901, James Stuart recorded a series of conversations with John Kumalo and four other informants, among whom were his assistant Ndukwana kaMbengwana, Solomon Mabaso, and Josiah 'John Africa'. According to Stuart's notes, at the time of the interviews John Kumalo was about 63 years old, 'an important headman at Roosboom' near Ladysmith, and a '*kholwa*' (literally, 'believer'), an African Christian convert.[88] While we learn little about Solomon Mabaso from Stuart's notes, Josiah 'John Africa' told Stuart that he had arrived in Ladysmith from the Transvaal in 1860 and either referred to himself or was referred to by Stuart as a '*rumuthsa*' (literally, 'interpreter').[89] Stuart notes that while he was known by Europeans as 'John Africa', Africans called him Josiah.[90] Over the course of their conversations and in different constellations, Stuart and his informants covered a wide range of topics, including black African

85 See, for example, Aplern, 'What Africans Got for Their Slaves'; Brauner, *Kompanien, Könige und caboceers*, 273–393.

86 Comaroff and Comaroff, *Of Revelation and Revolution*, 218–49 at 241.

87 Ruether, 'Heated Debates Over Crinolines', 361. See also Ross, 'The Top-Hat in South African History'.

88 *The James Stuart Archive of Recorded Oral Evidence*, 215–72 at 215. Regarding *amakholwa*, see Etherington, *Preachers, Peasants and Politics in South-East Africa, 1835–80*.

89 See *The James Stuart Archive of Recorded Oral Evidence*, 225. Webb and Wright note that '[*i*]*rumutsha* (*ihumusha*) seems to have been used to denote a town dweller who had to a greater or lesser extent broken his links with traditional authority'. Ibid. 268, n. 36. Contemporary dictionaries translate *rumutsha*/*ihumusha* as 'to interpret'/'interpreter'. See Mate, *Kleines Deutsch-kaffrisches Wörterbuch*, 25 ('dolmetschen'); Bryant, *An Abridged English-Zulu Word-Book*, 178 ('interpreter').

90 See *The James Stuart Archive of Recorded Oral Evidence*, 227.

attitudes towards colonial government in the Colony of Natal, black African adolescents' changing relations to their families, and religion. In the context of 'the subject of "The poor: are there observable in Natal any tendencies towards poverty?"', the informants and Stuart shared their views regarding, for example, the relation between land ownership and poverty in the Colony of Natal. Moreover, during a subsequent meeting, Stuart recorded two opinions shared by Mabaso and Kumalo that approached poverty from a different angle. Mabaso argued that

> natives [were] reduced to poverty by their own tastes. A man is taught to take to clothing; this creates for him a certain standard of living up to which he, from fear of being ridiculed by others, strives to live. Thus it is due to the advent of Europeans that there is this tendency to spend one's means merely for the sake of being like others; they bring all manner of goods which increase the desire to spend.[91]

According to Mabaso, poverty among black Africans was linked to what Arjun Appadurai terms the 'capacity to aspire', to wants that 'are never simply individual (as the language of wants and choices inclines us to think) [but] are always formed in interaction'.[92] Following Mabaso's testimony, interaction between black Africans and Europeans increased black African desire to consume European commodities 'for the sake of being like others', and Europeans specifically. This notion, moreover, appears encapsulated in a term used by Kumalo: according to Stuart, Kumalo spoke 'of clothing and other things made by Europeans as *ngwaqubulungu*'[93] (literally, 'striving to be like a white man').[94] Given the difficulties of establishing the specific connotations of this term in the James Stuart records, as noted by Colin de B. Webb and John B. Wright, I hesitate to overinterpret the literal translation in this context. Moreover, according to Kumalo, the presence of Europeans and European commodities—even if the literal translation of *ngwaqubulungu* is considered—did not lead to poverty among all black Africans. Kumalo, according to Stuart, disagreed with Mabaso that

> the articles brought to this country by Europeans are a cause of poverty, on the ground that *kolwas* and raw natives, i. e. those who are in the habit of purchasing European clothing and whatnot and those who rarely buy, the poorer are undoubtedly the raw natives, those who have not yet learned the need of the articles referred to.[95]

91 Ibid. 251.
92 Appadurai, 'The Capacity to Aspire', 67.
93 See *The James Stuart Archive of Recorded Oral Evidence*, 251.
94 Ibid. 271, n. 77.
95 Ibid. 251.

First, it is noteworthy that in contrast to Mabaso, Kumalo's observation appeared structured by notions of what Josiah had elsewhere described as the 'many classes in Ladysmith: there was the *kolwa*, the *rumutsha* ... the *isigqokwa*, and the ordinary kraal native.'[96] While the social differentiation implied in these terms, as David B. Coplan argues, was to 'some extent ... more apparent than real', they were meaningful to Kumalo in distinguishing consumption patterns in relation to European commodities and determining that consumption of the latter was not, in fact, the primary reason for poverty among black Africans.[97] Second, implied in the characterization of the 'raw natives ... who have not yet learned the need of the articles referred to' is the observation that, depending on the scope of interaction with Europeans, not all black Africans desired European commodities.[98] Finally, Mabaso and Kumalo spoke of interactions between Africans and Europeans in these contexts in terms of 'teaching' and 'learning'—terms that imply a hierarchical structure and unequal power relations.

During the last part of the conversation, Kumalo turned to Stuart, asking him for his opinion on the relation between poverty and class with regard to black Africans in Natal. While Stuart agreed with Kumalo about his characterization of the different consumption patterns of African Christian converts on the one hand and other black Africans on the other, he pointed out that 'yet, there are but few natives in Natal, even the rawest, who do not purchase, and what is more, are not in the habit of purchasing European goods; every man, for instance, is required to have a coat and a pair of trousers when he enters a town.'[99] Stuart's reference to colonial clothing regulations is particularly instructive, as various proclamations, bylaws, and ordinances aimed at black Africans stipulated dress codes from at least the 1850s onwards. Individuals passing through or entering towns or cities—in the words of a law passed in the Colony of Natal in 1880—were to 'be decently clothed ... with some garment or garments, extending from neck to knee.'[100] Colonial sumptuary laws, Hlonipha Mokoena argues, were in part responsible for black South Africans' hybrid dressing styles, which often included articles of second-hand military dress.[101] As Keletso E. Atkin's vivid description of black African town workers' attire illustrates, articles of second-hand military clothing were often combined with elements of traditional dress, and appropriated in ways that

96 Ibid. 229. According to Webb and Wright '[*i*]*sigqokwa* (from the verb *ukugqoka*, "to wear") was probably used to denote a person who wore European-type clothing.' Ibid. 268, n. 36.

97 Coplan, 'The Emergence of an African Working-Class Culture', 358.

98 See *The James Stuart Archive of Recorded Oral Evidence*, 251.

99 Ibid.

100 *The Laws of Natal, 1879–1880*, 1324–5 at 1324.

101 See Mokoena, 'The Rickshaw Puller and the Zulu Policeman', particularly 132–3; Atkins, *The Moon is Dead! Give Us Our Money!*, 141–2.

left newly 'arrived strangers ... flooded with feelings of revulsion ... acute self-conscious distress', or amazement.[102]

These sentiments are mirrored in contemporary European travel writing, in which European reactions ranged from ridicule, repulsion, and mockery, to amazement, and even admiration.[103] Black Africans' appropriations of European fashions in hybrid dressing styles caught the attention of, for example, Harold T. Tangye, who notes in his travel account *In New South Africa* (1900) his feeling of alienation while passing through Johannesburg, whose citizens he perceived as a 'collection of nationalities and men of various ranks. There are Chinese, Japanese, Kaffirs of many kinds, Hindoos, French, German, Dutch, and English.' The dance of a group of Africans appeared 'strange, incomprehensible', and the dress of one black African particularly noteworthy: 'There is ... the Kaffir with an old, red, military coat, a striped shirt hanging underneath, a rainbow-coloured umbrella, and not even an apology for trousers—his arms, too, being adorned with apparently ornamental fixtures in the shape of brass rings.'[104] Other European travel writers gave insight into their reasoning and their attempts to contextualize the phenomenon of black Africans adopting and appropriating second-hand military dress. In the winter of 1871, Anne M. Wilkinson was awaiting letters from England. 'The mail arrived last Friday', she eventually replied to her friend on 22 July, 'our letters were only forty-nine days from England.' Pleased with what Wilkinson considered a reasonable postal shipping time, she added that there was

> something very pleasant in expecting the post on Saturday, and looking over the hill for the old Kafir postman—from Rorke's Drift—in his red coat. I think that all the old army red coats are sent out to Natal, for the Kaffirs wear them. In towns they are obliged by law to wear something, and these coats are nice and warm. A great many of our Zulus have them ... though by far the greater number have simply their tails.[105]

Wilkinson and other Europeans frequently pointed out that colonial clothing regulations stipulated dress codes for black Africans, which partly accounted for their noteworthy dressing styles. However, Wilkinson also noted that colonial military authorities provided second-hand military clothing to black Africans and emphasized the material qualities of European military dress. Similarly, Edgerton

---

102 Atkins, *The Moon is Dead! Give Us Our Money!*, 141. In addition, see Mokoena, 'The Rickshaw Puller and the Zulu Policeman', 133.

103 See, for example, Geary, 'Political Dress'; Klopper, 'Gentlemen at Leisure'; Comaroff and Comaroff, *Of Revelation and Revolution*, 241–6; Ruether, 'Heated Debates Over Crinolines', 373–4.

104 Tangye, *In New South Africa*, 94–5. See also Vincent, *Actual Africa; Or, the Coming Continent*, 295–6.

105 Wilkinson, *A Lady's Life and Travels in Zululand and the Transvaal during Cetewayo's Reign*, 103–4.

K. Laird, for example, argued that Zulus, apart from 'the ordinary attire in their native wilds … on nearing town … must wear clothes, and this generally consists of a short shirt, or an old soldier's jacket, of which they are very fond.'[106] As indicated in Laird's account, it is not only the reference to second-hand military dress in connection with colonial clothing laws that features prominently in travel accounts published between *c.*1880 and 1900 but also the implication of male black Africans' preference for (British) second-hand military dress over other items of clothing, and travel writers and other observers tried to make sense of what many of them perceived as a distinct 'curiosity'.

Material quality was—as in Wilkinson's account—construed as one incentive for the appropriation of, for example, second-hand military coats by black Africans. Trade commissioner S. W. Whitham, who visited several South African cities in the early twentieth century at the request of the South African Trade Committee, claimed that the black African was 'shrewd enough to know that originally such uniforms [had] been made from the very best of materials, and little he cares what the colour may be provided he is kept warm in the bitterly cold nights.'[107] In contrast to Whitham's claim of black Africans' disregard for specific colours, however, some European observers argued that black Africans were, in fact, particularly 'fond of a red military coat'.[108] Red coats and 'grey great coats with brass buttons', Anthony Trollope claimed in the first volume of his travel account *South Africa* (1878), were in demand among Zulus in Pietermaritzburg:

> I have said of the Kafir that he is always dressed when seen in town, but that he is dressed like an Irish beggar. I should have added, however, that he always wears his rags with a grace … The rags are there, but it seems as though the rags have been chosen with as much solicitude as any dandy in Europe gives to the fit and colour of his raiment … One fellow will walk the street with an old soldier's red coat on him and nothing else, another will have a pair of knee breeches and a flannel shirt hanging over it … Old grey great coats with brass buttons, wherever they may come from, are in request and though common always seem to confer dignity.[109]

What stands out in Trollope's account is his comparison of black African practices of self-fashioning with dandyism. The figure of the dandy emerged in eighteenth- and nineteenth-century France and Britain, and although often associated primarily with a distinct fashion trend, dandyism functioned 'as a symptom of

106 Laird, *Incidents of Travel in South Africa*, 129. In addition, see Derham, *A Visit to Cape Colony and Natal in 1879*, 56: 'The Zulus are very fond of a red military coat or a long military overcoat'.

107 Whitham, *Report on the Textile and Soft Goods Trade of South Africa*, 43.

108 Derham, *A Visit to Cape Colony and Natal in 1879*, 56.

109 Trollope, *South Africa*, vol. 1, 317–18.

changing social, political, cultural and economic conditions.'[110] While dandyism among European working-class men involved mimicry of aristocratic dressing styles, it was not merely a transgression of class boundaries but a more fundamental critique of social conventions. In British South Africa, the figure of the dandy emerged in the context of mine labour, the emergence of a black African working class, and the rapid growth of the 'truck trade' during the late 1870s and early 1880s. Perceptions of black African mine workers clothed in European dress as 'Dandy Swell' by whites, Zine Magubane argues, were an expression of 'racial and economic anxiety, envy and hatred'.[111] Through his projection of the sartorial excess associated with European white dandyism onto black African appropriation of European dress, Trollope appears to acknowledge black Africans' practices of dressing in their careful consideration of fashions and self-conscious choice of style.[112] Still, and while bodily performativity (the 'graceful' wearing of dress) might distract from the material qualities of the clothing, it is, in Trollope's account, the clothes that dignify, not the black African who is dignified. James Mackinnon, for example, argued that black African men 'are often to be seen nearly nude, but, when possible, are very fond of wearing an English soldier's cast-off uniform. It may be tattered beyond recognition, but their pride is immense, as they swagger about with the air of a general.'[113] The disapproving undertone in Mackinnon's account speaks not only to his unease at seeing the British uniform decontextualized (appropriated in a non-military context); his remarks on bodily performativity suggest he perceived the appropriation of British second-hand military dress by black Africans as an objectionable appropriation of the social status of a British army official. In this respect, Mackinnon's attitude was similar to that of the British military and colonial authorities in South Africa, whose efforts to legislate against and prosecute black Africans increased in parallel with the consumption of second-hand military dress by black Africans. Indeed, as Sandra Klopper points out, British military and colonial authorities 'went to enormous efforts to prevent Africans from appropriating discarded uniforms and other military insignia.'[114]

In March 1878, a black African referred to by British colonial officials as 'a native named Vumazonke' pleaded guilty in a case brought against him at the magistrate court in Pietermaritzburg. According to the prosecution, Vumazonke had purchased 'a pair of boots, a great coat and a tunic from Private M. Evoy of The Buffs'. The case appears to have been processed swiftly: according to the court magistrate Robert I. Finnemore, the offender admitted to having purchased the

---

110 Miller, *Slaves to Fashion*, 8.

111 Magubane, 'Mines, Minstrels, and Masculinity', 280. See also Mnisi and Ngcongo, 'Looking Back to Look Forward'.

112 For an analysis of the semiotics of the 'dandy' and the 'fop', see Miller, *Slaves to Fashion*, 8–9.

113 Mackinnon, *South African Traits*, 196.

114 Klopper, 'Gentlemen at Leisure', 330–1.

boots. Vumazonke's employer testified to the offender's character, and although he too stated that other items of clothing (a great coat and a tunic) had been bought by another black African, Vumazonke was sentenced to pay a fee amounting to triple the value of all the articles of clothing, a sum of roughly £2.50. Finnemore concluded that 'to take away the property so purchased and to fine the native ... [was] sufficient punishment to detain other natives from having dealings with soldiers.' Given the circumstances, Finnemore pointed out, there was 'nothing "extraordinary" about the case'—except that the opinions on the sufficiency of the punishment inflicted on the offender differed significantly.

After sentencing, an adjutant who had followed the case in court complained that his opinion and evidence on the case had not been heard. The commanding officers he addressed on the matter agreed that consequently the 'punishment by the Magistrate in this case [had not been] in any way adequate to the crime'. The dispute over Vumazonke's case eventually reached the colonial secretary: 'Owing to the general practice among the natives of this colony of wearing cast off military uniforms the facility given to badly disposed soldiers for disposing their kits is very great', the colonel commanding the troops in so-called Natal and the Transvaal argued, and demanded 'from the Natal Government ... their assistance in putting a check upon a very serious and disgraceful military offence.' The colonial secretary's reply and final word in the matter reached army officials three weeks later:

> [I]f the prisoner had been a white man the case might have called for consideration in respect to the amount of punishment, but ... considering the circumstances ... that for a Native, unaware of the gravity [?] of the offence committed by the soldier and himself, also and accustomed to purchase articles of Military clothing from Store-Keepers and other white persons—punishment inflicted cannot be called very insufficient.[115]

The difference in opinions expressed in the aftermath of the case is symptomatic of the growing tensions between consumers, British military authorities, and colonial authorities during the late nineteenth century. The adoption of second-hand military dress by black Africans had already been criticized by, for example, Cape colonial authorities in the 1830s and had been increasingly objected to by military and colonial authorities since the mid nineteenth century, when the presence of British soldiers in South Africa intensified.[116] Despite military legal provisions such as the Mutiny Acts and, from 1881 onwards, the Army Acts, which prohibited civilians from purchasing, pawning, and receiving army clothing, guns, ammunition, and other army stores, British soldiers stationed in South Africa frequently

115 All quotes here from NASA NAB, CSO vol. 636, no. 1184/1878.

116 See NASA WCARS, GH vol. 23/11, no. 54/1837.

disposed of their worn-out military clothing through barter with black Africans.[117] Theophilus Shepstone—the highly influential Secretary for Native Affairs in Natal between 1856 and 1877—had already drawn attention to various instances of 'natives attempting to buy clothes of soldiers' in 1864, requesting that the magistrates caution black Africans on the subject.[118] Five years later, Shepstone warned 'Chiefs and Native people ... that to purchase necessaries and regimental clothing from soldiers [was] a punishable offence', adding that after this notice 'no plea of ignorance [would] be admitted at any expense or mitigation of the punishment.'[119] While prosecutions of black South Africans for the appropriation of British second-hand military dress continued throughout the following decades, the dispute reached a peak during the early and mid 1890s, when some colonial and military authorities attempted to introduce the Uniforms Act—enacted in Britain in 1894—in British South Africa.[120]

Witnesses before and members of the Committee on the Uniforms Bill in Britain had discussed the appropriation of British second-hand military dress primarily, but not exclusively, as a British domestic phenomenon: the participants of the committee not only acknowledged the existence of 'a large and remunerative market for showy uniforms in South Africa' but also considered the appropriation of British second-hand military clothing by black Africans unproblematic, 'as long as', Redvers H. Buller stressed, they had 'bare legs'.[121] Since bare feet and—by extension—bare legs were typically viewed as signs of subordination, Buller appears not to have viewed the adoption and appropriation of British second-hand military dress by black Africans as a threat to colonial social order that manifested, most visibly, in dressing styles and clothing.[122] After the passing of the Uniforms Bill in Britain, copies of it and requests by the imperial government to adopt this, or similar regulations, were sent to colonial governments including the British Bahamas, Barbados, South Africa, and India.[123] While the British colonial governments of the Bahamas and Barbados apparently agreed to enact the legislation

117 Section 85 of the *Mutiny Act 1871*, c. 9, for example, stated that any 'person who shall knowingly detain, exchange, or receive from any soldier or deserter ... any arms, ammunition, medals ... clothes, or military furniture, or any provisions, or any sheets or other articles used in barracks ... or regimental necessaries, or any article of forage ... and shall not give a satisfactory account how he or she came by the same, or shall change the colour of any clothes as aforesaid, shall forfeit for every such offence any sum not exceeding twenty pounds, together with treble the value of all or any of the several articles of which such offender shall so become or be possessed.' See also *Army Act 1881*, 336, section 168.

118 NASA NAB, 1/LDS vol. 3/3/2, no. H2/1864.

119 NASA NAB, 1/LDS vol. 3/3/3, no. H13/1869. See also NASA NAB, 1/WEN vol. 3/2/3, no. W444A/1900.

120 See chapter 1.2.

121 *Report ... on the Uniforms Bill*, 5–7, Ev 84–118 at 5, Ev 112.

122 See Ferguson, 'Footnotes on *Trilby*', particularly 131.

123 See TNA, CO 28/238, no. 13025, fols. 505–7, and TNA, CO 23/241, no. 5939, fols. 120–1.

with minor modifications, in British India and most British colonial governments in South Africa the adoption of the Uniforms Act 1894 or similar legislation was heavily objected to. According to British colonial officials, Rajas and Maharajas in British India frequently introduced British or British-style military dress among their troops,[124] and although British Indian colonial authorities thought it 'not desirable that any drunken Eurasian or Soldier who may take service with a small Rajah or any native for that matter shall burlesque H. M.'s commission by wearing the dress prescribed for Officers holding it', the wearing of British second-hand military uniforms by non-military individuals was not prohibited. While the appropriation of British military dress by, inter alia, Indians was not undisputed, it apparently remained unrestricted and unprosecuted during the nineteenth century. As a colonial official argued in August 1895: 'I imagine that people who wear cast off uniform in this country, if they think of anything at all beyond the fact that it is warm and cheap, think they are honouring themselves by wearing it. If so, it would be a pity to put it into their heads that they are insulting us.'[125]

In British South Africa, too, most colonial government authorities opposed the introduction of the proposed legislation. An attempt to pass the bill in the Cape Town House of Assembly in the summer of 1895, for example, failed miserably: most Cape Town politicians considered the proposed legislation, in the words of one MP, 'a "rubbish" little Bill.' Although the majority of MPs agreed that 'the real object [of the Uniforms Bill] was to prevent the feelings of the men in the Army being hurt', the responsibility was thought to '[lie] in the hands of the Imperial Government not to sell the uniforms' in the first place. Furthermore, MPs suspected that the 'Bill would work hardly, for there were many tradesmen ... who had old uniforms in stock.'[126] According to the Cape colonial MPs, the circulation and distribution of British second-hand military clothing had, by the mid 1890s, reached an extent that seemed beyond colonial control: 'In the country the uniforms were worn right and left, and even on farms some persons might be seen wearing them', while storekeepers held large numbers of uniforms in stock, and black Africans in colonial government employment were given, for example, second-hand uniforms of the British Royal Artillery.[127] To some Cape colonial politicians, however, the main concern over the proposed prohibition was not the potential limitations of law enforcement but the more fundamental question of restricting black African consumption:

> Suppose a law were passed that shepherds' plaid trousers ... or black hats ... should not be worn they would resent it, but that would not be doing more injustice than

124 See NAI, Foreign Department General – Part B, Proceedings November 1876, file nos. 75–6.

125 See NAI, Legislative Department – Part B, Proceedings October 1895, file nos. 54–5.

126 *Debates in the House of Assembly, in the Second Session of the Ninth Parliament of the Cape of Good Hope, 2nd May to 3rd August, 1895*, 14–5.

127 Ibid.

> to ask that those people who had these uniforms should not be allowed to wear them ... In this colony for the last fifty or sixty years this clothing had been worn, and there had been no idea that a single individual in the British Army had been brought into contempt.[128]

To the MP, the adoption of British second-hand military clothing by black Africans did not differ from the adoption of other forms of European dress: the black hat or top hat, for example, initially worn by elite white males in South African urban centres, was increasingly appropriated by Afrikaner and black African elites towards the end of nineteenth century.[129] Finally, in the Colony of Natal, colonial ministers argued in a similar manner that '[s]econd-hand uniforms are imported in large quantities by shop-keepers in the Colonies' largely unaltered, bearing their distinctive facings, buttons, badges, and other British military insignia. As long as the War Office allowed for the exportation and distribution of second-hand military clothing in British South Africa, ministers reckoned, legislation such as the Uniforms Act would hardly prevent black Africans from its consumption and appropriation.[130] Even initial adoptions of the Uniforms Act by some colonial governments were repealed shortly afterwards. In the Colony of Southern Rhodesia, for example, 'it was considered unfair, while uniforms continued to be fully exposed for sale, to punish ignorant natives for wearing them'.[131] Similarly, in the Bechuanaland Protectorate (Botswana), the resident magistrate of Mahikeng argued in 1899 that the legislation merely targeted black African consumers, and thus 'the person who actually wears the clothing in question, but in the case of natives, he really is more sinned against than sinning: he sees old clothing offered for sale, and being unaware of the Proclamation, he obtains the garment and then finds that it is illegal to wear it.'[132] The dispute over the introduction of the Uniforms Act in British South Africa and the rise in prosecutions show that military and colonial authorities invested considerable energy in attempting to curb the circulation of second-hand military clothing in British South Africa. Yet these developments also reveal how limited these efforts were. Second-hand military clothing continued to move through local trading networks and into everyday use—shaped more by the choices of consumers than by the intentions of colonial officials, thus underscoring the significance of African consumer demand and the degree to which practices of acquisition and use eluded colonial control.

---

128 Ibid. 24.

129 See Ross, 'The Top-Hat in South African History'; Klopper, 'Gentlemen at Leisure'.

130 NASA NAB, CSO vol. 1499, no. 1059/1895. See also NASA WCARS, CO vol. 8294, no. X2955.

131 TNA, WO 32/9118.

132 TNA, DO 119/289.

2.3 Competing for Black African Consumers: 'Truck Trade' and Second-Hand Military Clothing, *c.*1890–1902

FIGURE 2.3 Inside Emagusheni Trading Store (1970), photograph by Lance James.

Photographs taken of Emagusheni Trading Store's interior shortly before the buildings and property were sold to the Xhosa Development Corporation in 1970 by Brian Gallagher show a storeroom almost overflowing with manifold commodities: tinned foods and textile goods are neatly arranged on high shelves behind a long U-shaped counter. Large pots and other commodities can be seen hanging from the roof, a few chairs and buckets are placed in the storefront next to what appear to be some of the building's supporting beams, leaving enough space for potential customers to browse the store (Fig. 2.3). Stock book entries dated July 1887 reveal an equally wide range of diverse commodities offered by O'Donnell and his business associates at Emagusheni Trading Store: goods ranged from household items (such as pans, kettles, cups, bottles, and plates), food items (particularly flour, sugar, coffee, and pickles), and alcohol (encompassing different types of brandy, whiskey, and beer), to tools (such as axes, nails, hoes, plough shares, picks, and knives), toiletries, and medicines, as well as a wide range of beads, textiles, and items of clothing in particular. Hosiery, about twenty different types of shirts, handkerchiefs and blankets in varying sizes and colours, trousers, suits, and undervests, waistcoats, braces, and tunics—to name the main types of clothing—filled the store.[133] Second-hand military items of clothing, while less numerous, were continuously in stock at Emagusheni Trading Store between 1885 and 1892: the stock book entries list, for example, military overcoats, pouches, greatcoats, red tunics, and army sandals.[134]

According to British trade observers and colonial authorities, black African consumer demands increased and changed significantly towards the end of the nineteenth and the early twentieth century. While official statistics such as the *Blue Books* give some indication of the expansion in black South African consumption, these were—as the Secretary for Native Affairs for the Colony of Natal Frederick R. Moor explained in 1904—merely estimates: '[T]hese figures are very crude, they are only approximate', Moor argued, and added: 'There is lots of stuff which is not included there that the Native does consume. For instance, he consumes a lot of European clothing which is not shown in these amounts. I think those amounts merely indicate what is known as Kafir truck.'[135] The categorization of commodities intended for the trade with black Africans as 'truck', Moor's comment indicates, was by no means clear-cut and was certainly subject to change, pointing to European misunderstandings of African consumer preferences as well as the shifts in these. Henry T. Lowry, for example, who had traded in the Cape Colony since 1890, argued that traders were not selling 'such a quantity ... of what we call "Kafir truck." That is the red Native trade used to be done years ago: Ochre, Beads, Wire, and so on; that has fallen off very much of late years. [Black Africans] are going in more for clothing and groceries.'[136]

Reports on the changing black African consumption patterns differed between, for example, urban centres and the countrysides; however, European observers agreed that by the end of the early twentieth century, black African consumption had increased significantly, with 'hundreds of stores' now depending 'solely on the Kafirs for their existence. And which yield their owners a good livelihood.'[137] *The British and South African Export Gazette* estimated by the end of the nineteenth century that, in addition to the approximately 979 businesses and firms specializing in drapery and outfitting within the British South African textile trade, '3,000 or more storekeepers [were] scattered throughout the country, a por-

133 Judging from the handwriting, Josiah P. Bouvarie recorded the store's stock roughly every three to four months between 1885 and 1889. See KCM 95/11/15. For a list of goods carried by traders in nineteenth-century colonial Zimbabwe, see Burke, *Lifebuoy Men, Lux Women*, 64.

134 See KCM 95/11/15. See also KCM 95/11/64 for an entry in the Emagusheni Trading Store account books 1892–1894 dated 30 June 1892 which lists, among other commodities, '3 Police G. Coats 5/6' and 'M. G. Coat 7/9'.

135 *South African Native Affairs Commission*, vol. 3, 228, Ev 20965.

136 *South African Native Affairs Commission*, vol. 2, 1063–6, Ev 14439–93 at 1064, Ev 14457.

137 *South African Natives Affairs Commission*, vol. 5, 300.

tion of whose operations include[d] the sale of textiles of some sort, if only that rough and elementary kind included under the term of Kaffir truck.'[138]

In an article titled 'The Kaffir Trade. Its Extent and Future Importance', published in *The British and South African Export Gazette* in February 1903, an anonymous author argued that African consumers had, by the beginning of the twentieth century, received insufficient attention from British manufacturers, merchants, and storekeepers. According to the author, only a few British wholesale houses in South Africa had 'devoted their energies to the Kaffir trade alone.' 'For such houses', he went on, there was 'a business of unknown extent to be done—a harvest that requires but the reaping—but the workmen must be suited to, and understand the nature of, the crop.' The author claimed that while 'the purchasing value per head of native [would] never reach anything approaching that of the white, his numerical superiority may at least suggest a volume of trade which the commercial world cannot afford to ignore.'[139] Statements made by traders, colonial officials, and other Europeans before the South African Native Affairs Commission between 1903 and 1905 undermine the significance ascribed to black African consumption by the gazette's authors in the early twentieth century: as the Native Commissioner of Pietersburg, Colony of Transvaal (Polokwane, Limpopo Province) argued, black Africans' 'main item of ... contribution [to colonial revenue] in other forms than taxation is that he is a consumer. The great trade done in so-called Kafir truck fully bears this out.'[140] Yet long-time businessmen like Donald Strachan, who had become a managing partner of Strachan & Co. in Umzimkhulu in 1879, claimed in the early twentieth century that while black South African consumption had been 'increasing everywhere', it had been a 'quite recent development'.[141]

Contemporary trade observers noted significant changes and an overall expansion in black African consumption during the 1890s. Articles and reports published in *The British and South African Export Gazette* not only summarized, interpreted, and predicted changes in the 'truck trade' but, moreover, increasingly noted the shortcomings of British businesses and manufacturers in meeting black African consumer demand. While trade observers sometimes saw the lack of experience among British storekeepers as one reason why they struggled to adequately cater for African demands, British manufacturers and importers were held equally—at times even more—responsible for a development that characterized the African trade throughout the late nineteenth and early twentieth century: foreign competition (particularly Indian and, to a lesser extent, Chinese

138 *The British and South African Export Gazette*, 7/81 (7 Apr. 1899), 770.

139 *The British and South African Export Gazette*, 11/127, (6 Feb. 1903), 917–22.

140 *South African Natives Affairs Commission*, vol. 5, 298–300 at 298. For further examples, see ibid. 61, 128, and 346.

141 *South African Native Affairs Commission*, vol. 2, 1110, Ev 15210–3. See also ibid. 1223, Ev 16912–4; *Twentieth Century Impressions of Natal*, 646–8.

traders), many observers claimed, increasingly dominated the African trade and was perceived as a threat to the prosperity of British trade and economy. From its earliest issues, the gazette warned traders, merchants, and manufacturers of fluctuations in the African trade, drawing attention, in particular, to changes in consumption patterns among Africans: fashions among black African consumers, authors claimed in the December issue of the gazette in 1893, changed just as rapidly as among 'the Belgravian beauty or the Bond Street fop'.[142] As an author pointed out almost one year later, consumer demands also varied 'according to districts and tribes'. He further observed that '[s]ome manufacturers appear to find this peculiar trait rather difficult to realise. It is certain that they cannot comprehend that colourings in rugs, say, that are the thing for Basutoland, are quite useless in Natal or Johannesburg.'[143] Beads were often used as examples for rapid fashion changes: an article published in 1895 asking whether British manufacturers were meeting the requirements of South African buyers argued that 'the native trade [was] the most "tricky" one for passing fancies and fashions', giving an example of beads of a particular shade worth £1,500 that had been found to be 'absolutely unsaleable upon arrival'.[144] The 'value of observation as a market factor' could be distinctively felt in the African trade, and in this realm, many observers argued, British manufacturers and importers were gradually falling behind their competitors.[145] Simultaneously, authors continued to undermine the significance of the black African consumer as 'an economic factor': to the author of an article published in 1896, for example, the importance of black Africans for the colonial economy lay beyond the provision of labour: 'The Transkei native ... is a good customer of the Eastern Province importers over such matters as blankets [and] general truck goods'.[146] According to representatives of a British firm engaged in the South African textile trade interviewed by an author for the gazette in 1895, the 'truck trade' even offered 'better margins of profit than the business with the white population.'[147] The latter claim did not remain undisputed, but whether catering for African consumer demand was indeed more profitable than the trade with Europeans remains an open question.[148]

In several articles, authors argued that in contrast to British manufacturers, their foreign competitors showed '[m]ore tact ... in studying the peculiar tastes of the British colonies. The English were ... not particularly anxious to suit them-

142 *The British and South African Export Gazette*, 2/17 (1 Dec. 1893), 221. Regarding the semiotics of the 'fop', see Miller, *Slaves to Fashion*, 8–9.

143 *The British and South African Export Gazette*, 3/28 (2 Nov. 1894), 199.

144 *The British and South African Export Gazette*, 3/31 (1 Feb. 1895), 404–5 at 405. See also *The British and South African Export Gazette*, 2/17 (1 Dec. 1893), 220–1.

145 *The British and South African Export Gazette*, 7/83 (2 June 1899), 937.

146 *The British and South African Export Gazette*, 4/42 (3 Jan. 1896), 340.

147 *The British and South African Export Gazette*, 3/31 (1 Feb. 1895), 395.

148 *The British and South African Export Gazette*, 3/32 (1 Mar. 1895), 467.

selves to the requirements of the Colonial market.'[149] Watching foreign competition closely and publishing their observations regularly, the gazette's authors began to point out that unlike British manufacturers, their German and Belgian competitors were able to provide, for example, blankets of the make and quality in demand by black African consumers: 'The Continental make', an author pointed out in 1896, 'is looser and "woolier" ... than the English, and takes the Kaffir fancy more.'[150] In 1899, the gazette further reported that while manufacturers in Leeds recorded enquiries about coloured rugs, they were also pointing out that the trade in these commodities was decreasing owing to German competitors who were offering 'cheaper and inferior lines'.[151] Repeatedly, German and Belgian manufacturers were pinpointed as Britain's strongest competitors in the African trade because they were able to produce textile commodities according to African consumer demand and at lower prices than British manufacturers.[152]

In addition to foreign competition, storekeepers and merchants in British South Africa as well as British manufacturers perceived the growing number of Indian traders, particularly in the Colony of Natal, as a threat to British South African trade and commodity quality. Indian traders, an author argued in an article in 1895, 'brought about [the] demand for low-class Kaffir stuff.'[153] So-called 'free' or 'passenger' Indians began to immigrate to KwaZulu-Natal from the mid 1870s onwards, many of whom established themselves as petty traders, dealing in groceries and commodities in demand by Indians and black Africans. During the 1880s, Indian traders increasingly entered the retail and African trade. Their competition unleashed a growing wave of anti-Indian sentiment among Europeans that culminated in, inter alia, the passing of a series of racist laws.[154] The 1890s issues of *The British and South African Export Gazette* are filled with defamatory articles discriminating against Indian traders: as a commentator put it in 1894, reference had 'been frequently made in these columns to [their] lying, thieving, and dishonest practices'.[155]

In 1903, at the request of the South African Trade Committee, General Commissioner S.W. Whitham visited trading centres in British South Africa in order to gain insight into business methods, consumption patterns, manufacture, and

149 *The British and South African Export Gazette*, 6/62 (3 Sept. 1897), 99.

150 *The British and South African Export Gazette*, 5/53 (4 Dec. 1896), 216.

151 *The British and South African Export Gazette*, 7/82 (7 May 1899), 859.

152 See, for example, *The British and South African Export Gazette*, 4/42 (3 Jan. 1896), 364, and *The British and South African Export Gazette*, 7/78 (6 Jan. 1899), 499.

153 *The British and South African Export Gazette*, 3/32 (1 Mar. 1895), 467.

154 See Hiralal, 'Indian Family Businesses in Natal, 1870–1950'; Bhana and Brain, *Setting Down Roots*; Mertens, 'A Transnational History of Immigration Restriction'; Padayachee and Morrell, 'Indian Merchants and Dukawallahs in the Natal Economy, *c.*1875–1914'.

155 *The British and South African Export Gazette*, 3/25 (3 Aug. 1894), 30. Regarding competition by Chinese traders, see, for example *The British and South African Export Gazette*, 8/85 (4 Aug. 1899), 45.

trade conditions. His *Report on the Textile and Soft Goods Trade*, published on behalf of the National Industrial Association in London in 1903, largely confirmed that foreign competition had increased and even dominated the market in certain commodities, particularly in the context of the 'truck trade': German and Dutch printed cottons, for example, were popular among Afrikaner and black African consumers.[156] While imported rugs were, for the greater part, produced in Britain, Whitham observed that blankets—one of the most important commodities in the black African trade—were largely from foreign manufacture.[157] Overall, Whitham concluded that the textile trade in British South Africa was still in British hands, however the significance of Whitman's report lies beyond his observations and remarks on the textile and 'truck trade'. According to his account, Whitham had been specifically instructed to investigate the second-hand clothing trade.[158] The trade in second-hand military clothing had long been an integral part of the 'truck trade', and while it featured less prominently in the press and trade observations, it did not go unnoticed.

Towards the end of the nineteenth century, different outlets in British South Africa reported an increased demand for second-hand military clothing, particularly for military overcoats and tunics. A list of consumer goods for indigenous peoples in Eswatini compiled by a firm by the name of Wallerstein and Bremer, for example, included cotton goods, shirts, and 'old Military Overcoats and Tunics'. The firm's representative further stated that '[o]ther common clothings [had not been] very saleable' in 1890.[159] 'Military and police clothing [were] in request for all districts', an author remarked in an article published in the *The British and South African Export Gazette* in 1893 in its summary of past and present developments in the British South African textile trade, pointing out that, overall, the 'demand for second hand civilian clothing for the native trade ha[d] exceeded the supply'.[160] In contrast to many other commodities for which observers reported rapid fluctuations and changes, the demand for second-hand civilian and military clothing appears not only to have remained remarkably consistent throughout the nineteenth and early twentieth century but to have increased significantly during the mid 1890s. Yet, a trade observer claimed in an article in *The British and South African Export Gazette* in 1903, this demand was 'limited to a certain class among' black Africans. Lamenting what he regarded as storekeepers', retailers', and manufacturers' persistent ignorance of African consumer preferences, he argued that there had been

156 Whitham, *Report on the Textile and Soft Goods Trade of South Africa*, 42–3.

157 See ibid. 59–60.

158 See ibid. 43.

159 TNA, CO 879/33/1, *Africa Confidential Print. African (South) No. 393. Report on Swazieland by Colonel Sir. F. De Winton, R. A., K. C. M. G., C. B. (With Appendices and Correspondence)*, Colonial Office, Mar. 1890, 23.

160 *The British and South African Export Gazette*, 3/30 (4 Jan. 1895), 330–1 at 330.

> far too much haphazard buying indulged in, under the mistaken idea that anything is good enough for a 'nigger'. As an instance of this may be mentioned the case of a firm who, finding there was some inquire among the natives for soldiers' cast-off clothing, imported a tremendous quantity of it, sufficient almost to have garbed the entire native population in military attire, only to realize that … the majority [of black Africans] would not purchase the garments.[161]

To most contemporary trade observers, the rise in demand during the 1890s was closely tied to the opening of the mines and the growing employment of (migrant) black African workers. Under the heading 'Kaffir Clothing', *The British and South African Export Gazette* reported in 1893 that a Birmingham firm had dispatched 'in one order no less than 12,000 pairs of second-hand trousers to Johannesburg … intended for the mines.'[162] European travel accounts seem to substantiate this: Ralph W. Leyland, for example, describing the end of a work shift at the De Beer Co. mine in Kimberley in *A Holiday in South Africa* (1882), recalled that at '4 o'clock exactly a signal was given for men to leave work, and it was an amusing sight to see Kafirs coming up from the scene of their labours below … Some were clad in rags of blankets, others wore cast-off soldiers' coats, while many more appeared in nature's garb.'[163] By the mid 1890s, politicians, for example, were making similar observations: 'When the Diamond-fields broke out', an MP in the Cape colony argued, 'the natives fairly revelled in cast-off uniforms'.[164] The expansion of 'truck stores' near the mining centres transformed access to these commodities. While trading conditions differed significantly after the establishment of the so-called 'compound system', clothing was one of the key commodities sold to mine workers.[165] The increased demand for second-hand military clothing in particular was perceived by many trade observers as evidence of unmet needs. As one author noted in *The British and South African Export Gazette*

161 *The British and South African Export Gazette*, 11/127 (6 Feb. 1903), 917–22 at 919–20.

162 *The British and South African Export Gazette*, 2/16 (3 Nov. 1893), 163.

163 Leyland, *A Holiday in South Africa*, 114–15.

164 *Debates in the House of Assembly, in the Second Session of the Ninth Parliament of the Cape of Good Hope, 2nd May to 3rd August, 1895*, 15. See also Redvers H. Buller's testimony in connection to the Uniforms Act 1895, who stated in 1894 that 'old uniforms of all nations and old liveries are the principal dress of the coolies at the diamond fields, at Kimberley, for instance.' *Report … on the Uniforms Bill* 1894, 7, Ev 114.

165 See Harries, *Work, Culture, and Identity*, 66–8. *The British and South African Export Gazette* published a number of articles regarding the feared introduction of compounds at the mines in and around Johannesburg (which was eventually fought off). See *The British and South African Export Gazette*, 7/79 (3 Feb. 1899), 560 and 610; *The British and South African Export Gazette*, 7/81 (7 Apr. 1899), 742; *The British and South African Export Gazette*, 7/83 (2 June 1899), 913–14. In addition, Comaroff and Comaroff argue that labour migrancy 'and the urban experience … had the greatest impact on Tswana dress styles—in both the country and the city.' Comaroff and Comaroff, *Of Revelation and Revolution*, 249–52 at 250.

in 1899, affordable and adequate clothing for men 'working at great depths and in the wet' was largely unavailable.[166] Notably, the adoption of second-hand military clothing was not limited to (migrant) black African mine workers. In the early twentieth century, The Simmer & Jack Mining Co., Ltd. employed several Chinese workers at its mine in Germiston who were dressed in 'Service pattern jacket, riding breeches, puttees, and Slouch Hat'.[167] To contemporary trade commentators, the prominence of these garments in mining regions symbolized yet again the failure of British manufacturers, merchants, and storekeepers to adapt to evolving consumer expectations and to recognize the purchasing power of the emerging working class.[168]

Finally, the growing importance of black Africans as 'cash customer[s]' was welcomed in commercial circles for its perceived potential to raise profits, but it was equally thought to alter the dynamics of the 'truck trade'. In 1899, an author claimed in *The British and South African Export Gazette* that the spread of cash purchases deprived traders of advantages associated with barter: 'Some of my correspondents point out that owing to the Kaffir being placed in possession of money, there is no longer the possibility of making a profit on the produce formerly taken in exchange for goods.'[169] Cash transactions, however, did not eliminate opportunities for exploitation. Credit systems and the practice of 'bonsella' or 'ba-sala' (small gifts offered to African customers) were readily used by storekeepers for additional gain.[170] Moreover, bartering—especially exchanging second-hand military clothing for agricultural produce or labour—persisted. In 1906, a private who had purchased two sacks of second-hand military clothing from his regimental tailor intended 'to follow the goods to Meseru [Maseru, Leseotho] for use in bartering to natives in return for labour, etc., thereby enabling him to travel ... more cheaply.'[171]

An additional revealing perspective on the reach of the second-hand clothing trade emerges from Whitham's *Report on the Textile and Soft Goods Trade of South*

166 *The British and South African Export Gazette*, 7/83 (2 June 1899), 938–9.

167 NASA TAB, FLD vol. 179, no. 36/35. On Chinese indentured labour in the mining industry, see Richardson, 'The Recruiting of Chinese Indentured Labour for the South African Gold-Mines, 1903–1908'; Smith, 'Capitalism and War', particularly 67–70.

168 See *The British and South African Export Gazette*, 7/83 (2 June 1899), 938; *The British and South African Export Gazette*, 7/80 (3 Mar. 1899), 692; *The British and South African Export Gazette*, 3/28 (2 Nov. 1894), 199; *The British and South African Export Gazette*, 4/38 (6 Sept. 1895), 100; *The British and South African Export Gazette*, 8/95 (7 June 1900), 773. See also Harries, *Work, Culture, and Identity*, 48–80.

169 *The British and South African Export Gazette*, 12/136 (6 Nov. 1903), 503.

170 See Burke, *Lifebuoy Men, Lux Women*, 72–80. On 'ba-sala', see also *The British and South African Export Gazette*, 1/4 (4 Nov. 1892), 116; *The British and South African Export Gazette*, 2/13 (4 Aug. 1893), 17. On disputes between storekeepers and black African mine workers from 1913 onwards, see chapter 4.3.

171 See Burke, *Lifebuoy Men, Lux Women* 68–77; NASA TAB, DCU vol. 89, no. 1887/1906.

Africa (1903). His remarks on the second-hand clothing trade focused particularly on Durban, where he had inspected an importing firm dealing in a wide range of textile and soft goods and imported 'old clothing ... from Great Britain in immense quantities' that consisted for 'the greater part of cast-off uniforms, both military and police, which are sold to the natives or exchanged for produce.' Among Durban business owners, however, this trade in second-hand clothing was partly viewed as a source of unfair competition vis-á-vis cheaper lines of garments. One business owner, Whitham noted, argued that 'at the price this second-hand clothing was sold it greatly interfered with the legitimate trade with the Kaffir; that the Kaffir was sufficiently well off to pay a fair price for his clothing.'[172] Whitham's enquiries in King William's Town (Qonce, Eastern Cape Province) led him to similar conclusions regarding the scale of the trade, yet business owners there had not expressed the 'feeling as to the suppression or otherwise of this importation'.[173] As his report suggests, opinions among business owners in British South Africa diverged regarding the extent to which second-hand clothing imports interfered with the broader textile trade. Nevertheless, Whitham ultimately recommended prohibiting the importation of second-hand military clothing into British South Africa. His argument was not based on commercial considerations. Instead, he emphasized that the adoption and appropriation of British military dress by black Africans gave 'great offence to many colonists', adding that 'it did not tend to uphold the dignity of Great Britain to see a number of niggers masquerading in British soldier's uniforms, or policemen's overcoats and helmets. I must admit there is something in this gentleman's argument, for I have seen the nigger thus clothed.'[174] Throughout the 1890s, trade observers in *The British and South African Export Gazette* had rarely expressed outright criticism of the importation of second-hand military clothing.[175] The contents of Whitham's report and the timing of its publication indicate a marked intensification of criticism during and after the South African War (1899–1902), reflecting a notable shift in perceptions of African consumption and the distribution of second-hand military clothing.

172 Whitham, *Report on the Textile and Soft Goods Trade of South Africa*, 34–5.

173 Ibid. 43.

174 Ibid. 35–6.

175 For a notable exception, see *The British and South African Export Gazette*, 3/28 (2 Nov. 1894), 213: 'Mr. Grant Birch, a well-known Liverpool engineering merchant, has been touring through Zululand and the Transvaal. Amongst more agreeable souvenirs, he has brought back a strong feeling against the selling of cast-off British uniforms for Kaffir wear. Even in these days of the decadence, Mr. Birch has enough of the Englishman left in him to feel the desecration of employing the faded finery of our warrior to deck out Kaffirs. ... I hope Mr. Birch's protests will lead to the abolition of a peculiarly ignominious and twopenny-halfpenny piece of cheeseparing.'

2.4 Conclusion

Pausing on their way from Bethlehem to Harrismith in the South African Province of Free State, 'while doing a little cooking'—entertainer Charles H. Du Val notes in his book *With a Show Through Southern Africa* (1882)—his party was 'interviewed by half a dozen stalwart Zulus ... on their way to the Diamond Fields ... Each wore an old military coat, of nondescript kind, the long grey overcoat of the British infantry being their chief fancy. Curiosity-led', Du Val continues, he 'examined the buttons on one of their great-coats, a cast-off from the 94th regiment ... Taking the buttons in the front row downwards', the author describes having identified the

> 'Army Service Corps;' the '41st Prince Wales's Own;' the 'Devon Constabulary;' the 3rd 'Legion de Marche, Rhone;' the '42nd Old Black Watch;' and lastly, the harp and crown of the 'Royal Irish Constabulary:' all these varied forces represented on buttonholing the outer—well, chief—garment of the intelligent Zulu far away on the South African 'Veld.'[176]

Du Val's account captures the circulation of second-hand military clothing among black African consumers and underscores the attention these appropriations commanded. While merely indicative, the different buttons remind us of the rebuttoning practices that second-hand military clothing underwent in the workrooms of businesses like Mallett, Porter & Dowd, Ltd. The distribution of these commodities from British workrooms and exporters through wholesale importing businesses like Randles, Bros. & Hudson, local trading networks, and stores such as Emagusheni Trading Store highlights both the global and local embeddedness of these commodities. Between *c.*1860 and 1895, political transformations in Mpondoland intersected with competition for inland trade between the Cape Colony and the Colony of Natal, shaping the broader regional commercial environment. European traders, in turn, sought to influence Mpondo and colonial politics. The circulation of British second-hand military clothing along routes from London to Mpondoland illustrates the scope of the trade beyond major mining and urban centres while pointing to the constraints and flexibility of local trading networks, which remained remarkably stable against the background of preindustrial trading conditions.

The consumption and appropriation of second-hand military clothing by predominantly black Africans was contested throughout the late nineteenth and early twentieth century. Attitudes differed, not least, between Johan Kumalo and Solomon Mabaso. Colonial clothing regulations aimed at Africans restricted dressing styles while simultaneously enabling acts of appropriation, often perceived by Europeans as transgressions of social boundaries and colonial hierar-

176 Du Val, *With a Show Through Southern Africa*, 193–4.

chies.[177] Yet, the implementation of further restrictions on the sale and purchase of second-hand military clothing in British South Africa in 1895 failed not only because the primary producer continued to supply these garments but primarily because of the growing economic significance of black African consumption, which attracted an increasing number of 'truck traders'. Trade observers and commentary clearly mirrored contemporary anxieties over British economic decline while reproducing imperial imaginaries of 'new markets' abroad.[178] At the same time, they indicate that African consumers shaped trade patterns, influenced the flow and allocation of commodities, and forced traders to adapt to shifting demands.

At the site of consumption in British South Africa, the military and colonial authorities' attempts to regulate and restrict the circulation and appropriation of second-hand military clothing were primarily aimed at the preservation of colonial hierarchies and imperial authority. Yet, African consumers actively renegotiated, interpreted, and incorporated these garments, while local trading networks mediated access and responded to demand. The shifting landscape within which the social, symbolic, and economic significance of second-hand military clothing was continuously contested and redefined illustrates how authority, consumer agency, and distribution intersected, shaping correlating ascriptions of value and the legitimacy of these commodities.

---

177 See Posel, 'Races to Consume', 161; Callaway, 'Dressing for Dinner in the Bush'.

178 See Burke, *Lifebuoy Men, Lux Women*, 83–90 at 84. On the ensuing debate over British economic decline in the nineteenth century and the recurrence of 'declinism' as a theme in the long twentieth century, see, in summary, Tomlinson, 'Thrice Denied'.

CHAPTER 3

3 Imperial Public Health and the Second-Hand Clothing Trade

In 1903, London's press drew attention to an incident on board the *Cornwall*, a reformatory school ship moored on the Thames off Purfleet, Essex. The ship had been operated since May 1859 and was certified to accommodate up to 250 boys aged between 11 and 14 years who were taught nautical skills, tailoring, and carpentry while in detention. In an article titled 'A Grave Scandal', the *Daily Mail* reported on 21 May 1903 that 'eleven boys [had] been stricken down with enteric on board the ... ship as a result of sleeping in fever-infected blankets brought from South Africa'. According to the article's anonymous author, the outbreak of enteric (fever)—also known as typhoid (fever)—on the ship had been discovered six weeks earlier. Sanitary authorities had subsequently tested the drinking water on board and investigated various other means by which the boys could have contracted the disease. Finally, a few days prior to the publication of the article—and 'only by an inspiration', the author claimed—the blankets the boys had slept in were examined and found 'stained with blood and indescribably filthy in other respects ... swarming with typhoid bacilli.' The sale of the blankets to the ship's officials, the article further informed the readers, could be explained, but 'how the blankets, which [were] admittedly army blankets, ever got into the hands of the people who originally disposed of them, and how they reached the country at all, [were] matters attended by strange mystery and secrecy.'[1]

Over the following months, it became clear that very little about the *Cornwall* incident was strangely mysterious. In addition, much to the annoyance of the City of London's MOH William Collingridge, the local press ensured that few aspects of the outbreak on board the *Cornwall* and its aftermath remained secret: during the investigation into the circumstances leading to the typhoid fever outbreak, the British public learned from numerous newspaper articles that a much larger quantity of allegedly infected blankets had been distributed across the British Empire and beyond.[2]

1 *Daily Mail*, 2211 (21 May 1903). See also NASA WCARS, MOH vol. 87, no. 480/1903; Carradice, *Nautical Training Ships*. Even after typhoid fever became widely recognized and distinguished as a disease in 1869, the terms 'typhoid' and 'typhus' were often used synonymously. The term 'enteric fever' was frequently used by medical experts to avoid confusion. See Hardy, *The Endemic Streets*, 152–4. On the history of typhoid fever, see Steere-Williams, *The Filth Disease*.

2 As Collingridge pointed out, it had been his 'desire to avoid ... giving the publicity to the names of the different towns to which these blankets were distributed, and thus possibly injuriously affect ... their several claims to attraction as holiday resorts. It was regrettable, therefore, to find that some journalists had apparently no such scruples, and columns of the Press were filled

HTTPS://DOI.ORG/10.1515/9783112256503-004

The bacteriological examination of the infected blankets by Emmanuel A. Klein and his findings, referenced by the author in the *Daily Mail*, point to the long history of the development of Western European scientific knowledge on the origins and spread of diseases and reflect broader debates in British sanitary reform regarding material intermediaries during the second half of the nineteenth century. By the end of the century, the transformations and advances in scientific knowledge, including germ theories and laboratory-based research, gained influence across the British Empire. In 1891, the Cape colonial government established the Colonial Bacteriological Institute in Grahamstown, where the Scottish bacteriologist Alexander Edington studied animal diseases, including rinderpest, rabies, and horse sickness, as well as human diseases such as smallpox.[3] However, medical discourse and sanitary practices in British South Africa at the turn of the twentieth century remained highly racialized, and public health measures during the 1890s in reaction to the outbreak of bubonic plague in Cape Town in 1901 mirrored and furthered existing racism.[4] The juxtaposition of scientific advances and entrenched racial hierarchies reveals an uneven application of emerging medical knowledge in colonial contexts.

The blankets at the centre of the outbreak on board the *Cornwall* had initially been deposited by British soldiers returning to England after the end of the South African War, fought between the British Empire and the Afrikaner republics (South African Republic/Transvaal and Orange Free State) from 1899 to 1902. It provides the broader historical context of the *Cornwall* incident and the movement of these textiles while highlighting the connection between warfare and disease transmission.[5] The scope and intensity of media coverage of the South African War elevated many aspects of imperial warfare to new levels in the British and international public consciousness, including concerns about the health and well-being of British soldiers.[6] While the *Cornwall* incident did not mark a turning point in colonial public health measures and practices, the outbreak investigations in British South Africa highlight the contrasts in racially targeted public

with the fullest details procured by their agents scattered throughout the kingdom.' Collingridge, *Report of the Medical Officer of Health for the City of London for the Year 1903*, 29, Wellcome Collection at [https://wellcomecollection.org/works/u47fjz4m], accessed 3 Oct 2025.

3 See Madida, 'A History of the Colonial Bacteriological Institute 1891–1905'; Brown, *Mad Dogs and Meerkats*, 38–60.

4 See Swanson, 'The Sanitation Syndrome'; Deacon, 'Racial Segregation and Medical Discourse in Nineteenth-Century Cape Town'. See also Dubow, *Scientific Racism in Modern South Africa.*

5 See Omissi and Thompson, 'Introduction'.

6 See, for example, Morgan, 'The Boer War and the Media (1899–1902)'; Bender, *Der Burenkrieg in der deutschsprachigen Presse.* On the impact of the war on the British army, see Searle, '"National Efficiency" and the "Lessons" of the War'; Searle, *The Quest for National Efficiency*, 34–53; Strachan, 'The Boer War and its Impact on the British Army, 1902–14'; Thompson, *Imperial Britain*, 127–30; Steere-Williams, *The Filth Disease*, 224–70.

health practices while indicating subtle changes in the racialized perceptions of disease transmission among colonial medical officials.

Finally, the *Cornwall* incident and its aftermath reveal the deep entanglement of imperial public health and commercial interests. As, for example, Aidan Forth recently argued, 'while fueling the global circulation of labor and goods, imperialism also facilitated the transmission of microorganisms, escalating the speed and scope of epidemics and the concomitant urgency of disease control.'[7] Global commodity flows, including the trade in textile remnants such as rags and second-hand clothing, were affected by concern over disease transmission. In the early 1880s, the British Director of Army Contracts responsible for the resale of second-hand military clothing stated that 'the general dread of old clothing and rags, created by the fear of cholera ... had an ill effect upon the market' that had rendered 'cast-off uniforms ... nearly unsaleable.'[8] At the same time, national and imperial responses were significantly shaped by commercial interests. British government authorities in particular, Peter C. Baldwin argues, were keen to protect the empire's commercial interests from quarantine measures that could potentially harm trade.[9] The typhoid outbreak on board the *Cornwall* in London, remembered as 'the now historic case of the military blankets' by colonial officials in British South Africa became a recurring reference point in subsequent discussions of preventive disinfection measures and for the introduction of mandatory disinfection of second-hand clothing imported into British South Africa.[10] The *Cornwall* incident, subsequent investigations, and the evocation of the outbreak in the context of the introduction of mandatory disinfection illustrate how material objects like second-hand clothing operated as critical nodes, linking global commerce, imperial politics, and local public health imperatives and practices.

3.1 Fomites, Miasmata, and Germs: Second-Hand Clothing and British Sanitary Reform, *c.*1760s–1900s

'Among the odours of London', Charles J. B. Aldis—MOH of Belgravia, London—wrote in 1857,

> those emitted in rag shops, or the houses of marine-store dealers, are about the most dangerous. Such pestiferous spots contain fat of the worst description, which certain cooks have carefully collected until it becomes rancid, or almost unbear-

7 Forth, *Barbed-Wire Imperialism*, 74.

8 TNA, WO 33/42, *Report of the Director of Army Contracts for the Year Ended 31st December 1883* (1884, [A13] – 15wo), 13.

9 See Baldwin, *Contagion and the State in Europe, 1830–1930*, 201–11.

10 NASA NAB, DPH vol. 24, no. 306/1906.

> able, in their masters' houses, then they sell it at these places, where it is kept and produces one of the vilest stinks imaginable. Besides this, a dreadful smell proceeds from accumulated bones … Again, the musty smell from filthy rags, old clothes closely packed in the front shop and back parlour … may, altogether, produce what has been termed a 'deadly smell'.

Beyond the unpleasant olfactory experiences and inconveniences in everyday life allegedly caused by so-called 'rag and bone' or 'marine' stores, these businesses became increasingly associated with unsanitary conditions and were perceived as a threat to public health; Aldis, for example, considered the stores 'one of the many plague spots' in the city.[11] Used textiles and textile remnants such as second-hand clothing and rags occupied a peculiar position in public as well as scientific health discourse. In the mid 1850s, London citizens frequently complained about the 'effluvia & stench arising' from the 'considerable Traffic … in the most filthy description of rags and a manufactory of bones most pestilential' near their houses, lamenting the nuisance of bad smells and fearing potential health risks.[12] At the same time, the mid-nineteenth-century local second-hand clothing trade continued to flourish, not least because of the unavailability of some lines of cheaper ready-to-wear articles of clothing.[13]

To Londoners' mid-nineteenth-century noses and minds, the connection between bad smells and health risks as well as disease origin and spread seemed apparent: in many medical circles, decomposing biological material was thought to produce miasma, an airborne substance that was believed to cause the individual's body to decompose or ferment when inhaled. Miasma theory dominated the discourse on sanitation and sanitary practices for the greater part of the nineteenth century, with Edwin Chadwick—Britain's foremost mid-nineteenth-century sanitary and social reformer—as one of its biggest proponents. Particularly during the first half of the nineteenth century and according to many public health experts, sources of miasma such as excrement posed a greater risk to air than to water. Dumping sewage into rivers, for example, was preferable to letting it accumulate on solid ground, causing air pollution near houses. During the summer of 1858, particularly warm weather and the absence of winds and breezes highly intensified the already conspicuous smells of the sewage-laden river Thames, leading to what became known as the 'Great Stink' of London.[14]

---

11 Aldis, *A Letter to the Vestry of St. George's, Hanover Square, on Sanitary Work and Experience in Belgravia*, 10–11, Wellcome Collection at [https://wellcomecollection.org/works/jcseuwmk], accessed 3 Oct. 2025.

12 TNA, MH 13/261/412, fols. 836–7. In addition, see TNA, MH 13/261/336, fols. 657–60; TNA, MH 13/265/113, fols. 245–7; TNA, MH 13/265/198, fols. 478–80; TNA, MH 13/65/192, fols. 433–4.

13 See, for example, Ginsberg, 'Rags to Riches', 126–8.

14 See Barnes, 'Confronting Sensory Crisis in the Great Stinks of London and Paris', 103–32; Thorsheim, *Inventing Pollution*, 10–12. On miasma theory, see Wohl, *Endangered Lives*; Wor-

The idea that inanimate objects, such as clothing or furniture, could serve as intermediaries in the transmission of diseases has a long history. The Italian physician Girolamo Fracastoro—who coined the term 'syphilis' in 1530 for what had until then been predominantly known as, inter alia, 'The French Disease'—was neither the first nor the only medieval medical expert to consider clothing, wood, and other objects crucial to the transmission and spread of disease.[15] However, as Vivian Nutton points out, Fracastoro 'appears to have been the first to use the word *fomes* as a technical term for the substance deposited on these intermediaries and to describe the transferred infective agents as "seedlets of contagion"'. In his publication *De Contagione et Contagiosis Morbis et Curatione* (1546), Fracastoro proposed three methods of disease transmission: first, transmission through direct contact only; second, through direct contact and contact through so-called 'fomites'; and third, through direct contact, fomites, and from a distance. After its publication, Fracastoro's medical work presumably had little impact on medical discourse, but his theories and, in particular, his division of contagion was more widely discussed and adopted in medical circles from the 1560s onwards. Finally, while it was during the late nineteenth century that Frascatoro's theory on contagion had its biggest revival, his studies were known among physicians who read Latin texts throughout the late eighteenth and nineteenth centuries.[16]

In 1761, James Lind—the leading physician at the Royal Hospital Haslar in Gosport, Hampshire—noted that the labourers at the hospital who had to 'carry up the sick in their infected cloaths to the wards; and afterwards to bundle up, and bring away, every article of their apparel' contracted fevers more often than the nurses who tended to patients after the latter had been undressed. Based on these and other observations, Lind concluded that clothing, wood, furniture, and other objects could become 'strongly taintеd' with the 'seeds of an infection'. His definition of the latter illustrates that the terms 'seeds', 'miasma/ta', and '*fomes*/fomites' could be used interchangeably: 'Those seeds, more emphatically expressed by the *Greek* appellation Μιασματα, wherever imbibed, or to whatever materials they may adhere, I call the *source* (or, what is sometimes understood among physicians by the *Latin* appellation *Fomes*) of an infection.'[17]

The laundresses at the Royal Hospital Haslar were mentioned once again by Thomas Trotter—a Scottish naval physician—in his medical work *Medicina Nautica*, published in 1797: according to Trotter, the 'porters and people employed with the cleaning and fumigating the blankets and beds at Haslar' appeared to 'measure the danger by the badness of the smell'. In comparison to Lind, Trotter

boys, *Spreading Germs*. On public health politics under Edwin Chadwick, see Hamlin, *Public Health and Social Justice in the Age of Chadwick*.

15 See Pearce, 'Fracastoro on Syphilis', 135.

16 See Nutton, 'The Reception of Fracastoro's Theory of Contagion', 200; DeLacy, *The Germ of an Idea*, 8–10.

17 Lind, *Two Papers on Fevers and Infection*, 38–40.

believed to have identified 'the exhalations or excretions' of typhus patients as 'vehicles of contagion', with the resulting 'noxious matter' affecting both the atmosphere and fomites, including clothing and bedding. Moreover, he thought that when 'bed-cloaths, or body linen, but particularly silk or woollen cloth, [had] been exposed to these exhalations, and then heaped together for a length of time, the noxious effluvia are, as it were, multiplied, and will more certainly infect others, than they did at first.' In addition to his theory about contagious 'human effluvia',[18] Trotter used the term 'miasma' in reference to vapours emitted by 'stagnant water; or its decomposition, occasioned by animal or vegetable putrefaction'.[19]

Finally, in his study *Clinical Illustrations of Fever*, published in 1831, the Scottish physician Alexander Tweedie identified two different types of 'exhalations' as the main sources of fevers: first, 'effluvia or exhalations from the human body', and second, an 'exhalation from the ground, supposed to be the consequence of either animal or vegetable putrefaction. To this terrestrial poison the term *malaria* (bad air) has been given'.[20] Tweedie's views on the origin and spread of disease were not incompatible with a contagionist explanation of the mode of propagation through direct contact with infected persons or inanimate objects. Once again, sick labourers at a hospital who had not had direct contact with infected patients led to the insight that clothing could transmit disease. Tweedie noted that at the London Fever Hospital 'the laundresses, whose duty it is to wash the patients' clothes' were 'so invariably attacked with fever, that few women [would] undertake this loathsome, and frequently disgusting duty.' Like Lind and Trotter, Tweedie concluded that 'disease may be engendered by fomites in clothing'.[21]

Either explicitly or implicitly, all three physicians gave further consideration to measures to minimize the transmission of disease through clothing. Lind argued that airing textile articles had proven insufficient 'to destroy the latent seeds of disease' and recommended fumigating potentially contaminated clothing first (using, for example, gunpowder or tobacco smoke). Furthermore, in the case of clothing and linen admitted to laundresses, he advised that textile articles be first soaked in cold water, and 'never at first to be put in warm water, as it is danger-

18 Trotter, *Medicina Nautica*, 176–9, Wellcome Collection at [https://wellcomecollection.org/works/gmua488g], accessed 8 Oct. 2025.

19 Ibid. 193–4 at 193.

20 Tweedie, *Clinical Illustrations of Fever*, 54, Wellcome Collection at [https://wellcomecollection.org/works/b7xnqm9v], accessed 8 Oct. 2025. On *malaria* in its original sense (It.: 'bad air') in, for example, mid-eighteenth-century American medical discourse, see Baldwin, 'How Night Air Became Good Air, 1776–1930'.

21 See Tweedie, *Clinical Illustrations of Fever*, 56–7. For similar observations and conclusions on the transmission of disease via clothing, see, for example, Cormack, *Natural History, Pathology, and Treatment of the Epidemic Fever*, 115–18, Wellcome Collection at [https://wellcomecollection.org/works/d3etfy89], accessed 8 Oct. 2025.

ous for any person to receive the steam that may hence arise.'[22] Trotter considered fumigation useful as a preventative measure against 'sickness; but when contagion is established', he argued, 'a more powerful application of it, and other means must be adopted'. In direct reference to Lind, Trotter not only disagreed that fumigation was sufficient a measure in containing the spread of disease but considered some substances used in the processes harmful to individuals' health. He did not, however, advise against fumigation in general but rather recommended combining it with other practices such as increased personal hygiene, airing mattresses and bedding, disposing of clothing, as well as washing and fumigating 'serviceable apparel as … discovered the least filthy'.[23] Finally, Tweedie's recommendations were based on his view that social circumstances were predispositions to the cause and spread of fevers: he argued that in 'filthy abodes of the poor', where poverty led to insufficient nutrition and overcrowding to impure air, fevers tended to propagate more rapidly. Tweedie thus recommended isolating infected persons, practising general cleanliness, and ventilating sickrooms.[24]

Without referencing Fracastoro directly, Lind, Trotter, and Tweedie all applied the terms *fomes*/fomites in a similar technical sense. Although the three physicians differed in their overall approach to the causes and origins of diseases, based on their observations or statements given by hospital personnel, they drew attention to—what they perceived of as—a mode of disease transmission via inanimate objects, predominantly clothing. In addition, their medical studies illustrate that the terms 'miasma(-tic)' and 'contagious' were ambiguous, and that different underlying concepts of, and presumptions around, the causes, origins, and transmission of disease, were not necessarily incompatible. As part of their general objective, which was to understand the causes and spread of disease, late-eighteenth- and early-nineteenth-century physicians considered multiple explanations and readily redefined concepts and meanings.[25]

British mid-nineteenth-century sanitary reform, too, was largely informed by and derived from miasmatic approaches. Edwin Chadwick's often-cited statement in the context of a parliamentary committee on sewage in 1846 sums up the prevalence and influence of miasma theory on public health politics: 'all smell is,

---

22 Lind, *Two Papers on Fevers and Infection*, 52–4.

23 Trotter, *Medicina Nautica*, 432–8 at 438.

24 Ibid. 51–2 at 51.

25 These findings confirm Michael Worboys' results that rather than being overturned by the slowly emerging germ theories, the ambiguous meanings 'of miasmas were redefined until they were subsumed within a spectrum of contagious and infectious diseases.' While from the 1860s onwards the term 'contagious' began to be used to describe the transmission of diseases through close contact, inoculation, or touch, diseases that appeared to be transmitted at a distance seemed to have been described either as 'infectious' (transmission from an infected to a non-infected person) or 'miasmatic'. In the case of the latter, the environment (for example, soil) was thought to produce a 'poison' that affected humans. See Worboys, *Spreading Germs*, 37–8 at 37.

if it be intense, immediate acute disease, and eventually we may say that, by depressing the system and rendering it susceptible to action of other causes, all smell is disease'.[26] However, miasma theory had some vigorous opponents, including, for example, John Snow, whose famous Broad Street pump experiment strongly suggested that contaminated drinking water was the main cause of the cholera outbreak in Soho, London, in 1854. Following Snow's studies, and from the 1850s onwards, medical opinion on the transmission of cholera (and other diseases) began to change gradually, but the theory that polluted air caused and transmitted cholera and other diseases was not easily dismissed, and explanations based on or derived from miasma theory continued to circulate among medical experts until the end of the century.[27] Moreover, although scientists', physicians' and public health experts' theories of disease transmission diverged throughout the second half of the nineteenth century, they largely agreed on the possibility and probability of disease transmission through clothing. Even Thomas Southwood Smith, for example—a physician, sanitary reformer, and strong supporter of miasma theory who worked closely with Chadwick—argued in favour of the possibility of disease transmission through clothing. In his publication *A Treatise on Fever*, Southwood Smith claimed that 'febrile poison' originated from decomposing organic waste. In considering the question of whether it was 'capable of adhering to clothes, apparel, and other substances, in such a manner as truly to infect them, so that when applied to the bodies of the healthy ... the specific effect of the poison are produced', he argued that there was 'no reason why the question should not be settled with absolute certainty', proposing to use convicts in a series of experiments as a 'means of putting this question at rest'.[28] Furthermore, while medical experts and sanitary reformers differed in their conceptualization or theory of disease origin and spread, they found common ground in disinfection practices as a means of preventing the spread of disease. The British sanitationist approach to epidemic disease was, in the words of Peter C. Baldwin, 'a remarkably consistent and unified vision that combined social reform and public hygiene in a seamless whole.' While disinfection and isolation were considered 'classic contagionist measures', they were also supported and advocated by sanitationists as short-term measures that would no longer be needed once public hygiene had been perfected.[29] As a prophylactic measure, disinfection had already

26 *Report from the Select Committee on Metropolitan Sewage Manure*, 109, Ev 1503.

27 See Baldwin, *Contagion and the State in Europe, 1830–1930*, 147–8.

28 Southwood Smith, *A Treatise on Fever*, 366–8, Wellcome Collection at [https://wellcomecollection.org/works/upamv4b9], accessed 8 Oct. 2025. Furthermore, for direct references to the studies by Trotter, Tweedie, and Lind, see Murchinson, *A Treatise on the Continued Fevers of Great Britain*, 86–8, Wellcome Collection at [https://wellcomecollection.org/works/azkvqtq4], accessed 8 Oct. 2025. On Murchinson's influence on 1860s sanitary reforms, see Worboys, *Spreading Germs*, 37–8.

29 Baldwin, *Contagion and the State in Europe, 1830–1930*, 128–143 at 128.

been established by the mid nineteenth century. However, its prominence and scope increased considerably during the second half of the nineteenth century after the introduction of the Sanitary Act in 1866, which legally authorized state-sanctioned disinfection practices and led to an increase in the disinfection of domestic and private spheres by local authorities. Local sanitary authorities could now disinfect (private) property at the request of a medical practitioner.[30]

The infrastructure for disinfection measures aimed at household second-hand clothing, bedding, and other textile goods was provided by the construction of so-called 'disinfection chambers' across the city. The Sanitary Act called for the construction of 'a proper place, with all necessary apparatus and attendance, for the disinfection of woollen articles, clothing or bedding which [had] become infected'.[31] Following these provisions, several of London's districts authorities initiated the establishment of disinfection chambers during the early 1870s, where clothing and other household textiles were disinfected free of charge.

FIGURE 3.1
Public disinfectors (right) and James S. Dickson, Inspector of Nuisances (left), with an iron carriage for the disinfection of clothing in a dry heat disinfection chamber (*c.*1877).

In the City of London, for example, MOH Henry Letheby reported in 1872 that a mortuary and disinfection chamber had been constructed in Golden Lane; after a short time, Letheby claimed, both facilities had already proved to 'have been of the greatest service to the poor, especially during the recent epidemic of small-

30 See Mooney, *Intrusive Interventions*, 124–5.

31 Michael, *The Sanitary Acts*, 81. On the disinfection chamber in the City of London, built in 1872, see Letheby, *Report on the Sanitary Condition of the City of London*, 54–7, Wellcome Collection at [https://wellcomecollection.org/works/qbfwxph4], accessed 8 Oct. 2025.

pox; for from the month of February of last year until the end of September … there have been 3,350 articles of clothing and bedding disinfected and returned to the owners.'[32] These provisions and, consequently, the increase in disinfection practices went hand in hand with the development of disinfecting appliances, chemicals, and procedures. Between the 1830s and 1890s, laboratory experiments and technological innovation led by individual entrepreneurs contributed considerably to the refinement of disinfection processes.[33] In their publication *Street Life in London* (1877), John Thomson and Adolphe Smith dedicated one of their chapters to the so-called 'public disinfectors' in London. The photograph accompanying Smith's articles was probably taken in the yard outside the building where the disinfecting oven was situated in Hanover Square (Fig. 3.1).[34] It shows the iron carriage of a dry heat disinfector as part of a disinfection apparatus—a type of disinfector developed by George Fraser that became particularly popular in London and beyond. Fraser's dry heat disinfector and similar models that entered the market in the early 1870s became widely used after the introduction of a (semi-)portable version. While dry heat had been known for its disinfecting properties since at least the 1830s, it was unsuitable for the disinfection of bulky items such as mattresses or carpets. Furthermore, in the 1880s scientists concluded that, in practice, the disinfection apparatus thermometers' temperature display was unreliable. Disinfection by dry heat was gradually replaced by steam disinfection, with Washington Lyon's portable steam disinfector—patented in 1880 and manufactured by the company Manlove, Alliot, Fryer and Co. in Nottingham—being one of the most widely used disinfectors from the mid 1880s onwards (Fig. 3.2).[35]

32 Ibid. 54–7 at 57. On Letheby's role in downplaying the significance of contributions from the laboratory, see Mooney, *Intrusive Interventions*, 136–7.

33 See ibid. 132–42. However, and as Rebecca Whythe shows, the rise of disinfection as a prevention measure was accompanied by the marketing of a wide range of disinfectants, some of them designed to be deadly. While disinfection was thus, on the one hand, meant to 'manage the risks and dangers of infectious disease … [it] also created risks and dangers of its own.' Whythe, 'Public Health and Public Safety', 128. See also Whythe, 'Disinfection in the Laboratory'.

34 Thompson and Smith, *Street Life in London*, 16–18 at 17.

35 See Mooney, *Intrusive Interventions*, 139–41.

FIGURE 3.2 Washington Lyon's portable steam disinfector, manufactured by Manlove, Alliot, Fryer and Co., Ltd. (*c.*1893).

Despite the medical arguments for the role played by clothing and other inanimate objects in disease transmission, and despite the large-scale disinfection measures aimed at private households and personal textile belongings, public health measures targeting the second-hand clothing trade remained conspicuously absent throughout the nineteenth century and beyond, although the typhoid outbreak and subsequent bacteriological examination confirmed existing theories. Shortly before the *Daily Mail* reported the outbreak on board the *Cornwall* in May 1903, the MOH for the Port of London informed London's medical authorities about the incident and the alleged source of the boys' infection: the bacteriological examination referred to by the article had been carried out by Emmanuel A. Klein, a German histologist who had begun to focus on bacteriology when he immigrated to Britain, where he worked on a wide range of diseases including typhoid fever.[36] In his reports (extracts of which were published in the *Report of the Medical Officer of Health for the City of London for the Year 1903*), Klein confirmed he had found 'innumerable colonies of bacillus typhosus' in 'old stains of urine' on the sample of blankets he had received from the *ship*.[37] Klein's findings, however, were significant beyond his confirmation of the bacillus on the blankets: his examination was believed to have led to new insights into the viability of *Salmonella enterica serovar typhi* outside the human body. As the MOH for the City of London William Collingridge stressed in his report, Klein's enquiries

36 See Bulloch, 'Emmanuel Klein'. Regarding Klein's contribution to bacteriological science, see Steere-Williams, *The Filth Disease*, 172–223.

37 Collingridge, *Report of the Medical Officer of Health for the City of London for the Year 1903*, 27.

'established the important fact that the bacillus typhosus can retain activity in infected articles for so long a period as six months', while previous observations and experiments had estimated the bacilli's viability on textile surfaces at three months only.[38]

Klein's examination appears to have been regarded as a matter of course both by the press and in medical circles. There were neither any objections to his approach, nor were his findings debated; on the contrary, Klein's results were picked up and acknowledged shortly after their publication by, for example, Louis C. Parkes and other scientists interested in questions of the viability and longevity of (typhoid) bacilli outside the human body.[39] Given the state of early-twentieth-century medical knowledge, the consensus around and acceptance of Klein's laboratory findings might appear unsurprising. However, until Louis Pasteur's and Robert Koch's revolutionary micro-biological findings in the early 1880s, the medical debate over what would eventually become widely accepted as germ theory in the late nineteenth century had been highly controversial. Until the very end of the nineteenth century, germ theories were doubted and ridiculed by some medical experts.[40] In addition and as Jakob Steere-Williams shows, British epidemiology experts only began to interact and engage with bacteriological science in the 1880s and 1890s; even after and despite the important discoveries by Koch and other European scientists, laboratory evidence largely 'continued its backseat status' in Britain.[41] The cautious approach among British epidemiologists towards bacteriological science and laboratory evidence can be explained, first, by the lasting confusion over and the difficulty of bacilli as laboratory objects. Second, epidemiology, and especially epidemiological methods in outbreak investigations, had—in the words of Steere-Williams—'more cultural capital than laboratory-based medical science.'[42]

The *Cornwall* incident and Klein's findings nevertheless gave new impetus to considerations of the role of the local second-hand clothing trade in the transmission of disease. Antony Roche—an Irish public health professor—commented in the medical journal *The Lancet* in 1903 that the outbreak on board the ship had 'created considerable alarm which may do good by directing professional and public attention to ... our pawn offices and second-hand clothes shops', which he considered a 'very common' source of the spread of infectious diseases.[43] Suspi-

38 Ibid. 29.

39 Louis C. Parkes picked up on Klein's results shortly after their publication; see Parkes, 'Enteric Fever and Infected Blankets', 297. See also Stimson, 'The Longevity of B. Typhosus Outside of the Human Body', 187.

40 See Baldwin, *Contagion and the State in Europe, 1830–1930*, 183–6; Steere-Williams, *The Filth Disease*, 176–84.

41 Ibid. 177–84 at 182.

42 Ibid. 176–91 at 176–7.

43 Roche, 'The Infected Blankets'.

cion that the local circulation of second-hand clothing contributed to the spread of infectious diseases had been voiced by British medical authorities in London since the early 1850s, and criticism increased considerably from the late 1870s onwards. Initially, and once again, local MOHs were particularly concerned about rag and bone or marine stores and pointed towards the 'nuisance and danger to health from these shops' that had troubled MOH Charles J. B. Aldis almost twenty years earlier.[44] The provisions of the Sanitary Act 1866 allowed for the prosecution of individuals who sold infected bedding, clothing, rags, or other things without previous disinfection.[45] However, disinfection as a prophylactic measure was not mandatory, and local sanitary officials frequently complained about the inefficiency and limitations of the legislation. During the 1870s, sanitary officials began to refer 'the question of the probability of articles of second-hand clothing offered for sale by stall-keepers and others, acting as carriers of infection' to higher authorities: in the case of Bethnal Green, the Sanitary Committee, however, thought it 'impossible to decide if articles so exposed [were] ... laden with the germs of infectious disease'—an assessment that illustrates both the limits of microbiological research in the late 1870s as well as the limits of control that sanitary and municipal authorities were able to exert over the trade in textile remnants and second-hand clothing.[46] In his report to the Local Government Board in 1878, Edward Ballard complained that sellers of second-hand clothing and rags made no enquiries

> as to the source of rags offered for purchase, many of them are probably infected ... Health officers know how inefficiently the law operates to prevent the sale of infected articles to people who deal in rags and old clothes. Now and then it happens that an offender is caught and punished, but for one such case how many hundreds every year transmit with impunity such infected things to the shop of the marine-store dealer, in ignorance or in wilful contempt of the risk of so doing![47]

---

44 'Report by Dr. Ballard on the Effluvium Nuisances Arising in Connexion with Various Manufacturing and Other Branches of Industry: Part III', in *Eighth Annual Report of the Local Government Board 1878–79*, App. VI, 42–320 at 304–5.

45 Michael, *The Sanitary Acts*, 89. In addition, local MOH occasionally issued cautionary bills to prevent the sale of infected articles. See, for example, *Parish of Lambeth: Medical Officer's Report*, 28, Wellcome Collection at [https://wellcomecollection.org/works/c5w8tn2s], accessed 8 Oct. 2025.

46 *Parish of St. Matthew, Bethnal Green, in the County of Middlesex: Account in Abstract of the Receipt and Expenditure for the Year Ending 25th March 1879*, 59, Wellcome Collection at [https://wellcomecollection.org/works/gke9hcdk], accessed 8 Oct. 2025.

47 *Eighth Annual Report of the Local Government Board 1878–79*, App. VI, 42–320 at 304–5. See also the sanitary report for Paddington for 1874–5 by William Hardwicke, *Paddington: Report of the Vestry*, 26, Wellcome Collection at [https://wellcomecollection.org/works/vjtk3hw2], accessed 8 Oct. 2025.

However, against the hopes or expectations of some medical authorities, sanitary officials, and public health experts such as Roche, the local second-hand clothing trade remained exempt from further regulations beyond the provisions of the Sanitary Act 1866 and the occasional issuance of cautionary bills even well after the *Cornwall* incident.[48] As the MOH of Warrington stated in an article published in the medical journal *Public Health* in 1915, while 'the spread of infectious disease by second-hand clothing is undoubted ... [f]urther research is necessary, not only into the etiology of the infectious diseases, but also into the length of time infection will linger in clothing.'[49] The lack of research and the limits of control, public health officials and experts maintained, hindered the introduction of prophylactic disinfection measures, which continued to be perceived as highly effective in the prevention of disease transmission and spread through used textiles and textile remnants. Concerned not only with the transmission of infectious or contagious diseases but also the spread of vermin such as lice, the MOH for Hackney purchased several parcels of second-hand clothing in 1914 from second-hand clothing shops, so-called 'costers' stalls', and rag shops for the purpose of examination. Most of the clothing contained lice nits, and while the MOH admitted that for local authorities 'to prevent the sale of secondhand verminous clothing [was] a ... difficult problem to solve', he too shared his frustration about the lack of obligatory disinfection of second-hand clothing: 'it is quite clear that if all secondhand clothes [were] submitted to disinfection the problem would be solved ... The question of the sale of unclean clothes is surely not beyond the range of Public Health preventive measures.'[50]

3.2 From Mobile Bodies to Moving Things? Disinfection Practices in Early-Twentieth-Century British South Africa

The outbreak of typhoid fever on board the *Cornwall* and subsequent bacteriological findings by Emmanuel Klein were followed by an investigation involving MOHs in Britain and British South Africa, the War Office, the Colonial Office, and colonial government authorities in British South Africa. They began to reconstruct the distribution of, it would turn out, 250,000 army blankets sold in British South Africa, 80,000 of which could have led to the typhoid fever outbreak in London. According to the MOH for Cape Town, the number of blankets had initially

48 See, for example, the cautionary bill issued in Lambeth in 1876. *Parish of Lambeth: Medical Officer's Report*, 28.

49 Joseph, 'Some Remarks on Second-Hand Clothing and the Spread of Infectious Disease', 270.

50 *Report on the Sanitary Condition of the Hackney District, for the Year 1914*, 130–3 at 132.

> amounted to 500,000, with the result that any organized method of dealing with them, or even of properly storing them, became impossible … A certain number of them were washed by the Army Washing Contractors and have been taken into stores or re-issued to the Troops at present in South Africa, but the bulk of them have been sold.[51]

For a brief moment, the well-established and globally connected British South African trade in second-hand clothing surfaces from the archives: over 200 MOHs and 69 firms in London and the provinces were involved in reconstructing the distribution of the potentially infected army blankets, 20,000 of which 'had been sold to 338 customers, distributed over 207 towns in the United Kingdom and 19 Metropolitan Boroughs.'[52] In addition to the number of blankets distributed in Britain, colonial authorities tracked 500 blankets 'to various ports on the West Coast of Africa'.[53] In June 1903, an article in the *Daily Mail* claimed that a portion of the blankets exported to England had been re-exported to Pretoria (Tshwane), Kingston, Calcutta (Kolkata), Colombo, as well as two towns in Chile and Peru.[54] In Cape Town, the city that had been identified as the central node for the redistribution of these blankets, communication about the typhoid outbreak was received shortly after its discovery, and colonial administrative authorities immediately initiated their enquiry into the distribution of the potentially infected blankets across British South Africa. By mid June 1903, colonial officials had ascertained that in addition to the blankets in question bought by traders in the proximity of Cape Town's city centre in Maitland, Woodstock, Simonstown, and Uitvlugt (Ndabeni), a considerable number of blankets had been sold to merchants in Port Elizabeth (Gqeberha) and distributed across the eastern Cape Colony, to the Orange River Colony, and the Transvaal Colony.[55]

Second-hand clothing imports in British South Africa had been increasingly associated with the spread of infectious diseases towards the end of the nineteenth century. In November 1893, the Inspector General of Customs, Pretoria, Colony of Transvaal (Tshwane, Gauteng), confronted the State Secretary of British South Africa with—he would soon learn—an unpopular opinion. He argued that British colonial authorities had obvious reason to prohibit the importation of second-hand clothing in general and avoid the purchase thereof from the neighbouring colonies:

> There is no doubt that the various infectious diseases prevailing among the natives are partly caused by used uniforms, liveries, and other second-hand clothing that

51 NASA WCARS, MOH vol. 87, no. 480/1903.

52 Collingridge, *Report of the Medical Officer of Health for the City of London for the Year 1903*, 26.

53 *City of Westminster. Report of the Medical Officer of Health for … 1903*, 38, Wellcome Collection at [https://wellcomecollection.org/works/g2w4mge2], accessed 8 Oct. 2025.

54 See *Daily Mail*, 2232 (13 June 1903), 5.

55 See NASA WCARS, MOH vol. 87, no. 480/1903.

> transmit infectious diseases prevailing among soldiers and prisoners ... I am of the opinion that any doctor familiar with European conditions, especially with infectious diseases in the army, agrees with me.[56]

The contemporary Secretary of the Colony of Natal Robert I. Finnemore and his medical board strongly disagreed with the Inspector General: Finnemore stated he was 'not aware of a single case where disease of any kind [had] been traced to such importation'. In addition, for his 'Government to prohibit such importation, or even to impose harassing restrictions' on the second-hand clothing trade, Finnemore argued, 'would be to strike a serious blow at [the] native trade not only in the Colony, but with Zululand, Swaziland and other places in South Africa'.[57] Finnemore's strong objection to the Inspector General's suggestion is just as striking as his ignorance of other connections drawn in the letter: while records suggest that a considerable amount of imported second-hand clothing was, indeed, army clothing, the Inspector General made a direct connection between disease-stricken European soldiers' bodies and the transmission of infections to Africans through imported European worn-out military clothing articles. However, the implication that military activities and wars were infecting British bodies, and that their tainted belongings were driving the global transmission of diseases and affecting Africans, lay, in the eyes of most colonial authorities of the late nineteenth century, outside the logic of disease origin and spread. Accordingly, the contention that imperial public health was threatened—first and foremost—by mobile indigenous bodies was not dismissed after the turn of the century. Nonetheless, the typhoid epidemics in British India and British South Africa and the infamous *Cornwall* incident shortly afterwards shifted attention—if only for a brief moment—away from indigenous peoples to mobile British soldiers and imperial warfare as drivers of global disease spread, thus contradicting the colonial logics (which were characterized by racialized conceptualizations of disease transmission) and revealing uneven distribution in sanitary infrastructure.

During the South African War, British military camps were designed and believed to provide protection for soldiers from what were considered filthy surroundings and from what colonial and military authorities perceived as disease-harbouring indigenous bodies. Here, infected bodily fluids, clothing, and bedding underwent complex and meticulously planned disinfection procedures.[58] At Gen-

56 NASA NAB, CSO vol. 1383, no. 5980/1893: 'Het is niet te betwyfelen dat de verschillende besmettelyke ziekten heerschende onder de naturellen gedeeltelyk verorzaakt worden door de gebruikten uniform, liverei an anderen tweede hands kleederen, die de besmetting van onder de soldaten en prisoniers heerschende ziekten overbrengen. ... Ik ben van opinie dat eenige doctor met Europeesche toestanden, vooral van aanstekelyke ziekten in het leger, bekend in deze zal overeenstemmen'.

57 Ibid.

58 See Steere-Williams, *The Filth Disease*, 262–3; Steere-Williams, '"Coolie" Control'.

eral Hospital No. 6—a military hospital established in Naauwpoort (Noupoort, Northern Cape) in February 1900 and moved to Johannesburg six months later—Colonel Brisbane W. Somerville-Large and his staff had set up a typhoid fever division. Detached from the rest of the camp and the medical division, the typhoid fever division was provided with its own administration, medical staff, and a distinct disinfection infrastructure. Two disinfection sheds provided for the separate sterilization of excrement and linen. The step-by-step instructions for excrement sterilization—the collection of urine and faeces in buckets and bed pans, mixing with disinfectants, boiling, burying, and covering—exhibit the 'excremental obsessions' of early-twentieth-century medical and army officials in colonial settings.[59] Camp authorities and medical and nursing staff also, however, paid great attention to the disinfection of textiles. Clothing used by patients suffering from typhoid fever was soaked in a solution of mercuric chloride in large wooden barrels for half an hour, wrung out, and hung out to dry before it was washed. Bulky items such as mattresses and textile articles that would have been damaged or otherwise spoiled by boiling and soaking were sterilized by heated steam, presumably in a two-wheel portable disinfector manufactured by The Tresh Disinfector Co., Ltd.[60]

The efforts devoted to disinfection and sterilization at General Hospital No. 6 were not unique.[61] By the time the hospital was set up in Johannesburg, the typhoid epidemic in British South Africa had already proven disastrous to the health of British soldiers. With Bloemfontein at the centre of the largest outbreak of typhoid during the South African War, British officials reported that 1,000 troops had died from the disease in the first half of 1900.[62] Somerville-Large noted that the typhoid fever division of the camp had reached its capacity within one week in Naauwpoort and was extended from 57 to 350 beds over the course of four months, 'during the whole of which time they were kept constantly filled, fresh cases at once taking the place of those disposed of'. Despite low inoculation numbers and labour shortage, Somerville-Large argued that the mortality rate of 8 per cent (relating to all patients admitted to the hospital in both locations) compared 'most favourably with corresponding age period mortality of cases treated in the hospitals of London and other large cities.'[63] Notwithstanding the

59 Ibid. 50–3. See Wellcome Collection, RAMC/480/2, *Report. No. 6. General Hospital South African Campaign, 1900 & 1901*, 186–8.

60 See ibid. 190–2.

61 For examples of disinfection procedures in other British military hospitals, see Steere-Williams, '"Coolie" Control', 50–3.

62 Due to the lack of documentation of typhoid deaths by the British army or the British Board of Health it is impossible to reconstruct how many British soldiers died of the disease. See Steere-Williams, *The Filth Disease*, 250–4.

63 Wellcome Collection, RAMC/480/2, *Report No. 6. General Hospital South African Campaign, 1900 & 1901*, 170–8. On the invention of typhoid fever inoculation and its use in the South African War, see Steere-Williams, *The Filth Disease*, 242–70.

success that Somerville-Large attributed to his staff's efforts and extensive disinfection procedures, the typhoid epidemics in British India and South Africa had subtly led some colonial authorities to the conclusion that typhoid fever was, in fact, an imported disease.[64] This insight and advances in Western conceptualizations of diseases translated into the aforementioned meticulous disinfection and sterilization procedures at British military camps, undertaken largely (and ironically) by Africans or Indians.[65] At General Hospital No. 6, Africans worked at the disinfection shed for infected clothing and removed, buried, and covered sterilized excrement, while colonial knowledge about disease transmission through infected mobile bodies and their belongings continued to be viewed predominantly as being caused by, in the words of a local sanitary official, the 'gregarious habits' of non-white peoples.[66]

In the outbreak investigations connected with the typhoid infections on board the *Cornwall*, however, the movement of troops and soldiers' belongings took centre stage. Just as the typhoid epidemic among British troops in South Africa had, in the words of Steere-Williams, brought the disease 'to a new level of public consciousness, elevating typhoid from local and national to imperial concern', the circulation of potentially typhoid-infected blankets raised questions of disease transmission connected with imperial warfare and British soldiers' bodies.[67]

The blankets had been deposited by soldiers on their way home to England after the demobilization of British troops. Overwhelmed by the large number of blankets handed in by the soldiers upon departure, the military authorities sold a considerable number of the blankets to local merchants who in turn distributed them across the Western Cape, Eastern Cape, and other South African provinces.[68] In the context of the subsequent outbreak investigation in British South Africa, and in the words of the MOH for Cape Town, the British colonel responsible for enquiries into the distribution of blankets from their location of deposit, however,

64 See ibid. 239.

65 Steere-Williams shows that in a military hospital in the Colony of Natal, British authorities imposed a racial hierarchy preferring indentured Indians over Africans. See Steere-Williams, '"Coolie" Control', 50–3.

66 *Cape of Good Hope: Report of the Medical Officer of Health for the Colony ... for the Two Calendar Years 1904 and 1905*, 122. See Wellcome Collection, RAMC/480/2, *Report No. 6. General Hospital South African Campaign, 1900 & 1901*, 190–2. See also the photographs of the so-called 'Enteric Excreta Sterilizer' (ibid. 25) and barrels for disinfecting linen (ibid. 189).

67 Steere-Williams, *The Filth Disease*, 227.

68 According to the MOH for Cape Town, military authorities estimated that each soldier would deposit four blankets, 'but in many cases a much larger proportion was handed in, being the surplus supplies belonging to the different contingents.' Furthermore, 'it would ... have taken over two years for the [Army Washing] Contractors to have washed the whole of these blankets.' NASA WCARS, MOH vol. 87, no. 480/1903.

> was inclined to pooh pooh the idea that any of these blankets could have been infected at the time they were sold, and what is rather strange, is possessed with the idea of the possibility of their having become infected whilst stored by the purchasers in South Africa or in England; and he is also of the opinion that the holds of the vessels in which they were exported were probably infected with Typhoid germs.

Astonished by the colonel's search for explanations, the MOH remained unconvinced by his proposals: it was a fact, the MOH argued, 'that a very large number of returning soldiers have been suffering from unrecognized Typhoid Fever and ... have been very liable to soil their blankets with alvine discharges.'[69] Over the course of the South African War, colonial district surgeons had increasingly begun to trace the origins of infectious disease outbreaks to British soldiers. The movement of troops and military hospitals, military campsites and soldier's belongings subtly appeared in the Cape Colony's public health reports as threats to black African health. In 1901, outbreaks of infectious diseases among black Africans were occasionally attributed to infected water, but the presence and movement of British troops, district surgeons suspected, were increasingly beginning to affect local outbreaks of infectious diseases.[70] Typhoid fever outbreaks were reported to have been caused by 'imported cases',[71] some of which were attributed to the presence of garrisons in towns or villages or were thought to have been 'possibly imported in course of military movements.'[72] To the district surgeon of Uniondale, the absence of the British army at or near the village accounted for the low typhoid fever cases: 'We have none of the evils wrought by a Military Camp, and the few that are here have not brought Typhoid Fever with them.'[73] In addition, district surgeons increasingly remarked that (former) military campsites, hospitals, and soldiers' belongings spread diseases which affected Africans. In 1902, an outbreak of smallpox on a farm situated in Paarl (Western Cape), the district surgeon suggested, had been caused by infected blankets that the individuals had received from the British so-called 'remounting station' nearby.[74] Another smallpox outbreak in Wellington (Western Cape) likewise occurred on a farm 'situated near the railway station, the probable source of infection', the responsible district surgeon argued, 'being some blankets given to some coloured women by passing troops.'[75] According to the district surgeon's report in Sutherland (Northern Cape), the withdrawal and relocation of troops did not diminish

69 NASA WCARS, MOH vol. 87, no. 480/1903.

70 See *Cape of Good Hope: Reports on the Public Health for the Year 1901*, 137 and 196.

71 Ibid. 50. See also ibid. 198.

72 Ibid. 167. In addition, see ibid. 128 and 197.

73 Ibid. 128.

74 See *Cape of Good Hope: Reports on the Public Health for the Year 1902*, 109–10 at 110.

75 Ibid. 110–1 at 111. In addition, see *Cape of Good Hope: Report of the Medical Officer of Health for the Colony ... for the Half-Year Ended 30th June, 1904*, 48.

the threat that British soldiers' disease-infected bodies posed to public health. Apart from the movement of infected bodies that carried diseases across the colony, abandoned British military campsites caught the attention of colonial medical authorities as loci of disease spread. In Sutherland, the district surgeon recorded seven cases of typhoid fever in 1903, five of which had affected Europeans and black African children. 'These cases', he argued, 'have probably arisen from old enteric stools which were cast all about in days of military occupation. It is very noticeable that most of these cases have occurred in the vicinities where camps were pitched from time to time during the war.'[76] According to the reports on public health in the Cape Colony, district surgeons did not confirm their assumptions through tests by, for example, the Colonial Bacteriological Institute in Grahamstown, which assisted MOHs, for example, in the bubonic plague outbreak investigations. While the MOH reports exhibit a growing acceptance of textiles as intermediaries in the transmission of diseases, textile remnants and second-hand clothing did not receive the attention as laboratory objects in bacteriological research that British medical experts continued to call for in the 1910s.[77]

Disinfection measures in British South Africa continued to be shaped by the contemporary view on disease spread by Western medical authorities, summarized by, for example, an American delagate at the *Conférence Sanitaire Internationale* (International Sanitary Conference) in Paris in 1894:

> The whole history of the movement of cholera and the modes by which it is transported, both over short and long distances, both by land and by sea, is filled with indisputable evidence demonstrating that in general cholera is very commonly imported by the rags and used goods of the people who leave an infected locality, although these people are in good health.[78]

---

76 *Cape of Good Hope: Report of the Medical Officer of Health for the Colony … for the Year 1903*, 149.

77 See chapter 3.1.

78 *Ministère des Affaires Étrangères: Conférence Sanitaire Internationale de Paris*, 268 [unless stated otherwise, all translations are by the author]: 'Toute l'histoire du mouvement du choléra et des modes par lesquels il est transporté, tant sur les petites que sur les grandes distances, tant par terre que par mer, est remplie de preuves incontestables démontrant qu'en général le choléra est très fréquemment importé par les hardes et effets à usage des personnes qui quittent une localité infectée, bien que ces personnes soient en bonne santé.' Recommendations to suppress the spread of cholera included '1. compulsory and rigorous disinfection of all used items of all pilgrims without distinction; 2. close observation five days before boarding; 3. a ban on boarding persons who are infected or may have been contaminated during this period.' ('1. la désinfection obligatoire et rigoureuse de tous effets à usage de tous les pèlerins sans distinction; 2. l'observation sérieuse de cinq jours avant l'embarquement; 3. l'interdiction d'embarquement des personnes qui sont atteintes ou peuvent être contaminées pendant cette période.').

Public health, the American delegate appears to confirm, was threatened by the possibility and probability of disease transmission through inanimate objects. However, the delegate was not concerned about the movement of objects but the mobility of indigenous bodies. Specifically, the global spread of diseases was strongly associated with Indian pilgrims, characterized by the delegate and other medical authorities as 'dirty and poor'.[79] The notion of causal connection between colonized bodies, disease, and materiality was widely shared by colonial administrators and manifested in the public health and disinfection measures in British India and British South Africa, for example, that were centred around, and contributed to the further colonization of, indigenous bodies.[80] Following the outbreak of bubonic plague in Cape Town in 1900/01, for example, the Cape colonial government rushed the construction of the so-called 'native location' Uitvlugt (Ndabeni), approximately six kilometres from Cape Town's centre, and moved 6,000–7,000 Africans to this segregated area.[81] In addition to the segregation, encampment, and surveillance of Africans and Indians in British South Africa, highly intrusive disinfection measures such as the 'dipping' of bodies in tanks—a common late-nineteenth-century veterinary practice—had been introduced by colonial officials in British India in the 1890s and in British South Africa shortly afterwards. During an outbreak of rinderpest in 1896/97, for example, 11,000 African migrant workers were 'dipped' in a disinfection solution in Bethulie, Orange River Colony (Province of Free State).[82] Whites (especially Europeans), who in many cases were affected by diseases more frequently, were largely spared these and other drastic measures like surveillance, segregation, and the destruction of personal belongings: after the outbreak of typhoid fever and diphtheria in Sutherland in 1903, for example, the district surgeon in charge of public health measures reported that '[a]mongst the whites no steps were taken to prevent the

79 Ibid. 'malpropes et indigent'.

80 See Arnold, *Colonizing the Body*; Mukarji, 'Cat and Mouse', particularly 511–12.

81 As Swanson argues, British colonial authorities' reactions to the public health crises were based on a highly racialized imagery of disease origin and spread that influenced colonial politics. Swanson termed this conglomeration of racial attitudes 'sanitation syndrome' and identified it as 'a major strand in the creation of urban apartheid' (Swanson, 'The Sanitation Syndrome', 387–93). His article contributed to an important shift in historiography towards problematizing science as metaphorical and has influenced numerous studies that confirmed his initial findings. However, Marc Epprecht and other historians warn that the concept of sanitation syndrome might lead to oversimplified narratives. See, for example, Epprecht, 'The Native Village Debate in Pietermaritzburg, 1848–1925', particularly 260–2. The forceful encampment of thousands of Africans and Indians in South Africa as part of the colonial 'plague campaigns' drew from British experiences in India, where medical officials such as William J. Simpson, the MOH of Kolkata, came to be considered a 'global plague authority'. The Cape colonial government recruited Simpson as Chief Medical Advisor; he was involved in moving Africans to Ndabeni and had several racially segregated camps built at, for example, rail stations. See Forth, *Barbed-Wire Imperialism*, 74–6 at 74, and 91–4.

82 See Steere-Williams, '"Coolie" Control', particularly 50–1.

spread of the disease ... Amongst the natives the infected houses were watched, and any person who entered an infected house had to remain there until the house had been disinfected after the recovery or death of the disease.'[83]

Without downplaying the role of the British colonial authorities' racialized conceptualizations of disease spread in underpinning the implementation of intrusive and destructive public health measures, these may also be interpreted as a reaction to and expression of the frustration felt by many colonial medical officials in the face of insufficient means by which to contain rapidly spreading diseases.[84] During the South African War, MOHs and district surgeons increasingly voiced their discontent regarding, in particular, the lack of isolation hospitals and disinfection appliances. Although the 'disinfection of infected articles' was viewed as 'one of the most important duties falling upon Local Authorities ... only a small portion of even the Urban Local Authorities [had] provided' the necessary facilities.[85] In the Cape Colony, disinfectors had been supplied to Cape Town (in Wynberg, Mowbray, and Simonstown), East London (KuGompo City), Port Elizabeth (Gqeberha) as well as the Maitland military camp close to Uitvlugt as a reaction to the spread and prevalence of bubonic plague around 1902.[86] Until 1905, when the native location in Uitvlugt was supplied with its own steam disinfector, clothing, bedding, and other articles were disinfected at the Maitland campsite each Friday.[87] Cape colonial government efforts to resell surplus disinfectors to colonial administrations in Pietermaritzburg, Bloemfontein, and Lesotho in 1901 were initially unsuccessful. In Pietermaritzburg, for example, colonial government administrators did not see the need to establish (partly additional) disinfectors after the spread of the plague had been contained in the Cape Colony.[88] Outside urban centres, disinfection practices without a standard disinfector were, in the words of the district surgeon in Oudtshoorn, 'lax in the extreme', with 'bedding and clothing ... either put out to the sun's rays or left alone.'[89]

The lack of disinfection facilities and appliances intensified destructive measures aimed at personal belongings and accommodation. After tracing the move-

83 *Cape of Good Hope: Report of the Medical Officer of Health ... for the Year 1903*, 149, Wellcome Collection at [https://wellcomecollection.org/works/ha7kxc6y], accessed 8 Oct. 2025.

84 See Steere-Williams, '"Coolie" Control', 50.

85 *Cape of Good Hope: Report of the Medical Officer of Health for the Colony ... for the Year 1903*, p. lxvi.

86 See NASA WCARS, MOH vol. 26, no. 185/1901.

87 See *Cape of Good Hope: Report of the Medical Officer of Health for the Colony ... for the Two Calendar Years 1904 and 1905*, pp. A75–A76.

88 See NASA NAB, DPH vol. 6, no. 138/1901; NASA WCARS, MOH vol. 26, no. 185/1901. Colonial government authorities of the Colony of Natal eventually purchased a disinfector from the Cape colonial government in 1903 in connection with the formation of the plague administration committee in Pietermaritzburg. See NASA WCARS, MOH vol. 14, no. 45/1903.

89 *Cape of Good Hope: Reports on the Public Health for the Year 1902*, 107–8. See also *Cape of Good Hope: Report of the Medical Officer of Health for the Colony ... for the Year 1903*, p. cxxxiv.

ment of an African with bubonic plague from East London to Whittlesea in the Cape Colony in 1905, for example, the additional district surgeon for the Kamastone Location ordered all houses the individual had slept in and all clothing inside them to be burned.[90] Simultaneously, district surgeons began to voice concerns as to the efficiency of these destructive measures. Regarding a number of smallpox cases in Hopefield (Western Cape), the additional district surgeon suspected that articles of clothing had been hidden in the hope of escaping destruction, arguing that 'it is pretty nearly certain that all the clothing handled by the infected persons cannot have been destroyed, and … that … the disease will break out afresh from the fomites of clothes which have escaped the vigilance of the guards and others.'[91] Discontent among MOHs and district surgeons increased with the growing resistance among Africans to the public health measures. Medical officials complained about Africans' reluctance to report infections and follow instructions:[92] 'Natives are no longer in the condition that they can be "bounced" into doing anything they are not naturally inclined to do, and they have already discovered that there is no "law" whereby they can be compelled to observe any directions that may be given to the keeping of quarantine and disinfection of clothing, excreta, and huts, and attention to directions.'[93] Consequently, district surgeons began to replace destroyed articles of clothing, increasing the cost of public health measures.[94]

The enquiries and investigation following the *Cornwall* incident mirrored the uneven distribution and inefficiency of these early-twentieth-century colonial disinfection and public health measures in British South Africa. When the blankets were ordered to be re-collected and disinfected, the lack of disinfection appliances in less urban areas led to the destruction of a portion of the potentially infected blankets, and most traders were eventually compensated for their losses

90 See ibid. 121–2. For further examples of the destruction of infected persons' property and accommodation, see *Cape of Good Hope: Report of the Medical Officer of Health for the Colony … for the Year 1903*, 59–60, 84, 131–2, 162–3, and 197–200.

91 Ibid. 91–2.

92 See ibid. 64.

93 *Cape of Good Hope: Report of the Medical Officer of Health for the Colony … for the Two Calendar Years 1904 and 1905*, 168.

94 See, for example, *Cape of Good Hope: Report of the Medical Officer of Health for the Colony … for the Year 1903*, 63–4. In the report for Humansdorp (Eastern Cape), the district surgeon claimed that since all clothing was 'replaced there was no dissatisfaction shown by any of the natives, who were left quite content', and argued that, hence, they 'would not have hidden any further outbreak.' See also ibid. 162–3; NASA NAB, CSO vol. 1523, no. 4819/1887. In addition, see, for example, *Cape of Good Hope: Report of the Medical Officer of Health for the Colony … for the Year 1903*, 131–2. In Simon's Town, an outbreak of smallpox cost the municipality £180. According to the district surgeon, this 'amount would have been much less had the Municipality a steam disinfector at its disposal for the purpose of disinfecting clothing, bedding, etc., instead of destroying by burning.' See also ibid. 197–200.

by the British Army Council.[95] In some instances, the task of disinfecting the blankets was assigned to traders and prospective consumers. In Willowvale (Eastern Cape), where a large number of blankets had been sold in the town and district, the colonial magistrate reported that 'natives [had] been instructed through their headmen to disinfect their blankets by submerging same in their dipping tanks.' Finally, local medical authorities and practitioners resorted to disinfectants like Jeye's Fluid or Izal—products that were known to be either inadequate in terms of thorough disinfection, or damaging to textiles.[96] The reliance on improvised and destructive methods, uneven provision of disinfectors, and delegation of responsibility to local populations continued to disproportionately affect Africans, highlighting how public health measures reinforced racial hierarchies while revealing the ambitions and limitations of early-twentieth-century disease control in British South Africa.

3.3 The 'Historic Case of the Military Blankets'[97] and the Disinfection of Second-Hand Clothing, *c.*1906–1910

By the end of the nineteenth century, across the British Empire and beyond, outbreaks of diseases like cholera and bubonic plague had led to temporary restrictions in the global trade of rags and second-hand clothing. The prevalence of bubonic plague in Mumbai and Karachi in 1897, for example, led British Indian colonial government authorities and Walter Hely-Hutchinson, Governor and Commander-in-Chief of the Colony of Natal between 1893 and 1901, to prohibit the importation of textile remnants at the ports of Mumbai (Chennai), Calcutta (Kolkata), Yangon, and Durban, and from any port under quarantine.[98] Simultaneously, Hely-Hutchinson and the Durban Medical Committee maintained that the 'principal danger' of the global spread of diseases was not posed by the commercial trade in second-hand clothing and rags but by 'the old clothing of the

95 See NASA WCARS, MOH vol. 87, no. 480/1903. In addition, see the 'Statement showing amounts paid in respect of claims relative to the sale of Infected Army Blankets', in *Army Appropriation Account 1903–1904*, 181, which lists compensation for the destruction of blankets, the costs of disinfection, and the 'deterioration in value of blankets resulting from process of disinfection' received by British district/borough councils as well as British and South African dealers. In total, compensation costs amounted to almost £ 2,794, with an outstanding claim by E. Cohen of £ 353 (see ibid.).

96 NASA WCARS, MOH vol. 87, no. 480/1903.

97 NASA NAB, DPH vol. 24, no. 306/1906.

98 NAI, Finance Department, Statistics and Commerce A., January 1897, file nos. 46–53. Similar prohibitions were introduced by representatives in France, Switzerland, and Spain; see NAI, Home Department, Sanitary Proceedings A., April 1897, file nos. 573–83, and NAI, Home Department, Sanitary Proceedings B., July 1897, file no. 101.

immigrants', echoing racialized colonial logics and concepts of disease transmission and spread.[99]

Following the *Cornwall* incident and subsequent investigations, however, colonial government administrations moved to implement prophylactic disinfection measures. In April 1906, almost three years after the typhoid outbreak on board the *Cornwall*, the MOH of the Colony of Natal was informed that the Cape colonial government was planning 'to put in force Regulations, under which second hand "clothing" imported into that Colony, shall undergo disinfection before removal from the Dock'. The MOH of the Colony of Natal was consulted not only for his opinion on the matter but 'particularly' for his 'knowledge of any instances in which infectious diseases [had] been traced to second-hand clothing, similar to', the Cape colonial MOH specified, 'the now historic case of the military blankets'. The MOH of the Colony of Natal enthusiastically supported the idea in his reply, stating that he could not 'imagine a more possible vehicle for the carrying of infectious matter than clothing.'[100] During the following years and on several occasions, the *Cornwall* incident became a recurring reference point in discussions regarding the introduction of regulations for the prophylactic disinfection of second-hand clothing prior to importing it into British South Africa.

The subsequent negotiation of a uniform disinfection process among colonial governments sought to mitigate the perceived risks of disease transmission through second-hand clothing imports while simultaneously reshaping the commercial trade. The push for the introduction of disinfection measures in the global commercial second-hand clothing trade was largely driven by MOHs and, notably, representatives of the Chambers of Commerce in Pretoria (Tshwane, Gauteng), Durban, Cape Town, and Johannesburg, who co-ordinated their efforts and turned to their respective colonial government administrations with the request 'that the importation of second-hand clothing be prohibited until the outbreak of cholera in Europe has been suppressed.'[101] Invoking the outbreak on board the *Cornwall* to legitimize their request, municipal authorities in Pretoria argued that their

> attention ... was drawn to the large quantities of second hand clothing being hawked about the city, and the danger of the spread of disease thereby unless submitted to inspection ... The Medical Officer for Health reported ... that, unless such clothing are carefully disinfected, there is danger that those who wear them may be infected with enteric fever and other contagious diseases ... The occurrence of

99 The Medical Committee thus recommended all immigrants' clothing to be disinfected on arrival in Durban, 'and all rags and dirty clothing ... burnt.' NAI, Home Department, Sanitary Proceedings A., April 1897, file nos. 573–83.

100 All quotes here from NASA NAB, DPH vol. 24, no. 306/1906.

101 NASA NAB, CSO vol. 1797, no. 7449/1905.

enteric fever following the use of second hand blankets sent from South Africa to England after the war, is sufficient proof of the danger.[102]

Despite these appeals, their requests to prohibit the importation of second-hand clothing met resistance from colonial government representatives. Trade restriction based solely on the possibility of disease transmission was deemed incompatible with the agreements of the Paris Convention for the Protection of Industrial Property, first signed in 1883. Ernest Hill, the MOH of the Colony of Natal, for example, argued that 'it would not be legitimate to prohibit the importation of second-hand clothing on this account, other than clothing from places definitely infected with cholera.'[103] The tension between concerns over the protection of public health and adherence to trade agreements illustrates the complex negotiation surrounding disease prevention which formed the backdrop to the co-ordinated regulatory response aimed at the second-hand clothing trade. In November 1906, colonial medical authorities convened at the Conference of the Principal Medical Officers for Health for the Different South African Colonies, where they agreed upon regulations for the prophylactic disinfection of second-hand clothing prior to importation.[104] Under these regulations, introduced first in the Cape Colony in May 1907, 'every consignment of body linen, wearing apparel, bedding or blanket, which [had] been in use and which [was] imported for sale or disposal' was required to undergo disinfection either at the port of shipment or at a port of entry in British South Africa.[105]

The introduction of these regulations quickly produced practical challenges and conflicts between colonial officials and commercial actors. In early October 1907, the Durban-based shipping agents Andrew Dickie & Co. addressed the sec-

---

102 *Pretoria Chamber of Commerce (Incorporated): Annual Report for the Year Ending December 31st, 1905*, 8. Furthermore, see 'Report of the Executive Committee to be Submitted to the Monthly General Meeting of Member to be Held on Tuesday, October 10th, 1905', in *Johannesburg Chamber of Commerce: Annual Report for the Year Ended 28th February, 1906*, [n. p.]; *The Forty-Fifth Annual Report of the Cape Town Chamber of Commerce (Incorporated) for the Year 1905–6*, 34.

103 NASA NAB, CSO vol. 1797, no. 7449/1905.

104 See, for example, *Cape of Good Hope: Report of the Medical Officer of Health for the Colony … for the Calendar Year 1907*, pp. x–xi. In addition, and for another reference to the *Cornwall* incident, see the argumentation by the MOH for Cape Town in 1905: 'This second-hand clothing is … the discarded clothing and effects of European communities, much of it coming from Paris and Berlin, and although a very considerable quantity is condemned Army clothing, yet there is no doubt much of it consists of the effects of deceased persons who may have died of infectious complaints. And in this connection I may remind you of the serious outbreak of Enteric Fever in England in 1904, which was attributed by the Home Authorities to the importation into England and retail sale of Army blankets from South Africa infected with Typhoid germs.' NASA WCARS, T vol. 954, no. 6628/1905.

105 Personal belongings and luggage were exempt from the regulations. See NASA WCARS, GH vol. 35/58, no. 31/1907–1908.

retary of the Colony of Natal 'regarding the damages to second hand clothing' at the port of Durban. According to their clients, who ran a store under the name Lunz & Herman in Johannesburg's Commissioners Street, fifteen pairs of breeches and six officer jackets trimmed with leather had 'been so burned through fumigation that they [were] useless'. In addition to pointing out that the disinfection process carried out at the port of Durban apparently damaged leather goods, the shipping agents informed the colonial secretary that they had arranged for their next shipment to be sent to the port at Port Elizabeth, where second-hand clothing was not disinfected upon arrival.[106] Over the following weeks, Andrew Dickie, colonial government officials, and medical authorities in the Cape Colony and Colony of Natal engaged in extensive communication regarding the complaint, which provided a starting point for reconstructing the circumstances leading up to, and the immediate consequences of, the implementation of disinfection regulations in the global second-hand clothing trade. Notably, Dickie's complaint prompted colonial government administrators to confront the realities of intercolonial competition in British South Africa.

In business circles, news of the forthcoming disinfection regulations travelled fast: in June 1907, two firms redirected their shipments from Port Elizabeth to Durban after learning from their clients and agents that in Port Elizabeth 'for the future ... all second-hand clothing ... will have to be fumigated', while one firm's 'friends' replied 'that no such order will be enforced' in Durban. Over the following months, complaints by business owners about 'disparity of treatment at the different ports' in British South Africa increased, and a growing number of importers and shipping agents threatened customs offices at port cities with redirection of second-hand clothing shipments indefinitely. The shipping agent Payne Bros., for example, imported second-hand clothing on behalf of a trader in Johannesburg regularly through Port Elizabeth: 'Our client is a large general importer through this Port, and if he can import his second-hand clothing via Durban without any difficulty and expense of disinfecting the probability will be that he will divert the whole of his traffic through that Port.' The introduction of disinfection regulations, these disputes reveal, reshaped the distribution of goods in British South Africa, creating incentives for importers to strategically re-route shipments to minimize costs. The prospect of redirecting shipments to other ports was particularly unsettling for colonial (port) authorities in the Cape Colony, where the regulations for disinfecting second-hand clothing had been enforced first. Customs offices and colonial government administrations benefited from these imports through revenue from transit duties and carriage fees—there were fears that railway revenue in particular would be lost to other colonial government administrations. As pointed out by Cape Town's Controller of Customs, second-hand clothing imported through the port of the Cape Colony was 'practically en-

106 NASA NAB, CSO vol. 1843, no. 6895/1907.

tirely consigned beyond Cape borders and to the very heart of what has been styled … "the competitive zone".' In addition, he noted that many British South African importers and merchants 'who deal in second-hand clothing import other goods as well, so if we lose the carriage of the one we lose that on the other goods also.'[107]

The Cape colonial authorities' immediate reaction to these pressures appears to have been characterized by local improvisations and diversions from the disinfection regulations: as Dickie claimed, port authorities in Port Elizabeth resorted to disinfecting bales of second-hand clothing externally, leading to shipments now being redirected from Durban to Port Elizabeth.[108] In 1908, the British South African colonial government administrations eventually agreed on uniform regulations; however, due to trans-shipments in the second-hand clothing trade, disputes over disinfection procedures were not confined to British South Africa. When colonial authorities attempted to co-ordinate a uniform disinfection process with Portuguese colonial authorities in 1908, an MOH in British South Africa discovered that while Portuguese port authorities used 'a most up-to-date and efficient [apparatus] for the disinfection of cargo', they did not unpack the bales.[109] Moreover, the deviations of British colonial port authorities from initial agreements concerning disinfection procedures underscore the influence of economic considerations on public health policies and measures. The latter, ostensibly designed to safeguard health, were in practice readily compromised when they were perceived as threatening commercial interests. In addition, although colonial authorities emphasized their intention to minimize interference with the commercial second-hand clothing trade, the implementation of disinfection regulations reveals that they sought to derive financial advantages from the process.

By the early twentieth century, most second-hand clothing imported into British South Africa was pressed into bales and bound with hoop iron, while some consignments were shipped in 'cases lined with oil paper'.[110] Colonial medical officials largely agreed that it was 'impossible for steam to penetrate into such bales', rendering the exterior disinfection of clothing bales insufficient.[111] The bales thus had to be broken apart and the articles of clothing placed loosely in the disinfecting chambers or appliances—a process which, however, and as

107 All quotes here from NASA WCARS, T vol. 954, no. 6628/1905. Durban's Port Health Officer argued in a similar manner that 'although second hand clothing is an insignificant item in the cargo for this port, shippers and consignees might get in the way of sending other and more important articles by the same route.' NASA NAB, DPH vol. 28, no. 593/1907.

108 See NASA NAB, CSO vol. 1843, no. 6895/1907.

109 NASA TAB, GOV vol. 1146, no. PS33/1/1908.

110 *Cape of Good Hope: Report of the Medical Officer of Health for the Colony … for the Two Calendar Years 1904 and 1905*, pp. cxxxv–cxxxvii at p. cxxxvi. On packing in the second-hand clothing industry, see chapter 1.4.

111 NASA NAB, DPH vol. 24, no. 305/1906.

Dickie complained, 'greatly depreciate[d] the value quite apart from the damage from fumigation'.[112] Prior to the implementation of the disinfection regulations, the MOH of the Cape Colony predicted that the disinfection procedure, particularly breaking the bales apart, would lead to disputes with importers, because the latter would 'resent any process which compelled the breaking of the original packages.'[113] While Dickie's complaint primarily stemmed from damages inflicted upon leather goods through steam disinfection, the disinfection process increased overall costs for importers. In addition to the costs associated with acquiring new packing materials, importers or agents were required to provide workers for the (un-)packing of bales destined for disinfection and, to forestall further complaints, were expected to remain present throughout the disinfection procedure.[114] The operations involved in personal oversight, transportation, and handling of the clothing bales were imposed on importers and agents in addition to the official fees for the disinfection itself. Estimates of the actual costs of disinfection compiled by colonial medical officials initially varied according to local conditions and the facilities available at different ports, where disinfection chambers did not offer uniform capacity, prices of coal and labour differed markedly, and some ports lacked scales for weighing clothing. In Durban, for example, the Port Health Officer initially overestimated the capacity of the port authority's so-called 'Equifex disinfector', because they 'never had any means of weighing the load [and] had to guess it'. In addition, workers operating the disinfector were formally employed by the NGR, whose wages were fixed at a rate considerably lower than the amounts set by port authorities (s.8 per day instead of s.15). Eventually, MOHs and port authorities settled on a uniform charge of '7s. 6d. per 100 lbs. or under, with a minimum charge of 15s. for any one occasion' of disinfection of second-hand clothing, excepting shoes and boots.[115] The arrangement, however, disadvantaged importers dealing in smaller consignments, who were either required to pay a disproportionately high minimum fee of s.15 or delay the disinfection procedure until they found another importer or shipping agent with whom they could share both the load and the associated costs.[116]

Moreover, while disinfection by steam was widely regarded as a definitive method, practical experience revealed its limitations. After Dickie's complaint about the damages to leather clothing articles through steam disinfection, colo-

112 NASA NAB, CSO vol. 1843, no. 6895/1907.

113 *Cape of Good Hope: Report of the Medical Officer of Health for the Colony … for the Two Calendar Years 1904 and 1905*, p. cxxxvi.

114 NASA NAB, CSO vol. 1843, no. 6895/1907.

115 NASA NAB, DPH vol. 28, no. 593/1907.

116 Ibid.: 'No departure will be made in any instance from the minimum charge of 15/-, but when it is convenient, different consignees may arrange to have their several consignments disinfected on the same day, and the cost may be borne by them jointly … Importers of small quantities have no right to demand this concession.'

nial MOHs and port officials endeavoured to minimize the risk of damaging materials. The MOH of the Colony of Natal, for example, suggested building 'a special disinfecting box' or 'airtight cupboard ... with hooks and bars, that the articles can be hung separately'. On the one hand, while it remains unclear whether these plans materialized, they signal an inclination to devise immediate, practical solutions when issues arose, and reflect an attention to the interests of second-hand clothing importers and agents. Port authorities were directed, for example, that 'every care must be taken to prevent damage or deterioration to goods under disinfection'.[117] On the other hand, colonial authorities stipulated that they bore no responsibility for damages to commodities or equipment in the disinfection process, nor for injury to the workers involved.[118] Finally, the disinfection procedures slowed the trade in second-hand clothing, particularly in cases in which customs officials questioned the origin and legitimacy of disinfection certificates.[119]

These circumstances underscore the extent to which disinfection remained a locally negotiated and improvised procedure, shaped as much by administrative contingencies and sanitary principles as by correlating interests. As a result, the procedural complexities and locally contingent management of disinfection procedures inevitably translated into higher costs not only for importers and agents (particularly those dealing in smaller amounts of second-hand clothing) but most notably for consumers. Importers and agents passed disinfection fees on to traders, who subsequently adjusted retail prices. When the Durban-based agents Stranach, Glew & Co., for example, were asked to provide second-hand military clothing to a trader south of Estcourt in the Colony of Natal, they informed the buyer that one of the reasons for the unusually high prices for the items of clothing was the cost of disinfection, for which Stranach, Glew & Co. charged their potential clients 3d. per requested garment.[120]

Initially, the implementation of mandatory disinfection regulations required colonial governments to invest in labour, coal, and disinfection appliances. Officials calculated fees for disinfection with a profit margin, suggesting that colonial governments stood to benefit monetarily.[121] However, because disinfection at the ports of entry proved particularly disruptive for importers and agents, the majority of second-hand clothing destined for British South Africa was ultimately disinfected at the ports of origin. This shift redirected both labour and financial advantages from colonial government administrations to metropolitan exporters and disinfection facilities in Britain, exemplified by the Golden Lane disinfection

117 Ibid. See also NASA NAB, DPH vol. 29, no. 729/1907.

118 NASA WCARS, MOH vol. 418, no. H77/1909. On disinfection and the increase of risks, see Whythe, 'Public Health and Public Safety', 127–48.

119 See, for example, NASA SAB, DEA vol. 204, no. A10/16/X; NASA SAB, DEA vol. 204, no. A10/16/1X.

120 See NASA NAB, SNA vol. 1/1/392, no. 554/1908.

121 See, for example, NASA NAB, DPH vol. 28, no. 593/1907.

chamber in London. By the early twentieth century, local outbreaks of disease in private households—and thus the need to disinfect personal textile effects such as clothing and bedding—had largely diminished. Following the implementation of the disinfection regulations, the disinfection facilities were primarily used to treat second-hand clothing intended for export to British South Africa. Data from the *Reports of the Medical Officer of Health for the City of London* indicate that between 1908 and 1938 the disinfection chamber at Golden Lane was operated predominantly at the request of businesses exporting second-hand clothing to British South Africa, accounting on average for 91 per cent of all items of clothing disinfected (Fig. 3.3).[122]

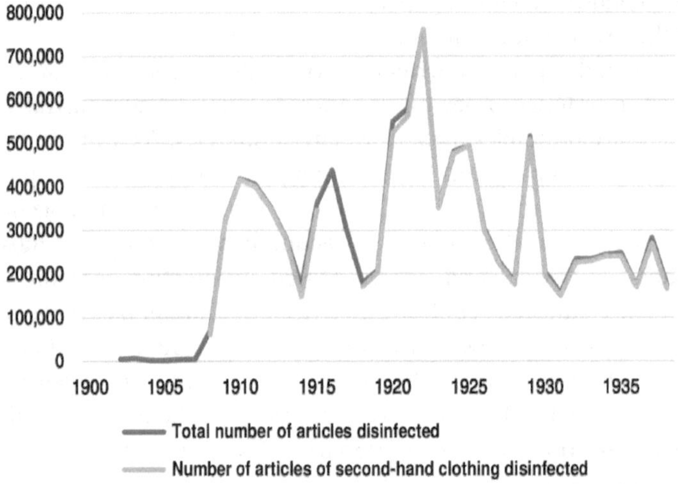

FIGURE 3.3 Number of textiles and articles of second-hand clothing for export to (British) South Africa disinfected at the Golden Lane disinfection chamber, London, 1902–38.

Finally, allowing disinfection to take place at the ports of origin enabled British South African importers to shift responsibility for compliance with the disinfection regulations onto British exporters. In practice, second-hand clothing intended for shipment was sorted, altered and repaired, and transported to disinfection stations before packing; it was then returned to warehouses, stored, and prepared for shipment once overseas orders had been received. Increasingly, exporters exploited loopholes in the provisions governing mandatory disinfection in

122 Fig. 3.3 is based on data from the *Reports of the Medical Officer of Health for the City of London* between 1902 and 1938 (graph by the author). The data is incomplete (for example, missing numbers for disinfected second-hand clothing for the years 1916 and 1917). From 1939 onwards, the reports do not list the destination of the second-hand clothing or the certificates issued.

the British South African second-hand clothing trade. Two decades after the regulations were introduced, colonial officials found that exporters had sent 'the same bale for disinfection several times and [used] the certificate for garments which [had] not been disinfected', thereby avoiding the additional costs associated with transportation and disinfection fees at the port of shipment. In addition, customs officials determined that, in some cases, bales of second-hand clothing disinfected in London contained more garments than were recorded on their accompanying disinfection certificates.[123] In effect, mandatory disinfection of second-hand clothing as a measure for disease prevention imposed by colonial authorities in British South Africa led to the reorganization of commercial practices, the redistribution of economic advantages, and the creation of new points of control within the British South African second-hand clothing trade.

3.4 Conclusion

Neither in Britain nor in British South Africa were officials involved in the investigations following the outbreak on board the *Cornwall* able to trace any other cases or outbreaks of typhoid fever to the re-exported, allegedly infected army blankets. Once the blankets reached consumers in British South Africa, colonial medical officials argued, it became impossible to trace their whereabouts. As military authorities in Cape Town noted, the blankets did not carry a distinguishing mark and were easily mistaken for other British military blankets distributed in the investigated regions, underscoring the limits of colonial public health surveillance in the context of transnational and transregional commodity flows. To some colonial and military officials involved in the search for, and the recall and destruction of, the blankets, the end of the investigation in British South Africa did not conclude the search for the source of infection. With the (false) promise that no 'blankets whatever nor any used textile stores [would] in future be sold in South Africa', a colonel stated in the aftermath of outbreak investigations in British South Africa that there was

> no reason for suspecting that any of these blankets were infected beyond the fact that some portion of them are alleged to have been found infected after having been stored by the purchasers in Whitechapel in England for some six months, probably in some insanitary warehouse, where doubtless blankets from many doubtful quarters were also stored.[124]

The global second-hand military clothing trade frequently generated ambiguity around responsibility, leading military, colonial, and metropolitan authorities to

123 See NASA SAB, DEA vol. 204, no. A10/16/1X.

124 NASA WCARS, MOH vol. 87, no. 480/1903.

contest one another's accounts and reasoning. While the British press sensationalized and scandalized the outbreak on board the *Cornwall*, the attribution of the disease origin to sources in British South Africa did not arise arbitrarily. Rather, it reflected prevailing epidemiological assumptions, racialized conceptualizations of disease spread and transmission, and heightened British anxieties in the context of the recent South African War. Amid the long contentious debates over disease origin and spread, Western European scientists, medical practitioners, and British sanitary reformers widely agreed on objects as intermediaries in the transmission of diseases. Towards the end of the nineteenth-century, laboratory research and germ theory validated these observational conclusions and renewed the emphasis on disinfection as a response to potentially disease-harbouring textiles. Yet, while these insights provided justification for regulatory interventions, the British second-hand clothing trade remained largely unaffected by policy interventions. In British South Africa, the outbreak investigations exposed the racialized conceptualizations of disease origin, spread, and transmission as well as the insufficiency of disinfection measures. While mobile indigenous bodies continued to be construed as the greatest threat to imperial public health, the typhoid epidemic among British troops in the South African War in combination with the *Cornwall* incident shifted colonial medical officials' attention to imperial warfare and the movements of troops as drivers of global disease spread. The reports by district surgeons reveal subtle changes in their perception of disease transmission and spread, which were increasingly attributed to British soldiers and their excrement, as well as to military camps and hospitals. While this gradual shift did not affect public health policy changes, colonial MOHs and, in particular, commercial actors elevated these considerations to the level of economic concern, with recurring reference to the *Cornwall* incident. In response to the intertwined sanitary concerns and commercial pressures, the colonial government administrations agreed on uniform mandatory disinfection regulations around standardized steam disinfection, certification, and supervision at their ports. By attempting to neutralize the health threat through technology and oversight, and to convert suspect second-hand clothing into safe and saleable commodities, colonial officials sought to mitigate epidemiological fears and commercial risks and stabilize supply chains. The benefits they were hoping for, however, did not materialize. The consolidation of disinfection processes at the ports of shipment in Britain left colonial officials in British South Africa with the regulatory burdens of inspection and the challenges of the resulting loopholes, which were readily exploited by British exporters.

The trajectory of the blankets underscores how the commodity status of second-hand military clothing was continually renegotiated as it moved between disposal chains, commercial redistribution, and colonial consumption. The *Cornwall* outbreak investigation illuminates the interfaces at which competing actors—MOHs, British military suppliers, local traders, storekeepers, importers and exporters, as well as colonial administrators—challenged and aimed to redefine the legitimacy of second-hand items of military clothing as commodities. Mandatory disinfection redistributed responsibilities and opportunities for profit. Rather than representing a linear episode of value addition, the allegedly infected army blankets at the centre of the typhoid outbreak on board the *Cornwall* and its subsequent investigation render second-hand military clothing contested commodities whose legitimization oscillated between consumer demand and commercial interests, colonial economic interests, and racialized assumptions.

CHAPTER 4

4 'Tariff Item No. 11': The Classification of a Contested Commodity

At the turn of the twentieth century, the circulation of British second-hand military clothing in British South Africa became a matter of sustained controversy across imperial and colonial administrative arenas. The intensity of these reignited debates is evident in a 1905 War Office investigation into 'the question of the sources of supply of old quasi military uniforms to the South African trade.' According to the author, military officials could not 'confirm the prevailing opinion that the War office system of disposing of worn out uniforms [was] responsible for the import into South Africa of Military garments or of garments of military pattern.' Instead, he attributed the phenomenon to market forces and South African consumers, asserting that the demand among black Africans for British military dress encouraged the production and distribution of

> quantities of imitation uniform ... both at home and on the Continent purely for export purposes, and in addition Police, Railway, and Post Office uniforms [were] renovated, embellished, and made up to represent old military garments to satisfy South African demand; moreover, worn out Continental and American uniforms [were] always available.

In addition, the report placed regulatory responsibility squarely with colonial governments in British South Africa, claiming that the 'only means of preventing unauthorised persons wearing articles of uniform or articles having the appearance of uniform' was 'to give effect to a measure similar to the Uniforms Act of 1894.'[1] Colonial officials responded sharply. In the Colony of Natal, the collector of customs swiftly exposed what metropolitan military authorities had concealed about long-standing disposal chains in the report:

> The War Office sells worn out uniforms to Old Clothes Contractors who cannot, under English law, dispose of them for wear in the United Kingdom, but can export them. That is the system, and as the articles which come to South Africa are, without even the shadow of a doubt, old worn out English uniforms, it is absolutely clear that the system <u>is</u> responsible for the import into South Africa of military garments ... No argument in the world can possibly lessen the responsibility of the system.[2]

1 NASA SAB, GG vol. 1509, no. 49/11.
2 Ibid.

While these exchanges were part of a longer trajectory since the mid 1890s, the South African War (1899–1902) intensified concerns. As the financial secretary of the War Office acknowledged, debates around the adoption and appropriation of British second-hand military garments by civilians had 'been revived with some force since the late war', when large quantities of British second-hand khaki uniforms—introduced in the Indian army in the 1860s/70s and in the British army towards the end of the nineteenth century—were disposed of in British South Africa.[3] Commercial and 'informal' circuits alike facilitated their distribution: army contractors, exporters and importers, traders, and storekeepers continued established trading networks, while battlegrounds, military camps, hospitals, and British soldiers provided additional sources of supply. The wartime expansion of modes of provision and the acceleration in mobility provoked not only renewed suspicion of second-hand clothing, contributing to the eventual introduction of mandatory disinfection, but also reignited debates about the adoption and appropriation of British second-hand military dress, with critics increasingly focusing on how these garments were embodied and performed by a wider range of consumers.

This renewed attention elevated the commodity within colonial tariff policy, which reshaped the British South African second-hand military clothing trade in the early twentieth century. The South African Customs Union Conventions preceding the establishment of the SACU in 1910 formed part of broader tariff reform debates in the late nineteenth and early twentieth centuries, in particular Joseph Chamberlain's campaign for tariff reform. The vision of an imperial customs union (*Zollverein*) emerged in the 1880s and came to imply a combination of free trade within the British Empire and protective duties on foreign imported goods.[4] Early attempts to establish a customs union in British South Africa were driven by the Cape colonial government in reaction to inter-colonial conflicts over trade direction, revenue benefits from trade (particularly transport tariffs), as well as struggles over access to markets following the development of mining centres. Over almost two decades, the terms of agreement and admission of members into the customs convention—first established by the Cape Colony and the Orange Free State in 1889—were repeatedly renegotiated.[5] By the early twentieth cen-

3 TNA, WO 32/9119. In addition, see NASA WCARS, CO vol. 8294, no. X2955. On the introduction of khaki uniforms in the British army, see, for example, Tynan, *British Army Uniform and the First World War*.

4 See Howe, *Free Trade and Liberal England, 1846–1946*, 191–229, particularly 213–22; Thompson, *Imperial Britain*, 81–96. According to Andrew S. Thompson, the influence of the German *Zollverein* on tariff reform should not be exaggerated. Its significance, however, 'was that it offered further evidence of the strength of commercial and economic association.' Thompson, 'Tariff Reform', 1042–3.

5 Bechuanaland, Basutoland, and Swaziland were admitted as members with diminished rights. See Martin, 'The Making of an Industrial South Africa'. Furthermore, see Colesky, 'A Comparative Study on Customs Tariff Classification', 24–38.

tury, it became apparent that the British colonies would not abandon their protective tariffs, which were oriented towards colonial fiscal policy rather than British economic interests. The colonial governments' refusal to reduce these tariffs led Chamberlain and his supporters to promote imperial preference, a policy that gained strong support in British South Africa, which was dependent on British imports and exports. Accordingly, the British South African general tariffs adopted at the customs union conferences in 1903/06 granted preferential tariffs to most British imports.[6] The negotiation of the tariffs highlights, on the one hand, how commercial interests—represented by European-style clothing manufacturers in British South Africa—exerted increasing influence over policies affecting the second-hand clothing trade. On the other hand, the tariff schedules for the first time assigned second-hand clothing a uniform category distinct from new garments and produced a formal classification system. The everyday practices of customs officials at the British South African docksides highlight the tensions in the theoretical 'taxonomic sway' of these tariffs, which were frequently contested in practice as customs officials grappled with the tangible and observable material characteristics of the imported goods.[7]

In response to marked increases in second-hand clothing imports towards the end and in the aftermath of the First World War, European-style clothing manufacturers and associated industry bodies advocated more vehemently for the prohibition of second-hand clothing imports, seeking to protect the production of European-style clothing in British South Africa. While import duties increased in response to manufacturers' demands, mining companies emerged as dominant actors in shaping tariff policy, exerting influence over the regulation of second-hand clothing imports well into the Second World War.

4.1 Pricing Prestige: British Second-Hand Military Clothing and the Question of Monetary Value, *c.*1899–1903

On 26 September 1903, the British military and naval gazette *Broad Arrow* published a reader's letter submitted to the editors from Umzimkhulu, Colony of Natal (KwaZulu-Natal), about a month earlier:

> The troops serving in this colony are greatly annoyed at the uses to which old Army uniforms are put out here. It is a common thing to see natives riding or walking about the country in the whole, or a portion, of full dress uniform of both officers and privates of British regiments. This is particularly distasteful to men in the military service, and it is even degrading to the regiments whose cast-off uniform is

6 See Howe, *Free Trade and Liberal England, 1846–1946*, 191–229, particularly 213–22; Thompson, *Imperial Britain*, 81–96; Thompson, 'Tariff Reform', 1042–3.

7 Hofmeyr, *Dockside Reading*, 39–44 at 42.

> thus made use of ... I feel sure that if the home authorities were aware of such irregularities ... steps would be taken to prevent British uniforms from being thus degraded.

The anonymous author did not limit his criticism to the adoption of British second-hand military clothing by black Africans but argued that it was

> a fact that storekeepers in this colony receive whole consignments of discarded uniforms ... and sell them to natives. There is no attempt made by the authorities to stop such a practice, in fact, in one case it is openly countenanced. In this instance a native policeman is allowed to perform his duties attired in a cast-off military uniform, although the Colonial Government provides a distinct uniform for all police.[8]

In addition to the well-established British South African trade in second-hand military clothing conducted by army contractors, importers, traders, and storekeepers, the South African War (1899–1902) further expanded both the availability of and the mechanisms for distributing these garments. As historians increasingly stress, the South African War was by no means a 'white man's war'; at least 100,000 black Africans were employed by the British army in various capacities, including as transport drivers, scouts, or blacksmiths, and were partly supplied with military dress either directly by the British army or through purchases of second-hand military clothing from local storekeepers and traders.[9] At the same time, colonial government departments continued to issue items of second-hand military clothing to black Africans in their employment, a practice which, while initially tolerated by colonial authorities, was increasingly criticized for leading 'to a great deal of abuse and ... [made] it difficult for the Police to check this'.[10] Moreover, the South African War brought a substantial increase in the number of British troops, military encampments, and stations across British South Africa, each of which generated additional channels for the distribution and disposal of second-hand military clothing. According to the British army clothing regulations, at military stations abroad, the so-called 'Senior Ordnance Store Officers' and commanding officers were responsible for arranging the disposal of soldiers' worn-out personal clothing as well as all worn-out public clothing. In principle, they were required to follow the same regulations applied at home stations, ensuring that purchasers altered all garments beyond recognizability as British army clothing. In practice, however, oversight of purchasers' actions remained limited.[11] The issue was compounded by the long-standing practice of the informal transfer of second-hand military clothing by British soldiers themselves, who were fre-

---

8 TNA, WO 32/9118.

9 Warwick, *Black People and the South African War 1899–1902*, 6–27 at 6, and 136–41.

10 NASA TAB, MGP vol. 13, no. 1624/1900.

11 See *Regulations for the Supply of Clothing and Necessaries to the Regular Forces*, 1894, 10. See also NASA TAB, DCU vol. 89, no. 1887/1906.

quently found to have sold or exchanged articles of military clothing and other necessaries with black Africans. This pattern is reflected in the rising number of prosecutions and convictions of black Africans for wearing 'condemned clothing belonging to Her Majesty's naval and military forces.'[12] In Ladysmith, Colony of Natal, for example, military officials reported in April 1900 that several black Africans 'found in possession of Military Clothing and Equipment ... [had] stated that Soldiers had sold these articles to them'. Commanding officers were subsequently instructed to warn soldiers accordingly: 'Every effort should be made to discover those who offend in this respect, and, if necessary, kits must be frequently inspected. Men convicted of making away with, or losing by neglect, Clothing, Equipment, &c., should be severely punished.'[13] Beyond concerns about soldiers' own role in the unauthorized sale of second-hand military garments, contemporary criticism of the adoption and appropriation of British second-hand military dress expanded considerably in scope. British military officials in South Africa emerged as the most vocal—and ultimately most influential—opponents of the distribution of second-hand military clothing, confronting the imperial government with demands to prohibit the export of these garments. Moreover, such criticism was neither limited to black Africans nor voiced solely by individuals with military affiliations.[14]

Over the course of the South African War and in its immediate aftermath, military officials frequently reported that Boer soldiers and prisoners of war (POWs) were found dressed in British military clothing. Upon his capture by British forces in late September 1901, the Boer soldier Martinus G. Schoeman, for example, explained to military officials that when his patrol arrived in the district twenty days earlier dressed in 'old clothes' of their own, they encountered a Boer commandant who had captured British soldiers and 'had a lot of clothing with him, so we went and asked him for clothes, as ours was very bad, so he gave me the clothing which I had on when you captured me ... There are a lot of our people wearing English uniforms.'[15] As a visual marker of distinction, military dress provided for the identification of opposing sides on battlefields, an attribute that, British military authorities argued, was disturbed by the adoption and appropriation of British military clothing by an enemy's soldiers and civilians. 'Is it not the most dangerous thing', a British commander asked three years after the end of the South African War in connection with a white transport rider who was found

12 TNA, DO 119/289.

13 NASA NAB, 1/WEN vol. 3/2/3, no. W444A/1900.

14 Ethnologist Dudley A. Kidd, for example, harshly criticized the trade in second-hand (military) clothing with black Africans. See Kidd, *The Essential Kafir*, 25 and 406; Kidd, *Kafir Socialism and the Dawn of Individualism*, 151–2 and 210. On Kidd in the context of racial science, see Dubow, *Scientific Racism in Modern South Africa*, 197–203.

15 NASA TAB, PMO vol. 39, no. PM2646/1901. On POWs dressed in British second-hand military clothing, see, for example, NASA TAB, PMO vol. 37, no. PM2551/1901.

dressed in 'a Khaki tunic with four patched pockets and brass buttons, such as worn by the member of Imperial British Army ... to allow irresponsible persons to wear uniforms such as prescribed for His Majesty's Naval and Imperial and Colonial Military Forces. The practice ... is a grave one, and in my opinion calculated to lead to international complication.' The former Boer soldier had received his clothing from his employer, who had recently supplied his white and black African transport drivers with some of the '200 khaki tunics and 200 pairs of khaki slacks' he had acquired from a storekeeper in Cape Town. Like many contemporary critics, the commander accused the second-hand clothing dealer of creating and increasing 'opportunities for crime' by supplying British second-hand military dress to civilians.[16] Perceived by military individuals as 'masquerade', adoption and appropriation of British military dress by non-military individuals was thought to not only further impersonation and fraud but to threaten the reputation and prestige of the British army.[17] This criticism of the second-hand clothing trade signals broader questions concerning the deployment of military dress and the normative expectations associated with it and its wearer—questions that are rendered more tangible in several instances of white civilians wearing British (second-hand) military dress.

At the same time, these questions extended beyond mere entitlement or legal permission but concerned the manner in which British military norms were performed and embodied. During and after the South African War, the wearing of British military dress by civilians in British South Africa was debated not solely as a matter of who could wear it, but of how; not merely of being allowed to dress according to established norms, but of enacting or failing to enact these norms bodily. The centrality of bodily performance to the symbolism of British military dress becomes evident in military authorities' perceptions of transgressive behaviour by whites. In a letter addressed to the Cape colonial secretary Thomas Graham in November 1900, a major reflected on the adoption and appropriation of second-hand military clothing by white civilians in British South Africa, claiming that men who dressed 'in uniform and wear often the badges of rank of officers, staff officers, etc. without any right [were] Gentlemen [...] sufficiently wanting in self-respect to do such a thing, [and] frequently [had] other failings, such as getting drunk'. 'It is much to be regretted', he added, 'that we cannot bring them to justice more easily.'[18]

The perhaps most instructive illustration of the significance of bodily performativity in relation to military dress is found in a report submitted by a lieutenant major to the head of the military police of the British forces. In November

16 See NASA WCARS, CO vol. 8294, no. X2955.

17 NASA WCARS, AG vol. 1635, no. 7514/1905.

18 Ibid.

1901, the lieutenant major recounts, he passed the prison in Pretoria, Transvaal Colony (Tshwane, KwaZulu-Natal) accompanied by a captain

> and was struck by a Man dressed in Kharki Uniform who stared at both of us as we rode by with his hands in his pocket: thinking that this man was a Soldier I decided to call his attention to the fact that it was subversive to discipline to stare at Officers with his hands in his pocket and not to attempt to pay the authorised compliment of a salute or of standing to attention. When I questioned the man he said (still with his hands in his pockets) that he was a Civilian ... As at the time the Kaffir Warders and Police whom I passed all without exception saluted I submit that this Warder should be dealt with on this subject and reminded that as a Reserve Soldier and as a Government Servant dressed in Uniform he is subject to Military Law.[19]

The stare, missing salute, posture, and practice of holding 'his hands in his pockets' diverged sharply from the passing officer's expectation, and little consideration was given to the fact that the man was a civilian permitted to wear military clothing in his position as a warder.[20] The officer's emphasis on these specific bodily practices underscores both the centrality of embodied performance to military identity and the role of military dress as a visual signifier of normative conduct. At the same time, the report illustrates that whiteness afforded individuals greater mobility between civilian and military identities, enabling them not merely to assume it but to inhabit military dress in ways that were legible—a flexibility rarely extended to black Africans in debates over the adoption and appropriation of British second-hand military clothing.[21] The set of military values ascribed to military dress entailed norms that had to be enacted both verbally and physically for their socially distinctive characteristics to be realized. From the perspective of British military authorities, the repetition of norms through bodily performativity was not only central to military training (the aim of which was to cultivate the embodiment of a set of military values); these norms also had to be reiterated continuously for their significance to be sustained. As Maren Wehrle argues, this linguistic or bodily enacted '*repetition* of norms ... is ... both the cause for its conserving and determining power, as well as for its inherent instabilities and changes.' Acts and practices perceived by the British military authorities as transgressive thus both reveal and challenge the norms themselves, exposing their fragility and the freedom not to enact them. As Wehrle concludes, in 'enact-

19 NASA TAB, PMO vol. 43, no. PM2895/1901.
20 Ibid.
21 See chapter 2.3, particularly Anthony Trollope's account.

ing norms, we thereby make them "real", but always retain the capacity to transcend them.'[22]

These concerns, in turn, reignited earlier debates over legal interventions and drove attempts to regulate the civilian adoption and appropriation of British second-hand military clothing in British South Africa. Given the overall increase in complaints and criticism regarding the wearing of British second-hand military clothing by white and black African civilians during and following the South African War, colonial government and military officials turned to the colonial law departments for guidance. They quickly discovered, however, that colonial statutes had no provision for legislation governing 'the wearing of cast-off uniforms'.[23] Meanwhile and in addition, Cape colonial government authorities briefly debated the implementation of trade restrictions but ultimately concluded, in the words of the law advisor to the Cape colonial government Malcome W. Searle, that it seemed 'anomalous to have any law on this subject at all, if ... His Government allows cast-off uniforms to be disposed of in such a manner that they can truly be offered for sale by traders.'[24] Finally, in April 1902, the matter was referred to the British Colonial Office and, subsequently, the War Office, where, over the following two years, military authorities grappled with the central question: what, precisely, was the prestige of the British army worth?[25]

'The wearing of old uniforms ... is a very old & troublesome question', the financial secretary to the War Office began his concluding discussion thereof in January 1904, and continued: 'I don't think there can be any doubt that so long as we allow the sale of old uniforms, as such, even under restrictions as to resale, we cannot be surprised if we find they are worn in the streets.' While the introduction of the Uniforms Act in 1894 had largely had the desired effect on the British domestic circulation of second-hand military clothing, it was the wearing of British second-hand military clothing by 'semi-naked natives' abroad and particularly in British South Africa that sparked a lengthy discussion between British colonial government representatives and War Office officials as to whether and how to reverse a process that had—to a certain degree—developed beyond imperial control.[26] To colonial government representatives, the solution to the 'degradation of the King's uniform by its sale to natives' appeared straightforward, and

22 Wehrle, 'Bodily Performativity', 139. Wehrle builds on and extends Judith Butler's recent broadening of her linguistic theory of gender performativity to include bodily action. See Butler, *Notes towards a Performative Theory of Assembly*.

23 See NASA TAB, LD vol. 631, no. 923/1904.

24 TNA, DO 119/289.

25 I use the term 'worth' in reference to David Stark because of its 'double connotation of an economic good and a moral good'. Stark, *The Sense of Dissonance*, 1–34 at 8. See also Aspers and Beckert, 'Value in Markets', 6.

26 TNA, WO 32/9119. On the introduction of the Uniforms Act in Britain and its limitations, see chapter 1.2.

—in the words of the collector of customs for the Colony of Natal—should have been 'arrived at regardless of any monetary consideration'. War Office officials, however, faced a complex and partly self-inflicted dilemma. First, the clothing systems of the regular British army, militia, and volunteer forces had come to rely financially on the resale of worn-out military clothing at multiple levels. As the financial secretary of the War Office put it, any alternative course in the disposal of British worn-out military clothing would have significant repercussions: 'The state would lose on Militia body clothing. The regular soldier would lose on his uniform ... The volunteers sell their old clothing [and] the loss of the right would be serious in the present state of Volunteer finances.'[27] These assessments of potential financial loss were themselves contested within the War Office, generating further uncertainty about how to proceed. Between 1873 and 1903, British military authorities calculated the monetary value of worn-out clothing primarily for the purpose of assessing potential charges against soldiers' and officers' accounts in case of the loss or destruction of military-issued clothing and equipment. The valuations fluctuated considerably over these decades: a worn-out great coat (without a cape), for example, initially issued to regular forces and the militia at home stations was valued at approx. 5–6s. in 1873, 7–9s. in 1880, and 6s. in 1882.[28] By the early 1900s, the same item was valued at approx. 3–5s. (1900), 3–4s. (1901), 3–5s. (1903), to 2–5s. (1904), depending—in all cases—on the rank and role of the military personnel concerned.[29] Contractors paid markedly lower prices for the worn-out clothing they collected, and profits from these sales fluctuated annually according to the quantities of clothing returned to the regiments' commanding officers.[30] Finally, the disposal system and assessment of its profits was further complicated by opaque and evolving accounting practices, already evident in the 1880s and early 1890s. Persistent adjustments to the army clothing system, and particularly the system of disposal of worn-out clothing, over roughly twenty years had, in effect, rendered official army statistics largely unreliable.[31]

With virtually no dependable financial data at their disposal, War Office officials weighed the financial implications of any proposed changes to the army clothing disposal system against highly uncertain and inconsistent estimates. The yearly proceeds of the sale of public second-hand military clothing in the early

27 TNA, WO 32/9118.

28 See 'Army Circular, 1st January 1874', in *Army Circulars 1874*, 21; 'Army Circular, 1st June 1880', in *Army Circulars 1881*, 23; 'Army Circular, 1st June 1882', in *Army Circulars 1883*, 13 and 27.

29 See *Prices of Clothing and Necessaries: Regular Forces and Militia* 1900, 5; *Prices of Clothing and Necessaries: Regular Forces and Militia* 1901, 141; *Price List of Clothing and Necessaries* 1903, 154; *Price List of Clothing and Necessaries* 1904, 125.

30 See the contract and the annexed schedule of prices for clothing articles for the army clothing contractor Samuel Moses & Sons, 1 July 1900 until 31 Dec. 1903. Per worn-out coat or cape and regardless of service and rank, for example, the contractor paid 4d. TNA, WO 32/9118.

31 See chapter 1.3.

twentieth century had amounted to approximately £ 25,000, and the total monetary value of soldiers' personal worn-out military clothing was estimated at £ 22,000. Annual losses—if the current system of disposal through army contractors were to be discontinued—were calculated for the public as well as for the individual soldier. Despite disputes over the aforementioned figures, military authorities ascertained that any alternative to the British army's contract-based sales of second-hand military clothing by tender would substantially reduce profits. In comparison with the current system of selling the clothing to army contractors, recycling worn-out military clothing, for example by turning the clothing into rags, was estimated to lead to an annual monetary loss of £ 10,000—a figure, the authorities admitted, that was a wild guess—while the value of contracts would be reduced by 50 to 75 per cent. Not yet included in this calculation was the additional 'cost of machinery & labour for the breaking up of uniforms'. Another proposal to obligate contractors with the transformation of second-hand military clothing into rags was quickly dismissed: 'What guarantee can we have that [the contractor] will carry out his bargain ...? We should be given a shiny inducement to dishonesty [and] I am afraid he would laugh at penal clauses.'[32] Distrust in the army contractor on the part of British army officials was likely rooted, first, in antisemitic sentiments that had already characterized the Director of Clothing's perception of auction sales of British second-hand military clothing during the 1880s.[33] Second, army officials were well aware that army contractors, in many cases, did not alter British second-hand military clothing beyond recognition prior to its resale. While contemplating possibilities to exert more control over army contractors, War Office officials realized that their options were limited, not least because of the overall dependence of the British army on contractors for the disposal of second-hand military clothing.[34] Third, beyond potential financial losses for the public, however, participants in the discussion feared that changes to the system of disposing of second-hand military clothing would once again cause 'serious dissatisfaction' among soldiers. A discontinuance of the contract-based sales by tender translated to an annual loss of £ 2–3 for the individual soldier. Given the precarious income situation of British soldiers—whose families, too, had come to depend increasingly on charitable aid over the course of the South African War—this consideration carried significant weight.[35]

Finally, the debates about the merits of the contemporary disposal system versus proposed alternatives were not driven solely by calculations of monetary value. For many military officials engaged in the decision-making process, the issue of how to dispose of second-hand military clothing was understood as funda-

32 TNA, WO 32/9119. See also TNA, WO 32/9118.
33 See chapter 1.3.
34 See TNA, WO 32/9119; TNA, WO 32/9118. See also chapter 1.3.
35 TNA, WO 32/9118. See Riedi, 'Assisting Mrs Tommy Atkins'; Thompson, 'Publicity, Philanthropy and Commemoration'.

mentally moral in a broader sense, a concern that could not be readily reduced to financial terms. War Office and colonial government authorities approached the issue by balancing potential financial implications against the concern that the adoption and appropriation of British second-hand military clothing by black Africans posed a threat to the prestige and public image of the British army, its soldiers, and imperial authority—in the words of a representative of the War Office, 'the wearing of the King's uniform by unauthorised natives ... [was] not only repugnant to the feelings of officers and men of His Majesty's forces, but ... politically injurious in so much as it tend[ed] to lower the prestige of the soldiers, and of white men generally.'[36] One colonel, for example, maintained that the estimated 'sum [of £10,000] is a moderate one, when the prestige of the Army and of the white man is at stake', while another official weighed possible monetary losses against 'the cost' of preventing 'the consequent degradation ... by semi-naked natives', which he believed would be 'sufficiently covered by the growing additional respect to [the] uniform.'[37] A third participant argued that British soldiers would willingly bear a reasonable expense to avoid 'the indignity of seeing a native wearing H.M.'s uniform'.[38] In his ultimately ambivalent summary of the discussion, the financial secretary of the War Office concluded that it was 'desirable to lose an appreciated portion ... to secure a free hand in the repression of an admitted abuse ... [My] view is that it is worth while but the point is quite debatable'.[39]

As this internal debate unfolded over the course of two years, War Office representatives simultaneously sought to negotiate what they regarded as a compromise with the colonial government representatives in British South Africa. In January 1903, Alfred Milner, Governor of the Transvaal and Orange River Colony, was informed that the War Office was 'now prepared ... to insert in future contracts of sale a Clause prohibiting the export of discarded uniforms to South Africa on condition', however, 'that the various administrations procure the passing of legislation forbidding the sale of such uniforms to natives.' While most colonial governments initially signalled their willingness to comply, the proposal drew strong objections from officials in the Colony of Natal. There, the collector of customs deemed the measures 'now made by the Home Authorities ... extremely weak and logically bad', arguing that the War Office appeared concerned 'only about South Africa. Surely the degradation complained of is equally great if British discarded uniforms are worn by the chiffonier and the gamin in Paris.' By November 1903, several colonial government representatives agreed that the sale of British second-hand military clothing should be prohibited

36 NASA WCARS, CO vol. 8294, no. X2955.
37 TNA, WO 32/9119.
38 TNA, WO 32/9118.
39 TNA, WO 32/9119.

> throughout the world, and not merely in South Africa. There is much force in [the] contention that it is of no avail to protect our uniform in South Africa, if it is dragged in the mud elsewhere ... [A]ll soldiers feel very strongly in this matter, and are agreed that both from a military and political point of view it is essential that the King's uniform should be treated with respect in every portion of the globe.

At the end of 1903, the debate between the War Office and the colonial governments in British South Africa appears to have reached an impasse. While War Office representatives continued to deliberate in the matter into 1904, colonial government representatives sought alternative solutions. In particular, they attempted to incorporate second-hand military clothing into the Customs Union Conventions preceding the establishment of the SACU in 1910. In the words of Albert H. Hime, Prime Minister of the Colony of Natal, adjusting tariff policy was 'the most convenient way' for the colonial governments to achieve their objective of prohibiting second-hand military clothing imports.[40]

4.2 The South African Customs Union Conventions and the Practices of Classification, 1903–1910

Before the controversies surrounding imports of second-hand military clothing re-emerged in the early twentieth century in the context of the Customs Union Conventions, the British South African colonial tariff environment—fiscal rates, classificatory categories, and administrative practices—shaped the conditions under which British second-hand military clothing entered colonial markets. Crucially, prior to 1903, most British South African tariff schedules did not distinguish between new and used garments. Between 1897 and 1902, in the Cape Colony and the Colony of Natal a uniform 5 per cent *ad valorem* duty was levied on all 'apparel and slops' imported for consumption, thereby classifying second-hand clothing within the same fiscal category as new clothing.[41] Within this context, colonial governments attempted in 1903 to include second-hand military clothing among the articles prohibited from import into British South Africa under the Customs Union Convention. However, according to the collector of customs of the Cape Colony, 'the matter was not discussed' by the delegates at the customs conference in Bloemfontein; they quickly dismissed it, noting that the views articulated since the mid 1890s still governed the issue. The continuous reluctance of British colonial authorities to assume local regulatory responsibility for the distribution of British second-hand military clothing reflects not only the hierarchical structure of imperial administrations but its limits. The War Office and the British army, colonial government representatives pointed out, were responsible for the

40 All quotes here are from TNA, WO 32/9118.

41 *Colonial Import Duties 1897*, 299; *Colonial Import Duties 1902*, 313.

global distribution of British second-hand military clothing, and it fell to them to prohibit its export.[42]

While the proposal to prohibit the importation of British second-hand military clothing failed in 1903, the issue gained new momentum in the years that followed. First, among colonial government representatives, concerns intensified following the outbreak on board the *Cornwall* and the subsequent outbreak investigation, which sparked debate over the risk of disease transmission through imported second-hand clothing. Second, and at the same time, the *Report of the Industries & Tariff Revision Commission* published between 1903 and 1905 introduced economic arguments linked to industrial policy and tariff reform. Third, the influence of commercial actors and associations increased. In 1905, the British South African chambers of commerce, while significantly shaping the discussion on the mandatory disinfection of imported second-hand clothing, began to advocate for a special duty on the import of these garments. The first proposition to impose a special duty on importers of second-hand clothing at the Congress of the Association of Chambers of Commerce in January 1905 was rejected by a narrow majority.[43] A second proposal initiated by the Pretoria Chamber of Commerce shortly before the Customs Union Conference in Pietermaritzburg in 1906, however, 'was carried by 15 to 4 votes'.[44]

Despite the extensive consequences of the Customs Union Convention agreements for importers, traders, and consumers, a striking feature of the records (which include conference minutes, documents, and reports) is the relative absence of substantive discourse on the very commodities affected. Against this backdrop, during a sitting of the Legislative Council at the Colony of Natal in June 1906, the motion to pass the Customs Union Convention Bill was interrupted by George Sutton, former Prime Minister of the Colony of Natal (1903–5), who had not attended the conference in Pietermaritzburg. Sutton questioned 'the reasons that influenced the recent Customs Conference to increase the duty on second-hand clothing.' He had 'not noticed any explanation of that change, if, indeed, any has been given.'[45] Indeed, the minutes of the assembly sittings are limited to brief summaries of topics and motions; however, the reports on which the delegates of the respective colonial governments based their discussions, negotiations, and recommendations are instructive.

The delegates of the Colony of Natal, for example, drew on the *Report of the Industries & Tariff Revision Commission*, which enquired into 'the question of the establishment and encouragement of manufacturing industries in Natal' and was

42 TNA, WO 32/9118.

43 *Johannesburg Chamber of Commerce: Annual Report for the Year Ended 28th February, 1905*, 19–20.

44 *Johannesburg Chamber of Commerce: Annual Report for the Year Ended 28th February, 1906*, 64.

45 *Debates of the Legislative Council of the Colony of Natal*, vol. 15, 112.

published in 1905. In fourteen sessions, the commission members interviewed 134 witnesses from almost every industry in the colony. Their final report comprised summaries of the evidence and general findings relating to different industries and fiscal policies as well as recommendations for the upcoming tariff reform.[46] Among other topics and issues, the commission focused on the manufacture of European-style clothing in the Colony of Natal, which had, in summary, 'not been taken up at all'.[47] A woollen textile factory in the colony had recently failed, and although commission members noted that certain British clothing manufacturers —for example, the Cardigan Clothing Co., Ltd. based in Leeds—had expressed interest in establishing production facilities in British South Africa, local industry representatives raised concerns.[48] A spokesperson for the master tailors of Pietermaritzburg contended that the development of the British South African tailoring trade was being significantly constrained by insufficient protection against foreign competition. In comparison to producers in British South Africa, he argued, manufacturers in Europe and British India enjoyed structural advantages, including markedly lower labour and raw material costs.[49] A merchant from Ladysmith contended that although black African demand for clothing and boots had been —and continued to be—on the rise, Indian competitors had increasingly 'been getting hold' of the British South African domestic market and were 'now catering for all classes of trade'. In addition, he asserted that demand for the cheapest forms of clothing was gradually diminishing; consumers would 'not now take slop clothing as they formerly did. They would rather pay a little more and get a better article.' A boot and shoe manufacturer advanced a stronger claim, stating that 'Arabs and other aliens [had] secured practically the whole of the coloured and Native trade ... they have filched the most desirable portion of our business—*i. e.*, the cash business.' In view of these developments, the manufacturer urged the commission to ensure that forthcoming tariff recommendations prioritized the protection of local industries. Storekeepers and merchants, he argued, should be compelled to purchase 'within the Colony as far as possible the bulk of those articles required by the Native.'[50] Drawing on such testimony, which echoed racialized narratives of non-European competition and reflected patterns identified in British South African trade commentary, the *Report of the Industries & Tariff Revision Commission* proposed a series of tariff regulations designed to restore to tailors in British South Africa the trade 'that [was] now being filched from them by this unfair class of competition'.[51] In relation to bespoke and second-hand cloth-

46 *Report of the Industries & Tariff Revision Commission*, 3. See also NASA NAB, PM vol. 101, no. 80/1906.

47 *Report of the Industries & Tariff Revision Commission*, 16.

48 See ibid. 17. For reference to the company, see Honeyman, *Well Suited*, 300.

49 See *Report of the Industries & Tariff Revision Commission*, 478–82.

50 Ibid. 291.

51 Ibid. 16.

ing, the commission recommended the imposition of a 40 per cent *ad valorem* duty on 'second-hand wearing apparel for both sexes, of every description, and of any material'. Notably, although these rates were exceptionally high compared to most other proposed duties, the commission did not recommend a prohibition on the importation of second-hand clothing.[52]

Building on the commission's recommendation, the delegates for the Colony of Natal approved most of the principles laid down in the report in early March 1906, including the proposed duty on second-hand clothing.[53] Yet, in the official records of the Customs Union Convention, the issue of second-hand clothing is absent from formal discussion. It appears, however, to have been addressed repeatedly in private conversations. Following the convention, Henry McCallum, for example—Governor of the Colony of Natal since 1901—recalled 'a conversation with ... Treasurer of the Cape Colony, who was staying with [him] during the ... Customs Conference': 'I pointed out to him that second-hand military clothing was still being landed in South Africa for disposal to natives with regimental buttons and military insignia intact ... [The Treasurer] informed me subsequently that he had brought the matter before the Conference and that the Members refused to take any action thereon.' Marginal notes referencing previous correspondence to the Secretary of State for the Colonies suggest that McCallum had repeatedly advocated for a prohibition on the importation of second-hand clothing into British South Africa, a strategy that had failed on multiple occasions.[54] Nevertheless, this and similar episodes underscore the significance of informal channels—dinner parties, clubs, and private meetings—as arenas of policy discussion and negotiation.

Building on both the formal and presumably informal policy discussions surrounding second-hand clothing, the debate continued into the legislative arena. During the previously mentioned sitting of the Natal Legislative Council on 28 June 1906, George Sutton eventually received a threefold explanation for the increased duty on second-hand clothing. The Minister for Railways and Harbours clarified that the measure had multiple purposes. First, the duty was intended to 'create some obstacle to a trade of this particular character', specifically the trade in second-hand military uniforms. Second, it was feared that second-hand clothing was introducing disease through its importation. Third, and adding a new argument to the debate, he claimed

52 For commodities considered 'unwholesome foodstuffs', for example, the commission 'suggested prohibitive Duties in the interest of public health'. Other commodities for which the commission recommended a 40 per cent *ad valorem* duty were those categorized as 'Advertising and Printed Matter'. Ibid. 30–46 at 30–7.

53 See NSA NAB, PM vol. 101, no. 80/1906.

54 Previous correspondence discussed the introduction of legislation similar to the Uniforms Act 1895 in British South Africa. TNA, CO 179/233.

> that dealing in second-hand clothing has for long been one of the means of occupation for one of the worst sweating class in the English metropolis ... And it was with a view to ... checking this somewhat nefarious traffic ... that it was decided to impose this special duty ... and so encourage the more genuine trade ... in cheap, but, nevertheless, first-hand clothing.[55]

Following the agreements reached during the customs union conference in March 1906 and the introduction of disinfection regulations for all imported second-hand clothing, importers were required to declare 'every consignment of second-hand clothing, no matter where its destination ... to the Customs at the Port of Entry'. Certified statements accompanying every consignment had to specify 'exactly of what it consisted', its place of origin, and provide proof of disinfection 'by a responsible Authority at the Port of shipment or place of origin of the package'.[56] Customs officials in the Colony of Natal received copies of the tariff regulations as per the Customs Union Convention in May 1906 'for their early guidance of classification' at the request of the collector of customs in Durban. Second-hand clothing was listed as tariff item no. 11, encompassing second-hand coats, vests, and trousers, for which a duty of 2s. per article was imposed.[57] While these detailed requirements aimed to ensure compliance, the taxonomy of the tariff regulations proved difficult to translate into clear operational guidelines and generated low-level disputes among customs officials and with importers over the interpretation of the tariff schedules, the classification of imported clothing along the guidelines, and the validity of certificates, reflecting ongoing tensions between regulatory intent and commercial practice.

The revision of the tariff regulations and schedules in 1903 and 1906, and the introduction of mandatory disinfection of imported second-hand clothing in 1907 significantly impacted the classificatory practices of customs officials at British South African ports. Each of these changes provided customs officials with a new set of guidelines. To determine whether imported clothing was new or second-hand, had been manufactured in Britain or elsewhere, and had been disinfected, customs officials checked and examined cargo marks and certificates accompanying consignments at the docksides. The Customs Union Convention of 1903 stipulated that all commodities not explicitly mentioned in the tariff schedules were subject to a general *ad valorem* duty of 10 per cent; however, importers could claim a rebate of 25 per cent for commodities of British manufacture.[58] Consequently, the principal concern of customs officials regarding second-hand cloth-

55 *Debates of the Legislative Council of the Colony of Natal 1906*, 112–13 at 112.

56 NASA TAB, EC vol. 92, no. 156/1906, *Regulations in Regard to the Importation of Second-Hand Clothing.*

57 NASA NAB, PM vol. 59, no. PM400/1906.

58 See NASA TAB, EC vol. 33, no. EC325/207/1903, *Customs Union Convention 1903*, art. 2: class 5, and art. 3a.

ing shipments was determining whether the clothing had been produced in Britain, a claim as frequently made by exporters and importers as it was questioned by customs officials because, in the words of a customs official in 1906, they 'could not possibly trace the original source of manufacture, even if they attempted to do so.'[59] After all, these garments had primarily originated from British soldiers' bodies rather than commercial factories. Customs officials therefore relied on clothing tags, tickets, and official marks as the most tangible indicators of origin. In one instance, a custom official examining a bale of second-hand clothing declared in East London as British-made found that on 'certain Apron Cloths were tickets with the words "Made in Holland" and some of the Second-hand Clothing had tags attached which read "Paris Nouveau," 38 Bould Rochechouart, and buttons J. Furlerer, Paris.' On the basis of these textual markers, the official deemed the garments of foreign manufacture and consequently denied the rebate to the importer.[60]

Notably, the condemned clothing mark—namely the double or inverted broad arrow introduced with the British army clothing regulations in 1881—was, in principle, to appear on all British second-hand military garments, presumably on the interior of the item.[61] In accordance with the regulations governing army contractors, second-hand military clothing was to be altered, prior to resale, to include its identification as former British army clothing. A representative of the army contractors Mallett, Porter & Dowd, Ltd. asserted that 'the labour put on the articles in England' in the course of processes such as relining and rebuttoning amounted to manufacturing operations undertaken domestically, thereby justifying the classification of British as well as foreign second-hand military clothing as products of British manufacture. According to the prevailing tariff regulations, 'at least 25 % of the value [had to be] represented by British workmanship to entitle goods to preferential treatment'.[62] Customs officials, however, argued that the imported bales under inspection contained a significant amount of second-hand military clothing of 'apparently French & German' origin. While an altered British second-hand military clothing article might have granted the exporters the rebate, the relined and rebuttoned foreign second-hand military garments were not British enough—rebates would 'not be allowed on Foreign Uniforms and second-hand clothes in general rebuttoned and relined in England.'[63] Nevertheless, as in

59 NASA TAB, DCU vol. 75, no. 638/1906.

60 NASA WCARS, T vol. 971, no. 771/1906.

61 See chapters 1.1 and 1.4. The clothing regulations 1881 specified that the double broad arrow mark was to 'be two inches long (each broad arrow one inch) ... and ... placed on such part of the article as [would] not prevent its sale by the Contractor or purchaser.' *Regulations for the Supply of Clothing and Necessaries to the Regular Forces*, 1881, 73.

62 NASA WCARS, T vol. 845, no. 3935/1903.

63 NASA TAB, DCU vol. 75, no. 638/1906. Similar disputes over this question arose in Kenya around 1930. See TNA, CO 533/404/9.

the case of clothing tags, the presence or absence of the inverted or double broad arrow mark facilitated the process of identification and classification at the British South African customs offices. Customs officials interpreted the marks as indicators of the country of manufacture and as a signifier that the garments were second-hand. This function became increasingly significant following the revision of the tariff schedule and regulations in 1906, both heightening the evidentiary role of visual markers and labels as instruments of categorization and intensifying disputes between customs officials, exporters, and importers.

Whether particular garments ought to have been classed as second-hand became a recurrent point of contention in the years following the introduction of the tariffs. Almost immediately after the revised schedule and regulations came into force, importers sought clarification from colonial government authorities in British South Africa. An importer in East London, for example, asked whether the regulations excluded 'Second Hand Overcoats as they [were] not mentioned in any way in the new tariff' and received a response that was as short as it was unequivocal: 'overcoats are coats and second-hand overcoats [would] consequently be liable to the rated duty'.[64] A similar dispute arose when an importer in Mbabane (Eswatini) reported that his agent had been required to pay the increased duty on second-hand clothing in Mozambique for 'remade waistcoats' and insisted that 'remade articles [were] not the same as second-hand' clothing. The customs officials who examined the waistcoats concluded that they 'had been turned and cleaned and otherwise repaired' and therefore classified them as second-hand.[65]

The incentives for commercial actors in the second-hand clothing trade to avoid the classification under tariff item no. 11 were significantly heightened with the increased duty on second-hand clothing. Although tariffs on other clothing articles also increased by roughly 7 per cent in 1906, the difference paled in comparison to the levy imposed on imported second-hand clothing items. Sampson Baughan, a London resident with ties to the British South African second-hand clothing merchant community, calculated in June 1906 that a shipment valued at approximately £155 would 'under the new tariff cost £206 … instead of £13' in duty.[66] As a result, customs officials encountered an increasing number of cases in which goods were deliberately entered under misleading descriptions. In one instance, agents for an importer in Johannesburg 'entered the contents [of two cases] as "New Clothing" … but on examination a large number of garments were found to be second-hand'. Customs authorities concluded that this was 'a deliber-

64 NASA WCARS, T vol. 1/986, no. 2510/1906.

65 NASA TAB, DCU vol. 97, no. 300/1907.

66 NASA TAB, DCU vol. 81, no. 1017/1906.

ate attempt to defraud the revenue and ... consequently seized the goods'.[67] In addition, importers and exporters sought to exploit exemptions for personal effects and for second-hand clothing intended for charitable distribution. In December 1907, an importer presented seventy-two garments in Port Elizabeth as the personal clothing of a resident in Johannesburg and argued that these were not intended for sale. The volume of clothing aroused suspicion among customs officials, who were subsequently informed that the purported owner was known to be a partner in the Johannesburg firm Lunz & Herman and currently involved in another dispute over damaged second-hand clothing at the port of Durban, a case already occupying customs officials in both the Cape Colony and the Colony of Natal.[68]

Notwithstanding the financial incentives to avoid the duty on second-hand clothing, disagreements over what ought to be classified as second-hand clothing were not confined to disputes between commercial actors and customs officials. They also emerged among customs authorities across the colonies themselves. Only a few months after the tariff regulations took effect in 1906, the collector of customs in Durban contacted the South African Customs Statistical Bureau in order to clarify which garments fell under 'tariff item no. 11':

> I shall be glad to have the views of the various Colonies as to what can be considered to come under this heading. Large quantities of second-hand overcoats, ulsters, etc., are being imported [in Durban] for sale to natives, both male and female, and I am doubtful whether we can collect duty under Item 11, especially when these articles are for women.[69]

His inquiry was circulated 'in the usual manner' among the customs departments of all colonial administrations in British South Africa, and the responses reveal a striking divergence of opinion. Some authorities maintained that second-hand 'overcoats and ulster whether for men or women should be classified under Item 11', whereas others questioned whether women's garments could or should fall within the category at all. The collector of customs in the Transvaal Colony argued that 'an overcoat or ulster [was] most certainly a coat' irrespective of the intended wearer's gender but conceded uncertainty as to 'whether women's draw-

---

67 NASA WCARS, T vol. 1084, no. 522/1907. See also NASA WCARS, T vol. 1106, no. 1704/1908; NASA WCARS, T vol. 1134, no. 3858/1908; NASA TAB, DCU vol. 89, no. 1840/1906; NASA TAB, DCU vol. 96, no. 284/1907.

68 See NASA TAB, DCU vol. 107, no. 1155/1907. On the amount of clothing 'in reasonable quantities' admitted duty free as personal clothing, see, for example, NASA TAB, DCU vol. 70, no. 355/1906. On the dispute over second-hand articles of clothing damaged through disinfection at the port in Durban and the involvement of the storekeepers of Lunz & Herman, see chapter 3.3.

69 NASA TAB, DCU vol. 97, no. 300/1907.

ers could properly be classed as trousers.'[70] Although customs authorities eventually agreed that overcoats—including those designed for women—should be treated as coats, the tariff schedule continued to embed strongly gendered assumptions into the classification of second-hand clothing. This ambiguity persisted into the late 1930s, when customs officials in Durban detained a shipment imported by representatives of The Barnett Clothing Co. consisting of nine bales of second-hand overcoats alongside an unspecified number of bales of '(Ladies) S. H. Overcoats'. The latter again generated protracted debate centred on the question 'as to what constitutes an overcoat.'[71] These classificatory uncertainties expose how binary gender assumptions, bureaucratic logics, and racialized commercial expectations intersected within customs offices. While the tariff categories appeared universal, they were based on military, male-coded garment types. Women's clothing destabilized these supposedly neutral categories, revealing how the tariff structure embedded gendered hierarchies. At the same time, the debates over classification occurred in a racialized commercial context where second-hand clothing was explicitly linked with black African consumer markets, and this influenced customs officials' assessments of which items merited duty collection, demonstrating that tariff enforcement was embedded within social and cultural logics.

Building on disputes over the classification of second-hand clothing, the practical work of customs enforcement at the British South African docks increasingly emphasized the materiality of the articles of clothing. In many cases, clothing—new and second-hand—was neither marked nor carried tags or tickets that could indicate its origin or status. Consequently, from 1906 onwards, customs officials relied on careful examination of the textiles, scrutinizing fibres, thread, and accessories such as buttons or badges, colours, and design features. Physical signs of prior use became critical for classification. Loose threads or holes near buttons, for example, suggested rebuttoning, while traces of relining often revealed remnants of earlier designs.[72] Evidence of previous ownership could also be found in the contents of pockets: forty-two jackets and coats were identified as railway uniforms based on the presence of 'buttons, braid and other marks of rank, still attached.' The inspecting customs official further noted that the uniforms exhibited 'distinct traces of wear; besides which were fragments of railway tickets, cigarettes and tobacco in the pockets.'[73] The emphasis on the materiality of clothing in customs inspections extended to consulting experts, particularly when customs officials faced uncertainty about the origin or status of the clothing. In 1906, a customs official tracking seven bales of second-hand military clothing reported to

70 Ibid.

71 NASA SAB, DEA vol. 204, no. A10/16/1X.

72 See NASA TAB, DCU vol. 75, no. 638/1906. See also Hofmeyr, *Dockside Reading*, 40–8; Piekacz, 'Beyond "Reading" Materials: Trace (on Trace) and Value'.

73 NASA WCARS, T vol. 1134, no. 3858/1908.

the director of customs in Pretoria, Transvaal Colony (Tshwane, Gauteng), that a shipment including five bales of military overcoats and two bales of cavalry coats from the warehouse of Mallett, Porter & Dowd, Ltd. posed classification challenges. Declared by the exporters to be British clothing, upon inspection many of the garments 'were found to bear no marks by which they could [have been] recognised as British and in fact appeared to be foreign':

> I found upon inspection that it was impossible for me to determine if the goods were of British or Foreign manufacture, & therefore I brought with me certain samples of military tunics, coats & civilian clothing with a view of getting an expert opinion. Enquiries at the military barracks resulted in a decision being arrived at in regard to the dark green tunic which is declared as of undoubted British origin, but there seems to be a doubt about the other articles, with the exception of the civilian clothes, which I believe are of British make.[74]

In this instance, military officials not only assisted in confirming the British origin of the tunics but implicitly verified that the garments were second-hand. When importers disputed customs classifications and declarations, customs authorities sought to assess the accuracy of declared values through third-party valuations. In October 1906, among eight cases of clothing entered at the port and customs office in Durban, one contained '32 Morning Coast and Vests' whose condition led the examining customs official to suspect they were second-hand. Samples of the garments were 'submitted to various Merchants which appeared to confirm this view'. While these third-party evaluations were frequently accepted by the parties involved, in this case the importer continued to insist that the garments were new. To resolve the dispute, the collector of customs eventually appointed two independent valuators—one representing the customs office, the other the importer. When they disagreed, a third valuator, 'appointed … as Umpire … placed a value of 6/- per Coat and Vest or £ 9-12-0 for the consignment', thereby confirming the under-entry for the customs office. Notably, although the material condition of the garments played a significant role in these determinations, it was not the only factor considered. As the collector of customs noted, all three valuators agreed that 'the original cost of the material and the making' exceeded the amounts reflected in their final assessments. Nevertheless, the final valuations were determined on the basis that the same lines of clothing could be purchased 'for the values as given by Oaths by them'.[75]

The inspection and valuation of second-hand clothing imported in British South Africa after 1906 demonstrates how customs officials relied on both material evidence and expert judgement. Customs officials examined textiles—fibres, threads, buttons, relining, and signs of wear—to determine their origin, status,

74 NASA TAB, DCU vol. 75, no. 638/1906.
75 NASA TAB, DCU vol. 89, no. 1840/1906.

and monetary value, effectively 'reading' these garments as texts. When the physical clues were ambiguous, they consulted military personnel, merchants, or independent valuators, combining observation with socially and institutionally mediated expertise. The valuation disputes show that materiality informed but did not determine fiscal decisions; final assessments were negotiated within bureaucratic frameworks. Together, these practices indicate that tariff enforcement was interpretative and labour intensive, requiring knowledge and mediation to translate the physical characteristics of clothing into the orderly tariff classifications. Finally, while the preceding examples illustrate customs practices and highlight inspection and expert consultation, they also point to the constraints of detection and limitation of enforcement. Deliberate misdescriptions of bales and cases, particularly when accompanied by fraudulent certificates, remained difficult to uncover. While archival records provide insights into the practices of classification and valuation at British South African docksides, they simultaneously indicate a larger realm of the undetected, unrecorded, and untraceable.

4.3 Struggles over Overcoats: Second-Hand Clothing Imports in South Africa, *c.*1910–1945

In 1920, the British Board of Trade launched its first comprehensive investigation into the British second-hand clothing retail and wholesale trade, including its export branches. Keen 'to obtain general information about every branch of the trade', investigators carried out 644 visits to retail and wholesale establishments, street markets, shippers, and packing businesses. The report provides valuable insights into the diverse sources of supply and local manufacturing processes as well as into the operations of businesses who engaged in both the domestic and transnational trade in second-hand clothing. At the same time, the investigators noted 'the reluctance of wholesale dealers to give information' and found that details regarding the export trade had not been 'easy to discover, and seem[ed] to be carefully guarded, as one retail establishment in Scotland informed the investigator that they were anxious to discover how to export their goods direct and save the loss of profit caused by going through certain London firms, but that so far they had absolutely failed.' In the final report, the Board of Trade concluded that most wholesale trade in second-hand clothing was concentrated in London's East End, from where substantial quantities were exported, predominantly to South Africa and India. Among the businesses visited was the army contractor Mallett, Porter & Dowd, Ltd., which continued to operate its warehouse in Caledonian Road, Islington, sorting, altering, and repairing second-hand clothing for export.[76]

76 TNA, LAB 2/668/TBD134/A/8/1920.

The timing of the investigation by the Board of Trade coincided with a record high in British South African imports of second-hand clothing. Up to that point, imports from Britain had fluctuated but risen steadily. In 1920, the South African Statistical Bureau recorded the importation of 1,118,426 items of second-hand clothing valued at £ 428,222, nearly triple the quantity and monetary value of the second highest level of recorded imports in 1916 and 1918.[77] Importation of second-hand boots and shoes, including British military footwear, similarly increased from 1916 onwards. Following complaints from footwear manufacturers in South Africa, imports of second-hand shoes were restricted in 1919 and formally prohibited in 1923.[78] By contrast, however, protests by European-style clothing manufacturers had little effect on imports of other items of second-hand clothing. A prohibition was not formalized until 1939, and even then, as detailed below, it made a notable exception.

Factory production of European-style clothing in South Africa emerged in the early twentieth century and expanded slowly yet steadily, particularly in Cape Town and Johannesburg. The outbreak of the First World War (1914–18) initially strengthened the position of clothing and textile manufacturers, as wartime disruptions sharply reduced imports from Britain. Growing demand for military garments and the availability of profitable government contracts further encouraged industrial expansion; however, as Iris Berger notes, these developments also 'produced numerous efforts at cost-cutting that included the payment of shockingly low wages' within the sector.[79] Despite manufacturers' concerns about the viability of the industry in the aftermath of the First World War, production continued to grow until the economic downturn in 1920/21, when factory owners com-

77 See *British South Africa: First Annual Statement of the Trade and Shipping of the Colonies and Territories Forming the South African Customs Union, 1907*, 6; *British South Africa: Third Annual Statement of the Trade and Shipping of the Colonies and Territories Forming the South African Customs Union, 1908*, 6; *British South Africa: Fourth Annual Statement of the Trade and Shipping of the Colonies and Territories Forming the South African Customs Union, 1909*, 6–7; *British South Africa: Fifteenth Annual Statement of the Trade and Shipping of the Union of South Africa, Southern and Northern Rhodesia, and South-West Africa, 1920*, 4; *British South Africa: Seventh Annual Statement of the Trade and Shipping of the Union of South Africa and of Southern and N. W. Rhodesia, 1912*, 4; *British South Africa: Ninth Annual Statement of the Trade and Shipping of the Union of South Africa and of Southern and Northern Rhodesia, 1914*, 3.

78 See, for example, NASA SAB, IMI vol. 15, no. I29/5; NASA SAB, BCP vol. 8, no. 33/90/45 (restriction of importation under the *Public Welfare and Moratorium Act 1917*); *Official Year Book of the Union of South Africa and of Basutoland, Bechuanaland Protectorate and Swaziland*, 581 (prohibition of importation under the *Customs and Excise Duties Act 1923*).

79 Berger, *Threads of Solidarity*, 31–2 at 32. Furthermore, see Nicol, 'A History of Garment and Tailoring Workers in Cape Town', 33–61; Feinstein, *An Economic History of South Africa*, 113–15; Honeyman, *Well Suited*, 81–2. On the history of the South African clothing industry with emphasis on non-white South African fashions, see Rovine, *African Fashion, Global Style*, particularly 191–230.

plained of a post-war depression and the persistent absence of protective tariff regulations.[80] By 1929, concern about foreign competition remained acute. A representative of the firm Jardin du Modes argued that high import duties on raw materials, combined with 'the great disadvantage by the payment of bigger wages than those paid in Britain' made it nearly impossible for producers to manufacture clothing 'of the same quality and at the same price as the landed cost of ... goods from overseas.' Such complaints formed part of a broader and increasingly vocal campaign among industry bodies. The British South African Industrial Council for the Clothing Industry—representing the Transvaal Manufacturers Association and the Witwatersrand Tailors' Association—and the Cape Chamber of Industries raised similar objections, particularly regarding the impact of imported second-hand clothing:

> We are grateful for the partial redress we have been granted by the Government in this matter by the imposition of higher duties on imported second hand garments, but we think that in the interests of our industry we are justified in asking for the total prohibition of the importation of second hand clothing ... [It] would lead to considerable expansion of our industry as the people buying now second hand garments would then satisfy their needs in buying local manufactured clothing.[81]

As clothing and textile manufacturers and associations increasingly advocated for the prohibition of second-hand clothing imports from the early 1920s onwards, importers and traders mounted counter-arguments. They contended that domestic producers had not yet developed the capacity to supply garments of comparable price and quality, particularly in the categories of second-hand clothing, that remained popular among consumers, including, though not limited to, black African buyers. A representative of S. Morris & Co, wholesale import merchants in Johannesburg, warned that a prohibition would present 'severe hardships to poor whites who usually purchase this class of commodity' and deliver 'a serious set-back to storekeepers throughout the Union who handle these articles.'[82]

Most notably, however, the post-war years had not only given rise to an expanding European-style clothing industry, but also to the emergence of a second-hand clothing industry. In 1930, trade observers estimated that 25 per cent of imported second-hand clothing was not distributed outright but was 'renovated' in local factories first. At least two firms based in Cape Town and Durban—A. Belikoff and Co., Ltd, wholesale importers of new and second-hand clothing, and

80 See Nicol, 'A History of Garment and Tailoring Workers in Cape Town', 90–1.

81 NASA SAB, RHN vol. 1297, no. 125/9/8. See also Nicol, 'A History of Garment and Tailoring Workers in Cape Town', 63 and 91.

82 NASA SAB, RHN vol. 1297, no. 125/9/8. On the increase of poverty among whites, the so-called 'poor whites' problem, during the first three decades of the twentieth century, see, for example, Feinstein, *An Economic History of South Africa*, 74–89; Seekings, '"Not a Single White Person Should be Allowed to Go Under"'.

Linder & Co. Ltd—employed between 80 and 200 workers. Second-hand garments (mainly jackets and overcoats) were 'fumigated overseas and renovated in the Union', predominantly by 'coloured' employees. Over the following decade, the number of such factories increased, established largely by importing merchants already active in the second-hand clothing trade. Representatives of the wholesale merchants, clothing manufacturers, and importers J. Catzel & Sons in Cape Town, for example—a business that specialized in 'second-hand jackets, and military clothing'—noted in 1939 that they had 'been dealing in this class of goods for over twenty years ... We also have a factory in which the repair of these garments is carried on, and our employees ... have been with us for a great number of years.'[83]

These industrial developments unfolded alongside sustained disputes over the regulatory framework governing the second-hand clothing trade. Between *c.*1920 and 1945, conflicts over the prohibition of second-hand clothing imports and tariff amendments were resolved largely between representatives of European-style clothing manufacturers and second-hand clothing importers, with few substantive shifts in the core arguments.[84] At a meeting with the British South African Board of Trade and Industries in 1930, for example, import merchants presented attendees with 'some samples of renovated second-hand jackets which were sold [in South Africa] at 9s. 6d., and of South African ready-made jackets sold at 15s., and pointed out the superior quality of the material of the second-hand garments as compared with the local product.'[85] In doing so, second-hand clothing importers continuously argued that rather than constituting a threat to the domestic European-style clothing industry, second-hand clothing represented an indispensable component in the clothing economy, particularly for lower-income consumers. However, while these disputes between European-style clothing manufacturers and second-hand clothing importers remained central, mining companies increasingly shaped the debate, recognizing that the availability and affordability of second-hand clothing for black African mine workers had direct implications for labour stability. Their intervention introduced a new layer of strategic concern, linking trade policy not just to industrial profit but to social

83 NASA SAB, RHN vol. 1297, no. 125/9/8. Meanwhile, a representative of the clothing manufacturers Jardin du Modes stressed in 1929 that they were employing twelve people, adding that they 'positively refuse[d] to employ any coloured labour in [the] factory and shall continue only to employ white labour' (ibid.). On the racial division of labour in South African factory work between 1900 and 1925, see Berger, *Threads of Solidarity*, 16–45. Regarding Linder & Co., Ltd., see NASA SAB, BIS vol. 31, no. BIS432.

84 It is important to note, however, that not all clothing manufacturer and tailor associations advocated for the prohibition of second-hand clothing imports. Regarding, for example, the Natal Clothing Manufacturers Association, see NASA SAB, RHN vol. 1297, no. 125/9/8.

85 Ibid.

and political control. Within this context, debates over second-hand military overcoats took on heightened significance.

In the interwar period, imported second-hand military overcoats were among the most profitable and in-demand garments in the second-hand clothing trade. A representative of S. Morris & Co., Ltd. explained that 'Officers' military overcoats' sold particularly well, 'as they could be relied upon to last for about 4 to 5 years.' Although more expensive than other second-hand overcoats, they remained more affordable than other European-style coats produced in South Africa. Following these assertions and after gathering further information—including an admission from European-style clothing manufacturers that indeed the industry could not produce cheaper overcoats—members of the British South African Board of Trade and Industries concluded that, regarding second-hand overcoats, restrictions of imports would have been 'a very expensive item to the country'.[86]

However, these concerns over the affordability of second-hand overcoats for consumers were primarily driven by mining companies' interest in controlling its workforce and avoiding unrest. Wholesalers of second-hand clothing distributed a large portion of second-hand (military) clothing to storekeepers near the mining centres. Black African mine workers' demand for second-hand military clothing had persisted since the mid 1890s, and conflicts between black African consumers and storekeepers in the 1910s and 1920s posed a significant threat to the economically and politically powerful mining companies. In a letter to the Board of Trade and Industries, the general manager of the Gold Producers Committee of the Transvaal Chamber of Mines argued that the committee was firmly opposed to the prohibition of second-hand clothing imports because its members were

> of opinion that the pressing need of the moment is a reduction of the native living cost, and that it is improper at this stage to contemplate any action likely to add to the cost of any article of common use by the native people ... [T]he prohibition of the importation of second-hand clothing ... would provoke and justify increased native unrest and dissatisfaction, and it is the view of the Committee that it would be unwise and unethical to take any such action as would intensify discontent and give vigour to the growing demands of the native people.[87]

These anxieties were rooted in a series of strikes and growing unionism.[88] Protests by black African mine workers had begun in 1913, and unrest intensified during and after the First World War, when prices rose rapidly while wages re-

86 Ibid.
87 Ibid.
88 See Johnstone, *Class, Race and Gold*, 180–4. On the *Gold Producers' Committee*, see Wilson, *Labour in the South African Gold Mines*, 47–8. For an overview on the rich literature on South African labour history, see Freund, 'Labour Studies and Labour History in South Africa: Perspectives from the Apartheid Era and After'.

mained low. Black African mine workers responded to the mining companies' refusal to raise wages by boycotting the trading stores at the Witwatersrand in 1918. Disputes between storekeepers and black African workers—particularly over the credit system—had already been noted in the *Report on the Native Grievances Inquiry* following the strike in 1913.[89] In 1918, reports connected to the boycotts indicated that miners were complaining about high prices, especially for clothing.[90] Following the boycott, black African mine workers repeatedly went on strike between 1918 and 1920, protesting low wages, rising prices, the job colour bar, and labour coercion. The continuous exclusion of black African mine workers from wage increases eventually culminated in a strike of 71,000 workers in twenty-one mines in February 1920. The ten-day strike did have an impact, though not in the way the protesters intended. Instead of conceding wage increases, mining companies

> expended large sums of money in order to contrive a reduction of the extortionate prices being charged to mine natives by profiteering shopkeepers. The effect of the Industry's action in 1920 served to check the upward trend of prices charged to natives for necessary articles, and has since assisted towards the maintenance of Reef trading operations on a reasonable price basis.[91]

Materially, Frederick Johnson argues, the arrangement between storekeepers and mining companies to reduce commodity prices was 'the only change which emerged from the strike'.[92] Moreover, according to the Transvaal Chamber of Mines, mining companies opened stores near mines where black African workers could purchase clothing and other commodities at cost price, because they believed it

89 See *Report of the Native Grievances Inquiry 1913–1914*, 62. The commission had been appointed 'to inquire into African grievances and into the compound system as a form of control over Africans.' Johnstone, *Class, Race and Gold*, 171. On different credit systems used by storekeepers in the 'truck trade' as a means to trick black African consumers, see Burke, *Lifebuoy Men, Lux Women*, 77–80.

90 For special reference to clothing, see *Report of the Special Commissioner Appointed to Enquire into the Boycotting of Rand Storekeepers by Natives*, 1: 'A consideration of the evidence already taken by me leads me at the present time to the belief ... that many of the storekeepers have no fixed prices, and in the first instance ask much more for an article, especially clothing, than they are prepared to take. Numerous instances of this were given by the witnesses, who argue, with reason, that the demanding by the storekeeper of a much higher price than he is prepared to take is a deliberate attempt to fleece the native, and that the inflated prices are not wholly due to war conditions.' On the boycott in general, see Johnstone, *Class, Race and Gold*, 173–4.

91 NASA SAB, RHN vol. 1297, no. 125/9/8.

92 Johnstone, *Class, Race and Gold*, 183.

> of highest importance ... that the great number of natives assembled here shall have no legitimate ground for discontent; and, while the Industry has no desire to enter permanently upon the business of soft goods dealers, the circumstances which compelled us to take this step have not been modified to the extent of justifying us in dropping it.[93]

By controlling prices and shaping workers' access to goods and purchasing options, mining companies transformed consumption into a mechanism of labour management to secure labour stability. Moreover, despite repeated requests by European-style clothing manufacturers, imports of second-hand clothing were not prohibited in the interwar period, reflecting the influence of mining companies in shaping tariff policy: in 1926, duties on imported second-hand clothing were increased to 3–4s. per item.[94]

Although the volume of second-hand clothing imports declined significantly during the following decade—by nearly 50 per cent for second-hand overcoats and roughly 65 per cent for second-hand coats, vests, trousers, and jumpers between 1934 and 1937—calls by European-style clothing manufacturers and associated industry bodies for the prohibition of second-hand clothing imports did not abate, and in fact intensified with the outbreak of the Second World War. The industry drew on its experience after the First World War, when substantial quantities of second-hand military clothing entered the South African market. A representative of the African Clothing Co., Ltd.—one of the earliest firms to establish a manufacturing facility in Cape Town in 1910/11—recalled shortly after the outbreak of the Second World War that

> after the last war importations of redundant military clothing were so considerable that many South African clothing manufacturers were ruined as they were unable to compete with this type of clothing. He felt that the matter should not be left over until the present war ended, because as soon as that happened every country with surplus war stores would be looking for markets in which to dispose of stocks and the Union market would be flooded before effective action could be taken to counter such importations.[95]

---

93 *Transvaal Chamber of Mines Thirty-First Report: Year 1920*, 67–8 at 68. See also ibid. 89.

94 See 'Customs Tariff of the Union of South Africa, Act 36 of 1926', in *British South Africa. Twenty-First Annual Statement of the Trade and Shipping*, 6–7. See also, for example, the recommendation of the customs tariff commission in 1934/36 in reaction to the request by the Transvaal Clothing Manufacturers Associations to increase the duty on imported overcoats: 'We consider that if the industry cannot be established or exist without a protective duty of 50 per cent., ad valorem, subject to a minimum of *10s.* per garment, it would be against the public interest to increase duties on overcoats for protective purposes.' *Report of the Customs Tariff Commission*, 59–60 at 60.

95 NASA SAB, RHN vol. 1280, no. 125/8/1. Regarding The African Clothing Co., Ltd., see also Nicol, 'A History of Garment and Tailoring Workers in Cape Town', 48–9.

Unlike earlier efforts, which yielded tariff amendments, these renewed interventions resulted in a policy shift. In June 1939, the government accepted the South African Board of Trade and Industries' recommendation to prohibit the importation of 'second-hand coats, jerkins, jumpers, vests, trousers and cloaks intended for sale in the Union'.[96] Although the import prohibition initially encompassed all categories of second-hand military clothing specified in the recommendation, second-hand overcoats were excluded from the list shortly afterwards. Once again, the Gold Producers' Committee—who had learned of the prohibition of second-hand clothing imports through the Government Gazette Notice—argued that the issue was 'of importance to the Mining Industry, inasmuch as Natives employed on the surface of the gold mines purchase to a considerable extent second-hand coats.'[97] Between 1939 and 1942, imports of second-hand overcoats predominantly from the United Kingdom and the United States fluctuated between approximately 90,000 and 200,000 items per year. Records further show that a proportion of these second-hand clothing imports was diverted to the South African Department of Defence. When the firm A. Belikoff & Co., Ltd. attempted to import 'a consignment of second hand British military overcoats' in 1939, customs officials seized the goods. Shortly afterwards, the importers received an offer from a representative of the Department of Defence, who explained that since the department was 'raising considerable numbers of coloured M. T. divers, native guards, Indian Services Corps, etc., such overcoats ... could probably be utilized for issue to members of one or other of these units.' Subsequently, all further importations of 'second-hand military overcoats, with or without buttons and badges' were to be reported to the Secretary for Defence.[98] Throughout the war, imports of most second-hand clothing items remained prohibited, although permits could be obtained for the importation of 'military, naval or air force uniform clothing (surplus war stores)', new and second-hand.[99] These regulations, shaped by the correlating and partly intersecting priorities of the clothing industry, mining capital, and the wartime state, not only defined the framework within which second-hand clothing circulated in South Africa during the 1940s but also created the conditions for post-war developments.

---

96 NASA SAB, RHN vol. 1297, no. 125/9/8. See NASA SAB, DEA vol. 204, no. A10/16/1X; 'Customs Tariff Amendment Act no. 39 (1939)', *Government Gazette: Union of South Africa,* 116 (22 June 1939), Government Notice no. 858, ii; *Official Year Book of the Union of South Africa and of Basutoland, Bechuanaland Protectorate and Swaziland* 1924, 581.

97 NASA SAB, DEA vol. 204, no. A10/16/1X.

98 Ibid.

99 NASA SAB, RHN vol. 1297, no. 125/9/8. See also NASA SAB, RHN vol. 1307, no. 125/10/11.

4.4 Conclusion

When news of the planned imposition of increased duties on second-hand clothing spread in the British South African mercantile community in the months preceding the revised customs tariff regulations of 1906, the measure was met with substantial opposition. British South African importers based in Johannesburg and elsewhere in the Transvaal Colony petitioned colonial authorities, insisting that they had 'purchased goods in the Markets of London to the value of £2000' shortly before the announcement of the new tariff and that the last shipment had left London at the end of May, leaving them 'no time to countermand the orders for' the consignments.[100] The petitioners' request for a delay was supported by the Durban Chamber of Commerce, whose secretary pointed out that similar concessions had been made by colonial government authorities to 'holders of stock of other articles much less seriously affected' by new tariff regulations, and resulted in the enforcement of the new duties being postponed until 1 July 1906.[101]

The concession constituted a limited victory for British South African importers, yet one that merely delayed the effects of the new regulatory environment. In the following months, British exporters of second-hand clothing, including Samuel Moses & Sons and Mallett, Porter & Dowd, Ltd., joined the protest. Addressing a petition to the colonial authorities, they argued that the increased duties threatened the economic prosperity and existence of British businesses and left consumer demand in British South Africa partly unmet: after forty years of their participation in the British South African second-hand clothing trade, the petitioners claimed, the 'South African Customs Convention has altered this condition of affairs ... the higher tariff has stopped the exportation of Second Hand Clothing, and consequently this source of Revenue to the Colony is stopped practically, besides inflicting great hardships on British subjects interested in the trade.'[102] Local accounts appeared to confirm these concerns. Importers and storekeepers in British South Africa reported a steep decline in the second-hand clothing trade in 1906. William G. Brown, a representative of a firm specializing in the 'truck trade' based in Durban, stated in 1907 that he used 'to deal ... considerably' in second-hand clothing but that 'the new duty' had 'stopped that trade'.[103] A trader in Moguntia, Colony of Natal, similarly remarked that he 'used to sell 20 garments a week before' the introduction of the 'excessive duty' on second-hand clothing, but by January 1908 he did 'not sell two a month.'[104]

100 NASA TAB, GOV vol. 974, no. PS21/10/1906.

101 NASA NAB, NT vol. 114, no. T1969/1906. See also, for example, NASA TAB, GOV vol. 974, no. PS21/10/1906.

102 NASA WCARS, T vol. 1/986, no. 2510/1906. See also NASA NAB, PM vol. 65, no. 634/1907.

103 *Report of the Royal Commission on Shipping Rings*, 82–7, Ev 2252–437 at 86, Ev 2394.

104 NASA NAB, NT vol. 131, no. T335/1908.

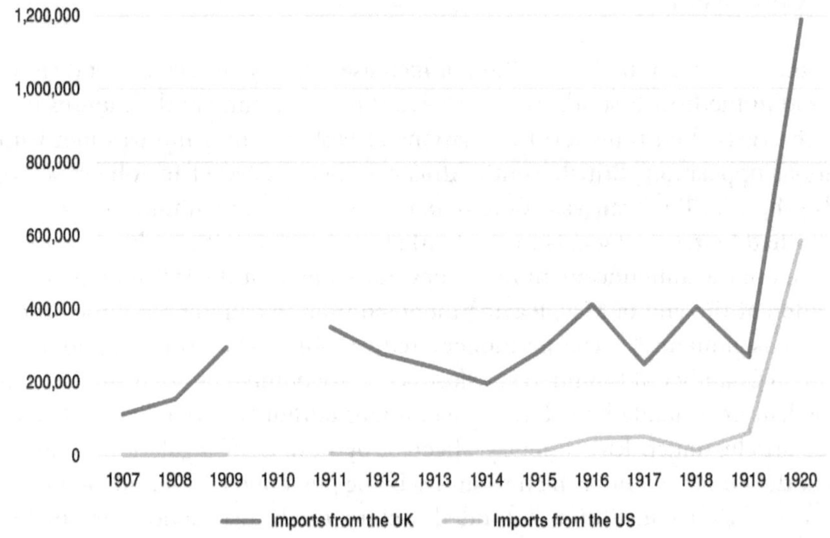

FIGURE 4.1 Quantities of second-hand vests, coats, and trousers imported into South Africa, 1907–20.

However, the statistical record complicates these accounts. Data compiled by the South African Customs Statistical Bureau show that between 1907 and 1920, imports of second-hand coats, vests, and trousers through the (British) South African ports and Maputo in Mozambique increased, albeit with significant fluctuations (Fig. 4.1).[105] Indeed, in the first two decades of the twentieth century, firms such as Mallett, Porter & Dowd, Ltd. and Randles, Bros. & Hudson continued to export and import British and other foreign second-hand military clothing, with South African demand for second-hand military overcoats particularly strong in the

105 Fig. 15 is based on the *Annual Statement of the Trade and Shipping of the Colonies and Territories Forming the South African Customs Union: 1907–1909*, first published in 1906, and the *Annual Statement of the Trade and Shipping of the Union of South Africa, and of Southern and N. W. Rhodesia: 1912–1920*. I have left out the import statistics for 1906 that distinguish between second-hand military clothing and apparel after May 1906 only (see *Annual Statement of the Trade and Shipping of the Colonies and Territories Forming the South African Customs Union: 1906*, no. 1, con. 5 [35]). No data was available to the author for the years 1910 and 1921–24. Since imports from India, Portugal, Denmark, France, Germany, and Holland—while noteworthy—were insignificant both in terms of quantity and value compared to imports from the UK and US, I have decided to not include them in the graph. The import duty of 2s. per second-hand coat, vest, or pair of trousers intended for sale in South Africa remained in place after the establishment of the SACU in 1910. See *Colonial Import Duties 1910*, 498.

mining centres.[106] Thus, while the petitions by importers and exporters appear, at first glance, to have overstated the effects of the increased duties, records indicate that retail prices for these articles rose in the twentieth century, affecting, in particular, consumers.

The developments traced throughout this chapter reveal how second-hand military clothing became a site through which competing economic, political, and administrative interests in (British) South Africa and Britain were renegotiated in the first half of the twentieth century. The events surrounding the introduction of increased duties in 1903/06 accordingly reflect a broader reassessment of the second-hand (military) clothing trade from multiple perspectives. The expansion of the modes of provision and distribution during the South African War, and the adoption of such garments by both black Africans and whites, intensified long-standing debates over their symbolic significance. Under increased pressure from colonial government officials in British South Africa, the War Office was forced to confront its disposal system, weighing monetary values against moral valorizations. The colonial authorities, in turn, weighed the future of the second-hand clothing imports against the backdrop of the slowly emerging European-style clothing industry in British South Africa, a sector that had been expanding since the early twentieth century. In the following decades, exemplified by the struggle over import prohibitions and second-hand military overcoats, further efforts by European-style clothing manufacturers to restrict imports proved unsuccessful, as mining companies increasingly mobilized control over access to these garments as a means of governing black African labour. Finally, the classification of second-hand military clothing under the tariff regulations elevated the role of customs officials in the negotiation of these garments' monetary value at the docksides. The notion of commensurability embedded in the tariff schedule was largely theoretical: determining provenance, distinguishing between new and second-hand articles, and estimating monetary value required interpretative judgements. Customs officials examined traces of wear, buttonholes, fibres, pocket contents, and clothing tickets, with the inverted or double broad arrow mark as the most unequivocal marker of British second-hand military garments. Paradoxically, in seeking to reduce the recognizability of army property and to prevent misuse, the British army had simultaneously furnished the second-hand clothing trade with an unmistakable brand.

106 See NASA TAB, DCU vol. 75, no. 638/1906; NASA SAB, DEA vol. 204, no. A10/16X; TNA, LAB 2/668/TBD134/A/8/1920.

CHAPTER 5

5 Conclusion

In September 2025, the European Parliament approved new measures to reduce textile waste across the European Union (EU). Extended Producer Responsibility schemes—to be set up by member states within thirty months—ought to ensure that producers selling textiles in the EU cover the costs of second-hand clothing and textile waste collection, sorting, and recycling.[1] The measures are part of the EU's Waste Framework Directive, which is embedded in the Circular Economy Action Plan. The latter is based on the concept of the 'circular economy' and related ideas that have been informing environmental and economic policies over the past two decades. In November 2024, for example, the UK government established a Circular Economy Taskforce, comprised of independent expert advisors, to develop a strategy for transition into a circular economy in England.[2] Central to the vision of contemporary concepts of circular economy is the idea of an economic system in which all resources, products, and materials are kept in circular flow through recycling, reuse, and remanufacturing, thereby minimizing waste and reducing environmental impacts.[3]

Yet critics argue that the vision of a sustainable economy as an endless recycling loop that decouples economic growth from environmental impacts and consumption vastly underestimates the challenges posed by global markets. With most products manufactured, distributed, purchased, disposed of, and recycled in different geographic locations, the implementation of a circular economy would require a comprehensive 'global reorganization of consumption and production' that ought to take into consideration the complex interrelationships between different material cycles. However, opponents point out that current Western European policies along the guiding principles of the concept of circular economy do not take sufficient account of global dependencies and exclude discourses from

1 See the press release by the European Parliament, 9 Sept. 2025 at [https://www.europarl.europa.eu/news/en/press-room/20250905IPR30172/parliament-adopts-new-eu-rules-to-reduce-textile-and-food-waste], accessed 27 Nov. 2025.

2 See the UK Government webpage *Terms of Reference: Circular Economy Taskforce*, 12 Dec. 2024 at [https://www.gov.uk/government/groups/circular-economy-taskforce], accessed 29 Nov. 2025.

3 For a comparative perspective on the concept of 'circular economy', from recycling programmes in the 1970s and 1980s to contemporary discourse, see Weber and Jaeger-Erben, 'Circular Economy'.

 | HTTPS://DOI.ORG/10.1515/9783112256503-006

the 'Global South'.[4] The 'end-of-lifecycle' circuits in the contemporary second-hand clothing trade provide prime examples of these interrelations and dependencies. Following temporary suspensions during the Covid-19 pandemic, several high-import countries in Africa, including Rwanda, Uganda, and Ethiopia, have announced and partially implemented a ban on second-hand clothing imports in an effort to revitalize and bolster their textile industries. In Kenya, one of the biggest importing countries in Africa, the government faces considerable backlash after renewing its proposal to ban imports in 2022 and 2025. Notably, Kenya imports second-hand clothing mainly from China and the US, and the most recent proposal is partly a reaction to new US tariffs that heavily affect Kenya's textile industry. Critics such as the Mitumba Consortium Association argue that the second-hand clothing industry supports the livelihoods of thousands of Kenyans and provides affordable clothing to low-income households.[5] The reliance on the second-hand clothing trade for economic opportunities and affordable commodities characterizes many countries that import second-hand clothing in high volumes.

At the same time, the influx of low-quality second-hand clothing as a consequence of the expansion in the 'fast-fashion' industry has led to, and continues to cause, severe social, economic, and environmental harm.[6] South Africa is both a case in point and diverges considerably from more recent developments in other African countries. In official statistics, South Africa appears as a small importer of second-hand clothing; between 1999 and 2003, the country absorbed 0.4 per cent of the monetary value of second-hand clothing imports worldwide. Since 1994, the South African government has imposed a series of heavy import restrictions and high tariffs.[7] Second-hand clothing imports are mainly reserved for charitable donations and require an import permit. While these restrictions appear to have significantly reduced second-hand clothing imports and mitigated the environmental consequences faced by many high-importing countries, second-hand clothing is still entering the South African market. As studies based on interviews with street traders in Durban, Pinetown, and Verulam show, second-hand clothing is imported illegally through Maputo, Mozambique, where imports are not

4 Corvellec, Stowell, and Johansson, 'Critiques of the Circular Economy', 425–6 at 426; Calisto Friant, Vermeulen, and Salomone, 'A Typology of Circular Economy Discourses', particularly 6.

5 See Mburu, 'Renewed Drive to Ban "Mitumba" risks Kenya, US Trade Ties'. See also Kibii, 'Fear of Political Consequences Frustrates Mitumba Ban'.

6 For Ghana, see, for example, Acquave et al., 'Consumer Attitude and Disposal Behaviour to Second-Hand Clothing in Ghana'.

7 See Brooks and Simon, 'Unravelling the Relationship between Used-Clothing Imports and the Decline of African Clothing Industries'.

restricted; most of these illegal re-exports and trans-shipments remain undetected by South African customs officials.[8]

The period explored in this study reveals a distinct landscape in which second-hand military clothing moved through imperial and colonial networks. Between *c.*1870 and 1910, second-hand items of British military clothing emerged as volatile commodities whose legitimacy was continually renegotiated at each interface of their trajectory—from soldiers' bodies and military storerooms, to the workrooms of second-hand clothing businesses in Britain, to importers, traders, storekeepers, and consumers in (British) South Africa. Reuse of 'part-worn' and 'worn-out' military clothing within the British army exposed tensions between correlating symbolic and monetary valuations, as second-hand military dress was simultaneously a marker of military discipline and imperial authority, a repository of individual value ascriptions, and a material resource that could either be redirected within the army clothing system or generate revenue by disposing of them into commercial circuits. In the workrooms of the second-hand clothing businesses, manual labour like sorting, repairing, and rebuttoning not only prepared garments for resale, but determined which items would continue to circulate. At the site of consumption in British South Africa, British second-hand military clothing was embedded within local trading networks, colonial regulations, and African adoption and appropriation, revealing that consumer agency mattered as much as metropolitan supply. By unsettling European notions of distinction, African consumers of second-hand military dress were disrupting colonial hierarchies, and towards the end of the nineteenth century, as Africans came to represent an expanding consumer base central to commerce, colonial authorities' increased attempts to regulate, prohibit, and police dressing practices through proposed sales restrictions proved ineffective.

During the South African War, and following an outbreak of typhoid fever on board a reformatory school ship near London allegedly caused by reimported second-hand army blankets, the outbreak investigations elevated second-hand clothing to a new level of public health concern. As colonial officials struggled to trace the blankets' distribution (revealing racialized assumptions about disease transmission and the limits of surveillance), attention shifted to global commerce and British soldiers as vectors of disease transmission and spread. Mandatory disinfection of second-hand clothing—introduced in British South Africa as an immediate consequence of these discussions—redistributed responsibilities and opportunities for profit, rendering disinfection a means to re-legitimate commodities. Finally, debates over second-hand clothing as a public health risk intersected with the re-evaluation of these commodities in the context of consolidating the SACU. Following the expansion of the modes of provision and supply of British

8 See Velia, Valodia, and Amisi, *Trade Dynamics in Used Clothing*; Mkhize, 'Exploring the Second Hand Clothes Trade'.

second-hand military dress in the context of the South African War, the adoption and appropriation of these garments by civilians re-intensified debates over their symbolic significance, culminating in the classification and categorization of second-hand clothing and the imposition of import duties. The efforts to impose commensurability through tariff schedules, classifications, and certificates highlight the interpretative and administrative work involved in assigning monetary value to, and reassessing the value of, these commodities.

The findings of this study highlight the contingency and instability of processes of commoditization and globalization. The nodes of the chain, including their endpoints, served as key sites of negotiation, highlighting the commoditization of British second-hand military clothing as an ongoing process of 'making' and 'unmaking'. At the same time, contestation and friction were central to redirecting the 'flow' of commodities between domestic markets, export channels, and imperial trading and colonial consumption networks. In Britain, the circulation of second-hand military dress outside the army clothing system in, for example, street advertising and theatrical productions prompted heightened regulation, trade restrictions, and increasingly specific requirements for the alteration of these garments by army contractors. The expansion of the export trade in British second-hand military clothing from the 1880s onwards was thus significantly shaped by shifting regulatory pressures and commercial incentives, redirecting these commodities towards overseas markets in British South Africa, where demand increased following the establishment of mining centres in particular. Debates over the adoption and appropriation of British second-hand military clothing by predominantly male black Africans intersected with commercial interests focused on extracting profit from African consumers, ultimately limiting the implementation of additional restrictions. The emergence of the materiality of second-hand military clothing as a site of contestation during and in the aftermath of the South African War culminated in the introduction of mandatory disinfection measures that reshaped the distribution of profits. Finally, the imposition of high tariffs on second-hand clothing turned the docksides and customs offices at South African ports into sites of low-level but persistent dispute as importers contested classifications and exploited ambiguities and loopholes in the tariff schedules and regulations, shaping how commodities entered or were diverted from ports and markets. At these micro-sites of contention and contestation, frictions were actually constitutive in global connectivity, for they generated fractures, disruptions, and redirections.[9] It is through the interplay and interwovenness of these processes of

9 On the production of global connectivity through friction, see Lowenhaupt Tsing, *Friction*. See also Beckert et al., 'Commodity Frontiers and the Transformation of the Global Countrysite', particularly 444–6, who consider frictions (competition and resistance) as a reaction to commodity regimes crucial to the understanding of historical change.

connectivity and dis-connectivity that globalization processes unfold.[10] Central to these processes, this study shows, is the agency of actors at the edges and margins of the chain, demonstrating that the expansion of the export trade and globalization of the second-hand clothing trade were actively shaped by African consumers, traders, and workers. 'Globalization from below' unfolded at multiple locations, challenging regulatory frameworks and colonial hierarchies and revealing how global processes were constituted through local agency and everyday practices, involving small-scale businesses such as those of storekeepers and market and street vendors.[11]

Capturing these multi-sited micro-locations across the historical records is challenging. Contemporary and historical studies of the second-hand clothing trade in its translocal, transnational, and global dimensions are complicated by disparate and fragmentary records. Incomplete statistical datasets and the absence of distinctions between trans-shipments and re-exports, for example, introduce and reproduce distortions in the representation of trade patterns.[12] In the present study, the patchiness of archival sources and colonial knowledge embodied by the records provides equally limited and distorted perspectives, emphasizing colonial and commercial priorities while leaving gaps, for example, in terms of documenting everyday practices and capturing consumer perspectives. Business records, including the Gallagher Family Papers on Emagusheni Trading Store, provide exceptionally rare and valuable insights into trading networks and the circulation of commodities, enabling the reconstruction of commodity chains as well as their disentanglement by linking producers, intermediaries, and consumers. As this study shows, the second-hand clothing trade was largely operated by small businesses whose activities and operations in Britain and South Africa continued well into the twentieth century. While the prohibition of most second-hand articles of clothing from 1939 might suggest that the import business in South Africa was short-lived, records indicate that companies adapted to trade restrictions and high tariffs after the Second World War. In 1958, Morris Belikoff (Pty.), Ltd.—once known as A. Belikoff and Co., Ltd.—established an associate company named Embelle Distributor (Pty.), Ltd. in East London (KuGompo City).

---

10 See Wenzelhuemer et al., 'Forum Global Dis:connections'. See also Cooper, 'What is the Concept of Globalization Good for?'.

11 Appadurai, 'Grassroots Globalization and the Research Imagination', 3. For the extension of 'globalization from below' to the economic activities of small-scale businesses, see Ribeiro, 'Economic Globalization from Below'. For micro-economic perspectives on global trade, see, for example, Magee and Thompson, *Empire and Globalisation*, chapters 2 and 4; Rischbieter, *Mikro-Ökonomie der Globalisierung*.

12 See, in summary, Brooks, 'The International Second-Hand Clothing Trade'; Brooks and Simon, 'Unravelling the Relationship between Used-Clothing Imports and the Decline of African Clothing Industries'. To address these limitations, scholars draw on print, radio, television media reporting, and field research. See, for example, Tranberg-Hansen, *Sulaula*, particularly 16–20.

In the following decades, the company continued to offer 'fully renovated, ready to wear, in standardised grades, brand labelled, steampressed and conveniently packed' civilian and military overcoats imported mainly from the US, UK, Canada, and Scandinavian countries.[13] These insights suggest directions for further research. First, in the newly emerging field of (post-)colonial business history there is a particular need for studies of small businesses and small-scale trading networks, adaptive strategies, and the intersection of 'legal' and 'illegal' trade from a long-term, transnational, and global perspective.[14] Second, interest in 'waste' has grown noticeably in historical research in recent decades. Historical approaches have since expanded, diversified, and begun to incorporate global perspectives. However, with notable exceptions in environmental history focusing on, for example, water pollution, few historical studies have integrated postcolonial perspectives.[15] In addition, the broadening of the understanding of 'waste' and 'disposal' to include practices of reuse, redistribution, and recycling risks flattening distinctions and obscures crucial developments and contexts, a conceptual challenge underscored by the findings of this study. The British domestic and the British South African trade in second-hand military clothing intersected with, for example, the trade in rags and other textile remnants. However, the emergence of a distinct trading network for second-hand military clothing was shaped by layered and multi-sited revaluations: authorities repeatedly debated whether recycling the garments was preferable to their reuse within, for example, the army clothing system or to their resale, while workers in sorting rooms influenced which items entered different streams of commercial reuse. Methodologically, histories of 'waste' would therefore benefit from closer engagement with approaches from the interdisciplinary field of discard studies and, in particular, from analyses of the changing processes and practices of valuation that precede acts of disposal.[16] Third, findings from contemporary second-hand clothing economies in the 'Global South' and recent historical contributions underscore the importance of pursuing this approach in comparative perspective. In Ghana,

13 NASA SAB, RHN vol. 1307, no. 125/10/11.

14 In commodity chain research, global value chain approaches have largely focused on a few multinational businesses. See, in summary, Hesse and Neveling, 'Global Value Chains'. On post(-)colonial business history perspectives with a focus on African countries, see, for example, Decker, *Postcolonial Transition and Global Business History*; Dimier and Stockwell (eds.), *The Business of Development in Post-Colonial Africa*. Since 2023, the network '(Post-)Colonial Business History' (PCBH), funded by the German Research Foundation (*Deutsche Forschungsgemeinschaft*), explores the interconnection between private businesses and colonial expansion and its long-term effects on capitalism. See the PCBH website at [https://www.uni-bamberg.de/en/hist-econ/pcbh-network/], accessed 27 Nov. 2025. See also Todzi, 'Colonial Business in Postcolonial Germany'.

15 See, for example, Wilhelm, *Environment and Pollution in Colonial India*; Müller, *The Toxic Ship*; Köster, *Müll.*

16 See Liboiron and Lewapsky, *Discard Studies*; Gregson, *The Waste of the World.*

for example, traders discard an estimated 40–80 per cent of the imported, pre-sorted second-hand clothing, illustrating different and disconnected valuation systems and underscoring the significance of sorting labour at the margins and edges of the second-hand clothing chain. These diverging valuation systems await exploration in historical perspective. In addition, a recent contribution by Marcel Charpy focusing on second-hand uniforms in the French-Senegalese context identified themes that partly resonate with the dynamics explored in this study: the parallels emerging from different imperial and regional settings suggest shared dynamics, while simultaneously raising questions about local adaptations and configurations as well as postcolonial legacies.[17]

It remains to be seen how the new EU measures and forthcoming import bans will affect the contemporary second-hand clothing trade. Far from providing a template for governance, this historical case study underscores the enduring complexity of commodity chains and flows, which are shaped by entangled economic, social, and regulatory forces across multiple sites. It highlights, not least, how policies, resistances, contentions, and perceptions at the edges and margins of the chains inevitably interacted with one another, changed dynamics, and produced unexpected outcomes. In these contexts, different actors and interests exercised varying degrees of influence and leverage. The study opens avenues for further historical research into how these interactions developed over the twentieth century and have reflected, produced, and reinforced global economic hierarchies and (in-)dependencies.

17 See Charpy, 'The Spoils of War'.

List of Illustrations

Fig. 1.1: Officer's full-dress tunic, British infantry pattern (*c*.1868). Source: National Army Museum, accession number NAM. 1974-09-72-1. Image Courtesy of the National Army Museum, London.

Fig. 1.2: Pattern for inverted broad arrow (1881). Source: *Regulations for the Supply of Clothing and Necessaries to the Regular Forces*, 1881, 73.

Fig. 1.3: Pattern for marks on first issued and part-worn reissued military clothing (1881). Source: *Regulations for the Supply of Clothing and Necessaries to the Regular Forces*, 1881, 72.

Fig. 1.4: C. Paul Renouard, *Recruiting the Sandwich Men: Accepted* (1894). Source: *The Graphic*, 1261 (27 Jan. 1894), 98. © Illustrated London News/Mary Evans Picture Library.

Fig. 1.5: C. Paul Renouard, *Recruiting the Sandwich Men: Rejected* (1894). Source: *The Graphic*, 1261 (27 Jan. 1894), 99. © Illustrated London News/Mary Evans Picture Library.

Fig. 1.6: Advertisement by Mallett, Porter & Dowd, Ltd. (1905–6). Source: *The British and South African Export Gazette*, 13/156 (July 1905), 1553.

Fig. 1.7: Rag-dusting machine manufactured by Bryan Donkin and Co., London (1890). Source: Watt, *The Art of Paper-Making*, 27.

Fig. 1.8: Advertisement by H. Möschke, Polokwane, Limpopo Province (1895/6). Source: *The Directory of Bulawayo and Handbook to Matabeleland 1895–1896*, 108.

Fig. 2.1: Sign next to the main road for Emagusheni Trading Store (1970), photograph by Lance James. Source: KCM 95/11/83. Credit: Killie Campbell Africana Library (University of KwaZulu-Natal).

Fig. 2.2: Detail of J. Fleming, *Sketch Map Shewing Districts and Principal Trading Routes in the Territories of Transkei, Tembuland, Griqualand East and Pondoland* (1899). Source: ibali Digital Collection, University of Cape Town. Credit: Talbot Maps, UCT Libraries, Special Collections.

Fig. 2.3: Inside Emagusheni Trading Store (1970), photograph by Lance James. Source: KCM 95/11/83. Credit: Killie Campbell Africana Library (University of KwaZulu-Natal).

Fig. 3.1: Public disinfectors (right) and James S. Dickson, Inspector of Nuisances (left), with iron carriage for the disinfection of clothing in a dry heat disinfection chamber (*c*.1877). Source: Thompson and Smith, *Street Life in London*, fig. 6.

Fig. 3.2: Washington Lyon's portable steam disinfector, manufactured by Manlove, Alliot, Fryer and Co., Ltd. (*c*.1893). Source: Rideal, *Disinfection and Disinfectants*, 39.

Fig. 3.3: Number of textiles and articles of second-hand clothing for export to (British) South Africa disinfected at the Golden Lane disinfection chamber, London, 1902–38. Graph by the author.

Fig. 4.1: Quantities of second-hand vests, coats, and trousers imported into South Africa, 1907–20. Graph by the author.

 | HTTPS://DOI.ORG/10.1515/9783112256503-007

Index of Abbreviations

BL	British Library
GCC	Global Commodity Chain
GHIL	German Historical Institute, London
GVC	Global Value Chain
HC	House of Commons
HMSO	His/Her Majesty's Stationary Office
IEG	Leibniz-Institut für Europäische Geschichte/Leibniz Institute of European History, Mainz
KCAL	Killie Campbell Africana Library, Durban
KCM	Killie Campbell Africana Library, Manuscripts Collection, Durban
MOH(s)	Medical Officer(s) of Health
MP(s)	Member(s) of Parliament
NAI	National Archives of India, New Delhi
NAM	National Army Museum, London
NASA NAB	National Archives of South Africa, Pietermaritzburg Archives Repository
NASA SAB	National Archives of South Africa, National Archives Repository (Public Records of Central Government since 1910), Tshwane
NASA TAB	National Archives of South Africa, National Archives Repository (Public Records of former Transvaal Province and its Predecessors as well as of Magistrates and Local Authorities), Tshwane
NASA TBD	National Archives of South Africa, Durban Archives Repository
NASA WCARS	National Archives of South Africa, Western Cape Archives and Records Service, Cape Town
NFCA	National Fairground and Circus Archive, University of Sheffield
PCBH	(Post-)Colonial Business History
POW	Prisoner of War
SACU	South African Customs Union
SAGNC	South African Geographical Names Council
SCAPA	National Society of Controlling Abuses of Public Advertising
TNA	The National Archives, London
UCT	University of Cape Town
UN	United Nations

 | HTTPS://DOI.ORG/10.1515/9783112256503-008

Bibliography

Archives

British Library, London

Ramsay Papers:
Add MS 46450

Personal and Official Papers of Sir Guy Fleetwood Wilson:
Mss Eur E224/47

Killie Campbell Africana Library, Manuscripts Collection, Durban

Gallagher Family Papers:
KCM 95/11/1 (c.1873–1987); KCM 95/11/5 (1882–1889); KCM 95/11/6 (1882–1899); KCM 95/11/7 (1883); KCM 95/11/8 (1884); KCM 95/11/13 (1885); KCM 95/11/15 (1885–1888); KCM 95/11/17 (1886); KCM 95/11/18 (1886); KCM 95/11/20 (1886); KCM 95/11/21 (1886); KCM 95/11/22 (1886); KCM 95/11/23 (1886); KCM 95/11/25 (1887); KCM 95/11/26 (1887); KCM 95/11/27 (1887); KCM 95/11/30 (1887); KCM 95/11/31 (1887); KCM 95/11/32 (1887); KCM 95/11/53 (1890); KCM 95/11/54 (1890); KCM 95/11/55 (1890); KCM 95/11/56 (1890); KCM 95/11/59 (1890); KCM 95/11/60 (1890); KCM 95/11/63 (1892); KCM 95/11/64 (1892–1894); KCM 95/11/67 (1895); KCM 95/11/68 (1895); KCM 95/11/69 (1895); KCM 95/11/71 (1905–1928); KCM 95/11/73 (1908–1921); KCM 95/11/80 (1883–1889, 1922–1984)

National Archives of India, New Delhi

Homc Department:
Sanitary Proceedings A, April 1897; Sanitary Proceedings B, July 1897

Finance Department:
Statistics and Commerce A, January 1897

Foreign Department:
General B, Proceedings November 1876

Legislative Department:
Part B, Proceedings October 1895

 | HTTPS://DOI.ORG/10.1515/9783112256503-009

National Archives of South Africa, Pietermaritzburg Archives Repository

Colonial Secretary's Office:
CSO vol. 636 (1878); CSO vol. 1383 (1893); CSO vol. 1499 (1895); CSO vol. 1523 (1887); CSO vol. 1797 (1905); CSO vol. 1843 (1907)

Department of Public Health:
DPH vol. 6 (1901); DPH vol. 24 (1906); DPH vol. 28 (1907); DPH vol. 29 (1907)

Natal Treasury:
NT vol. 114 (1906); NT vol. 131 (1908)

Magistrate and Commissioner, Ladysmith:
1/LDS vol. 3/3/2 (1864); 1/LDS vol. 3/3/3 (1869)

Magistrate and Commissioner, Weenen:
1/WEN vol. 3/2/3 (1900)

Postmaster General:
PMG vol. 68 (1898)

Prime Minister's Office:
PM vol. 59 (1906); PM vol. 65 (1907); PM vol. 101 (1906)

Public Works Department:
PWD vol. 2/37 (1897)

Secretary of Native Affairs:
SNA vol. 1/1/392 (1908)

National Archives of South Africa, National Archives Repository (Public Records of Central Government since 1910), Tshwane

Board of Control on Profiteering:
BCP vol. 8 (1920)

Board of Trade and Industries:
RHN vol. 1280 (1901); RHN vol. 1297 (1908); RHN vol. 1307 (1956–70)

Customs and Excise:
DEA vol. 204 (1928–42)

Industries Section, Department of Mines and Industries:
IMI vol. 15 (1917–18)

Office of the Governor-General of South Africa:
GG vol. 1509 (1910)

National Archives of South Africa, National Archives Repository (Public Records of former Transvaal Province and its Predecessors as well as of Magistrates and Local Authorities), Tshwane

Clerk of the Executive Council:
EC vol. 92 (1906)

Director of Customs:
DCU vol. 70 (1906); DCU vol. 75 (1906); DCU vol. 81 (1906); DCU vol. 82 (1906); DCU vol. 89 (1906); DCU vol. 96 (1907); DCU vol. 97 (1907); DCU vol. 107 (1907)

Foreign Labour Department:
FLD vol. 179 (1906)

Governor of the Transvaal Colony:
GOV vol. 974 (1906); GOV vol. 1146 (1908)

Secretary to the Law Department:
LD vol. 631 (1904)

National Archives of South Africa, Western Cape Archives and Records Service, Cape Town

Attorney General:
AG vol. 1635 (1905)

Colonial Office:
CO vol. 8294 (1903–6)

Government House, Papers Despatched to Secretary of State, London:
GH vol. 23/11 (1837); GH vol. 35/58 (1907–8)

Medical Officer of Health:
MOH vol. 14 (1903); MOH vol. 26 (1901); MOH vol. 87 (1903); MOH vol. 418 (1909)

Treasury Department:

T vol. 845 (1903); T vol. 954 (1905); T vol. 971 (1906); T vol. 1/986 (1906); T vol. 1084 (1907); T vol. 1106 (1908); T vol. 1134 (1908)

Museum of London Docklands, Port and River Archive

9.2.6; 21.7.4, Box 14

The National Archives, Kew

Colonial Office:

CO 23/241; CO 28/238; CO 179/233; CO 533/404; CO 879/33

Records Created or Inherited by the Dominions Office, and of the Commonwealth Relations and Foreign and Commonwealth Offices:

DO 119/289

Foreign Office:

FO 371/78; FO 881/7626

Metropolitan Police, Office of the Commissioner: Correspondence and Papers:

MEPO 2/351; MEPO 2/974

Ministry of Labour and Predecessors: Correspondence:

LAB 2/668

General Board of Health and Home Office, Local Government Act Office: Correspondence:

MH 13/261; MH 13/265

War Office:

WO 32/7039; WO 32/9118; WO 32/9119; WO 33/38; WO 33/42; WO 33/78; WO 377/7; WO 377/43; WO 395/1

Wellcome Collection, London

Royal Army Medical Corps Muniments Collection: Notes and Photographs of Colonel Brisbane:

RAMC/480/2

Official Reports and Government Publications

Aldis, Charles J. B., *A Letter to the Vestry of St. George's, Hanover Square, on Sanitary Work and Experience in Belgravia* (London: Rice's Library, Midland's Library, Rastall's, 1857).

Annual Report of the Chief Inspector of Factories and Workshops for the Year 1900, Cd., 668 (London: HMSO, 1901).

Annual Report of the Chief Inspector of Factories and Workshops for the Year 1904: Part I. Reports, Cd. 2569 (London: HMSO, 1905).

Annual Report of the Chief Inspector of Factories and Workshops for the Year 1905. Reports and Statistics, Cd. 3036 (London: HMSO, 1906).

Annual Report of the Chief Inspector of Factories and Workshops for the Year 1906. Reports and Statistics, Cd. 3586 (London: HMSO, 1907).

Annual Report of the Chief Inspector of Factories and Workshops for the Year 1907. Reports and Statistics, Cd. 4166 (London: HMSO, 1908).

Annual Report of the Chief Inspector of Factories and Workshops for the Year 1909. Reports and Statistics, Cd. 5191 (London: HMSO, 1910).

Annual Report of the Chief Inspector of Factories and Workshops for the Year 1911, Cd. 6239 (London: HMSO, 1912).

Army Act 1881, 44 & 45 Vict. (London: HMSO, 1881).

Army Circulars 1874 (London: HMSO, 1874).

Army Circulars 1881 (London: HMSO, 1881).

Army Circulars 1883 (London: HMSO, 1883).

Army Appropriation Account, 1881–82, HC 20 (London: Henry Hansard and Son, 1883).

Army Appropriation Account, 1883–84, HC 75 (London: Henry Hansard and Son, 1885).

Army Appropriation Account, 1903, HC 45 (London: HMSO, 1905).

Army Estimates of Effective and Non-Effective Services, for 1870–71, HC 36 (London: HMSO, 1870).

Army Estimates of Effective and Non-Effective Services, for 1873–74, HC 35 (London: HMSO, 1873).

Army Estimates of Effective and Non-Effective Services, for 1881–82, HC 46 (London: HMSO, 1881).

Army Estimates of Effective and Non-Effective Services, for 1882–83, HC 69 (London: HMSO, 1882).

Army Estimates of Effective and Non-Effective Services, for 1895–96 (London: HMSO, 1895).

Army: Return to an Address of the Honourable The House of Commons, dated 10 July 1889; for, Copies 'of Departmental Minutes Relative to the Army Contracts Department', HC 248 (London: HMSO, 1889).

British South Africa: Fifteenth Annual Statement of the Trade and Shipping of the Union of South Africa, Southern and Northern Rhodesia, and South-West Africa, 1920 (Cape Town, Johannesburg, Durban, Pretoria: Hortors Ltd., 1921).

British South Africa: First Annual Statement of the Trade and Shipping of the Colonies and Territories Forming the South African Customs Union, 1907 (Cape Town: Whitehead, Morris & Co., 1908).

British South Africa: Fourth Annual Statement of the Trade and Shipping of the Colonies and Territories Forming the South African Customs Union, 1909 (Cape Town: Whitehead, Morris & Co., 1910).

British South Africa: Ninth Annual Statement of the Trade and Shipping of the Union of South Africa and of Southern and Northern Rhodesia, 1914 (Cape Town: Whitehead, Morris & Co., 1915).

British South Africa: Seventh Annual Statement of the Trade and Shipping of the Union of South Africa and of Southern and N. W. Rhodesia, 1912 (Cape Town: Whitehead, Morris & Co., 1913).

British South Africa: Third Annual Statement of the Trade and Shipping of the Colonies and Territories Forming the South African Customs Union, 1908 (Cape Town: Whitehead, Morris & Co., 1908).

Cape of Good Hope: Debates in the House of Assembly, in the Second Session of the Ninth Parliament of the Cape of Good Hope, 2nd May to 3rd August, 1895 (Cape Town: 'Cape Times' Printing Works, 1895).

Cape of Good Hope: Reports on the Public Health for the Year 1901, Including Reports of District Surgeons, Local Authorities and Medical Inspectors, G. 66 – 1902 (Cape Town: 'Cape Times' Printing Works, 1902).

Cape of Good Hope: Reports on the Public Health for the Year 1902. Including the Reports of District Surgeons, Local Authorities and Medical Inspectors, G. 66 – 1903 (Cape Town: 'Cape Times' Printing Works, 1903).

Cape of Good Hope: Report of the Medical Officer of Health for the Colony on the Public Health and the Government and State-Aided Hospitals of the Colony. Together with Reports of District Surgeons and Local Authorities for the Two Calendar Years 1904 and 1905, G. 39 – 1906 (Cape Town: 'Cape Times' Printing Works, 1906).

Cape of Good Hope: Report of the Medical Officer of Health for the Colony on the Public Health and on the Government & State-Aided Hospitals of the Colony, Together with the Annual Health Reports of District Surgeons and Local Authorities for the Year 1903, G. 35. – 1904 (Cape Town: 'Cape Times' Printing Works, 1904).

Cape of Good Hope: Report of the Medical Officer of Health for the Colony on the Public Health for the Calendar Year 1906, G. 40 – 1907 (Cape Town: 'Cape Times' Printing Works, 1907).

Cape of Good Hope: Report of the Medical Officer of Health for the Colony on the Public Health together with the Health Reports of District Surgeons and Local Authorities for the Half-Year Ended 30th June, 1904, G. 35 – 1904 (Cape Town: 'Cape Times' Printing Works, 1905).

Cape of Good Hope: Report of the Medical Officer of Health for the Colony on the Public Health for the Calendar Year 1907, G. 33 – 1908 (Cape Town: Cape Times Ltd., 1908).

Cape of Good Hope: Reports on the Public Health for the Year 1902. Including the Reports of District Surgeons, Local Authorities and Medical Inspectors, G. 66 – 1903 (Cape Town: 'Cape Times' Printing Works, 1903).

Cape of Good Hope: Return of Papers on Pondo Affairs, in Compliance with a Resolution of the Honourable the House of Assembly Adopted on the 8th June 1880, A. 105 – '80 (Cape Town: Saul Solomon & Co., 1880).

City of Westminster: Report of the Medical Officer of Health for the Five Weeks Ending 4th April, 1903; Together with Statistics Relating to the First Quarter of the Year 1903, Wellcome Collection at [https://wellcomecollection.org/works/dgkufkwd], accessed 8 Oct. 2025.

Collingridge, William, *Report of the Medical Officer of Health for the City of London for the Year 1903* (London: Charles Skipper & East, 1904).

Courts-Martial Commission: Second Report of the Commissioners Appointed to Inquire into the Constitution and Practice of Courts-Martial in the Army and the Present System of Punishment for Military Offences; Together with the Minutes of Evidence and Appendix, 21421. – (2.) (London: HMSO, 1869).

Debates of the Legislative Council of the Colony of Natal, vol. 15 (Pietermaritzburg: P. Davis & Sons, 1906).

Eighth Annual Report of the Local Government Board 1878–79: Supplement Containing the Report of the Medical Officer for 1878, C. – 2452 (London: HMSO, 1879).

Factories and Workshop Act 1891, 54 Vict. (London: Eyre and Spottiswoode, 1891).

First Report from the Select Committee of the House of Lords on the Sweating System; Together with the Proceedings of the Committee, Minutes of Evidence, and Appendix, HC 361 (London: Henry Hansard and Son, 1888).

First Report of the Royal Commission Appointed to Inquire into the Civil Establishments of the Different Offices of State at Home and Abroad, with Minutes of Evidence, Appendix, &c., HC and HL C. – 5226 (London: HMSO, 1887).

Fourth Report and Special Report from the Select Committee on Army and Navy Estimates: Together with the Proceedings of the Committee and Minutes of Evidence, HC 239 (London: Henry Hansard and Son, 1887).

Fourth Report from the Select Committee on Army Estimates; Together with the Proceedings of the Committee and Minutes of Evidence, HC 269 (London: Henry Hansard and Son, 1888).

Hardwicke, William, *Paddington: Report of the Vestry, for the Year Ending 25th March, 1875* (London: Vestry Clerk's Department, 1875).

Johannesburg Chamber of Commerce: Annual Report for the Year Ended 28th February, 1905 (Johannesburg: The Argus Printing & Publishing Co., Ltd. 1905).

Johannesburg Chamber of Commerce: Annual Report for the Year Ended 28th February, 1906 (Johannesburg: The Argus Printing & Publishing Co., Ltd. 1906).

Letheby, Henry, *Report on the Sanitary Condition of the City of London, for the Year 1870–1871* (London: Judd & Co. Printers, 1872).

Ministère des Affaires Étrangères: Conférence Sanitaire Internationale de Paris. 7 Février–3 Avril 1894. Procès-verbaux (Paris: Imprimerie Nationale, 1894).

Natal Law Reports: Supreme Court. New Series, vol. 8, ed. by W. Broome (Pietermaritzburg: Munro Brothers, 1892).

Official Year Book of the Union of South Africa and of Basutoland, Bechuanaland Protectorate and Szwaziland: No. 7 – 1924 (Pretoria: The Government Printing and Stationary Office, 1925).

Parish of Lambeth: Medical Officer's Report (London: Samuel W. Gardener Machine Printer, 1877).

Parish of St. Matthew, Bethnal Green, in the County of Middlesex: Account in Abstract of the Receipt and Expenditure for the Year Ending 25th March 1879 (London: Forsaith Brothers, 1879).

Pretoria Chamber of Commerce (Incorporated): Annual Report for the Year Ending December 31st, 1905 (Pretoria: Pretoria Chamber of Commerce, 1905).

Public Stores Act 1875, 38 & 39 Vict. (London: HMSO 1875).

Regulations for the Supply of Clothing and Necessaries to the Regular Forces (London: HMSO, 1881).

Regulations for the Supply of Clothing and Necessaries to the Regular Forces (London: HMSO, 1894).

Regulations for the Clothing of the Army: Part I. – Regular Forces. Excluding the Special Reserve (London: HMSO, 1914).

Report from the Select Committee on Metropolitan Sewage Manure; Together with the Minutes of Evidence, Appendix and Index, HC 474 (London: HMSO, 1846).

Report from the Select Committee on Public Departments (Purchases, &c.); Together with the Proceedings of the Committee, Minutes of Evidence, Appendix and Index, HC 311 (London: HMSO, 1873).

Report from the Select Committee on Public Departments (Purchases, &c.); Together with the Proceedings of the Committee, Minutes of Evidence, Appendix and Index, HC 263 (London: HMSO, 1874).

Report from the Select Committee on the Uniforms Bill; Together with the Proceedings of the Committee, Minutes of Evidence, and Appendix, HC 212 (London: HMSO, 1894).

Report of a Committee of General and Other Officers of the Army on Army Re-Organization, HC and HL C. – 2791 (London: George Edward Eyre and William Spottiswoode, 1881).

Report of the Committee Appointed by the Secretary of State for War to Consider the Terms and Conditions of Service in the Army, HC and HL C. – 6582 (London: HMSO, 1892).

Report of the Committee Appointed by the Secretary of State for War to Enquire into Certain Questions that Have Arisen with Respect to the Militia and the Present Brigade Depôt System; Together with Minutes of Evidence, Appendix, and Index, HC and HL C. – 1654 (London: HMSO, 1877).

Report of the Departmental Committee Appointed to Inquire into the Conditions of Work in Wool-Sorting and Other Kindred Trades, C. – 8506 (London: HMSO, 1897).

Report of the Industries & Tariff Revision Commission, with Appendices and Evidence (Pietermaritzburg: P. Davis & Sons, 1906).
Report of the Native Grievances Inquiry 1913–1914, U. G. 37 – '14 (Cape Town: Cape Times Ltd., 1914).
Report of the Royal Commission on Shipping Rings, with Minutes of Evidence and Appendices, vol. 5, Cd. 4686 (London: HMSO, 1909).
Report of the Special Commissioner Appointed to Enquire into the Boycotting of Rand Storekeepers by Natives, U. G. 4 – '19 (Cape Town: Cape Times Ltd., 1919).
Report of the Customs Tariff Commission, 1934–35, U. G. No. 5 '36 (Pretoria: Government Printer, 1936).
Report on the Sanitary Condition of the Hackney District, for the Year 1914 (London: Chas. Straker & Sons, 1915).
Second Report from the Committee of Public Accounts; Together with the Minutes of Evidence, HC 284 (London: HMSO, 1895).
South African Native Affairs Commission 1903–05, vol. 2: Minutes of Evidence Taken in the Cape Colony (Cape Town: Cape Times Ltd., 1904).
South African Native Affairs Commission 1903–05, vol. 3: Minutes of Evidence Taken in the Colony of Natal (Cape Town: Cape Times Ltd., 1904).
South African Native Affairs Commission 1903–05, vol. 5: Index and Annexures to Minutes of Evidence together with Written Replies to Questions and Additional Memoranda by Witnesses (Cape Town: Cape Times Ltd., 1905).
The Employment of Women. Reports by Miss Eliza Orme, Miss Clara E. Collet, Miss May E. Abraham, and Miss Margaret H. Irwin (Lady Assistant Commissioners), on the Conditions of Work in Various Industries in England, Wales, Scotland, and Ireland, C. – 6894. – XXIII (London: HMSO, 1893).
The Forty-Fifth Annual Report of the Cape Town Chamber of Commerce (Incorporated) for the Year 1905–6 (Cape Town: S. A. 'Electric' Printing and Publishing Co., 1906).
Transvaal Chamber of Mines Thirty-First Report: Year 1920 (Johannesburg: The Argus Printing & Publishing Co., Ltd. 1921).
Uniforms Act 1894, 57 & 58 Vict. (London: HMSO, 1894).
War Department Stores Act 1867, 30 & 31 Vict. (London: HMSO, 1867).

Newspapers and Gazettes

Army and Navy Gazette: Journal of the Reserve and Auxiliary Forces (1885), *Berliner Börsenzeitung* (1879), *Daily Mail* (1903), *Daily Mirror* (1904), *Daily News* (1904), *Dundee Evening Telegraph* (1934), *East London Observer* (1927), *Gloucestershire Echo* (1900), *Government Gazette: Republic of South Africa* (2021), *Government Gazette: Union of South Africa* (1939–40), *Illustrated Times* (1866), *Islington Gazette* (1879), *Sheldrake's Aldershot and Sandhurst Military Gazette* (1884), *The British and South African Export Gazette* (1893–1903), *The Broad Arrow* (1869–77), *The Graphic* (1894), *The Kinematograph and*

Lantern Weekly (1912), *The Kokstad Advertiser and East Griqualand Gazette* (1970), *The London Gazette* (1881–1901), *The London Evening Standard* (1884), *The Tailor & Cutter* (1884–97), *The Times* (1906), *Western Mail* (1956).

Other Printed Sources

Barker, Mary A., *Colonial Memories* (London: Smith, Elder & Co., 1904).

Barker, Mary A., *Life in South Africa* (Philadelphia: J. B. Lippincott & Co., 1877).

Bryant, Alfred T., *An Abridged English-Zulu Word-Book* (Pietermaritzburg, Durban: P. Davis & Sons; Adams & Co., 1917).

Cormack, John R., *Natural History, Pathology, and Treatment of the Epidemic Fever, at Present Prevailing in Edinburgh and Other Towns* (London: John Churchill, 1843).

Derham, Walter, *A Visit to Cape Colony and Natal in 1879* (Privately Printed by H. Mardon, 1879).

Du Val, Charles H., *With a Show Through Southern Africa, and Personal Reminiscences of the Transvaal War*, vol. 1 (London: Tinsley Brothers, 1882).

Fracastoro, Girolamo, *De Contagione et Contagiosis Morbis et Curatione,* Libris III, Liber Primus (1546).

Kidd, Dudley A., *Kafir Socialism and the Dawn of Individualism: An Introduction to the Study of the Native Problem* (London: Adam and Charles Black, 1908).

Kidd, Dudley A., *The Essential Kafir* (London: Adam and Charles Black, 1904).

Laird, Egerton K., *Incidents of Travel in South Africa: Being an Account of a Three Month's Tour in the Cape Colony, Orange Free State, Natal, and a Ride into Zululand* (Birkenhead: Printed for Private Circulation, 1881).

Leyland, Ralph W., *A Holiday in South Africa: With Maps and Illustrations* (London: Sampson Low, Marston, Searle and Rivington, 1882).

Lind, James, *Two Papers on Fevers and Infection* (London: Plato's Head, 1763).

Mackinnon, James, *South African Traits* (Edinburgh: James Gemmel, 1887).

Mate, Phil, *Kleines Deutsch-kaffrisches Wörterbuch: Hülfsmittel für kaffrisch-Lehrende mit Specieller Rücksichtnahme auf Übersetzungen aus dem Deutschen in's Kaffrische* (Mariannhill: St. Thomas Aquins Buchdruckerei, 1891).

Michael, William H., *The Sanitary Acts: Comprising The Sewage Utilization Act, 1865, and the Sanitary Act, 1866 and Various Sections of Other Acts Incorporated Therewith, with an Introduction, Notes, and Index* (London: H. Sweet; Stevens and Sons, 1867).

Murchinson, Charles, *A Treatise on the Continued Fevers of Great Britain* (London: Parker, Son, and Bourn, 1862).

Rideal, Samuel, *Disinfection and Disinfectants (An Introduction to the Study of): Together with an Account of the Chemical Substances Used as Antiseptics and Preservatives* (London, Philadelphia: Charles Griffin and Company, Limited; J. B. Lippincott Company, 1895).

Southwood Smith, Thomas, *A Treatise on Fever* (London: Longman, Rees, Orme, Brown, and Green, 1830).

Tangye, Harold L., *In New South Africa: Travels in the Transvaal and Rhodesia* (London, Birmingham: Simpkin, Marshall, Hamilton, Kent & Co., Ltd.; Cornish Brothers, 1900).

The Directory of Bulawayo and Handbook to Matabeleland 1895–1896, ed. by Alexander Davis, facsimile reproduction of the 1896 edition (Bulawayo: Books of Zimbabwe, 1981).

The Islington Directory for 1874: Including Canonbury, Highbury, Holloway, Etc., Etc., Containing a Comprehensive Street Guide, and Alphabetical List of the Inhabitants, a Select Trade and Professional List, and Various Useful Local Information (London: William Trounce, 1874).

The Islington Directory for 1883: Containing a Comprehensive Street Guide, an Alphabetical List of the Inhabitants, a Select Trade and Professional List, and Various Useful Local Information (London: William Trounce, 1883).

The Islington Directory for 1894: Containing a Comprehensive Street Guide, an Alphabetical List of the Inhabitants, a Select Trade and Professional List, and Various Useful Local Information (London: William Trounce 1894).

The James Stuart Archive of Recorded Oral Evidence Relating to the History of the Zulu and Neighbouring Peoples, vol. 1, ed. and trans. by Colin de B. Webb and John B. Wright, Killie Cambell Africana Library Manuscript Series (Pietermaritzburg and Durban: University of Natal Press and Killie Campbell Africana Library, 1976).

The Laws of Natal, vol. 3: 1879–1880, ed. by William Broome (Pietermaritzburg: W. M. Waston, 1890).

The Natal Who's Who: An Illustrated Biographical Sketch Book of Natalians (Durban: The Natal Who's Who Publishing Company, 1906).

The New Army List, and Militia List; Exhibiting the Rank, Standing, and Various Services of Every Regimental Officer in the Army, ed. by Colonel H. G. Hart (London: John Murrey, 1869).

The Post Office London Directory for 1912, Comprising, Amongst Other Information, Official, Streets Commercial, Trades, Law, Court, Parliamentary, Postal, City, Municipal and Clerical, Conveyance and Banking Directories (London: Kelly's Directories, Ltd., 1912).

Thompson, John, and Adolphe Smith, *Street Life in London* (London: Low, Marston, and Rivington, 1877).

Trollope, Anthony, *South Africa*, vol. 1, 3rd edn. (London: Chapman and Hall, 1878).

Trotter, Thomas, *Medicina Nautica: An Essay on the Diseases of Seamen: Comprehending the History of Health in His Majesty's Fleet* (London: T. Cadell, Jun. and W. Davies, 1797).

Tweedie, Alexander, *Clinical Illustrations of Fever: Comprising a Report of the Cases Treated at the London Fever Hospital 1828–1829* (Philadelphia: Carey and Lea, 1831).

Vincent, Frank, *Actual Africa; Or, the Coming Continent: A Tour of Exploration* (New York: D. Appleton and Co., 1895).

Watt, Alexander, *The Art of Paper-Making: A Practical Handbook of the Manufacture of Paper from Rags, Esparto, Straw, and Other Fibrous Materials, Including the Manufacture of Pulp from Wood Fibre, with a Description of the Machinery and Appliances Used, to Which are Added Details of Processes Recovering Soda from Waste Liquors* (London: Crosby Lockwood and Son, 1890).

Whitham, S. W., *Report on the Textile and Soft Goods Trade of South Africa* (London: P. S. King & Son, 1903).

Wilkinson, Anne M., *A Lady's Life and Travels in Zululand and the Transvaal during Cetewayo's Reign: Being the African Letters and Journals of the Late Mrs Wilkinson* (London: J. T. Hayes, 1882).

Digital Publications, Resources, and Databases

Akese, Grace, Uli Beisel, and Muntaka Chasant, 'Agbogbloshie: A Year After the Violent Demolition', *African Arguments* (21 July 2022) at [https://africanarguments.org/2022/07/agbogbloshie-a-year-after-the-violent-demolition/], accessed 3 Oct. 2025.

Assael, Brenda, 'Sanger, George [*known as* Lord George Sanger]: (1825?–1911)', *Oxford Dictionary of National Biography* (3 Jan. 2008) at [https://doi.org/10.1093/ref:odnb/35940].

Dead White Men's Clothes at [https://deadwhitemansclothes.org/], accessed 10 Oct. 2025.

EU Parliament at [https://www.europarl.europa.eu/portal/en].

Hansard Online at [https://hansard.parliament.uk/], accessed 10 Oct. 2025.

ibali Digital Collections UCT at [https://ibali.uct.ac.za/].

Johnson, Sarah, 'Dead White Person's Clothes' Mount Up as Ghana's Kantamanto Market Struggles to Rebuild after Fire', *The Guardian* (24 Feb. 2025) at [https://www.theguardian.com/global-development/2025/feb/24/ghana-clothes-market-fire-kantamanto-rebuild], accessed 3 Oct. 2025.

Kibii, Eliud, 'Fear of Political Consequences Frustrates Mitumba Ban', *The Star* (21 Apr. 2025) at [https://www.the-star.co.ke/news/2025-04-21-fear-of-political-consequences-frustrates-mitumba-ban], accessed 28 Nov. 2025.

Libera, Malcolm, 'Goodbye East London and Graaff-Reinet—Big Name Changes Coming to South Africa', *Businesstech* (28 Jan. 2026) at [https://businesstech.co.za/news/government/849047/goodbye-east-london-and-graaff-reinet-big-name-changes-coming-for-south-africa], accessed 30 June 2026.

Liboiron, Max, 'Waste Colonialism', *Discard Studies* (11 Jan. 2018) at [https://discardstudies.com/2018/11/01/waste-colonialism/], accessed 28 Nov. 2025.

Mburu, Peter, 'Renewed Drive to Ban "Mitumba" risks Kenya, US Trade Ties', *Business Daily* (15 Apr. 2025) at [https://www.businessdailyafrica.com/bd/economy/renewed-drive-to-ban-mitumba-risks-kenya-us-trade-ties-5004330], accessed 28 Nov. 2025.

NAM at [https://www.nam.ac.uk].

NFCA, University of Sheffield Library Digital Collections at [https://cdm15847.contentdm.oclc.org/digital/collection/p15847coll3].

PCBH at [https://www.uni-bamberg.de/en/hist-econ/pcbh-network/], accessed 27 Nov. 2025.
Piekacz, Agnes, 'Beyond "Reading" Materials: Trace (on Trace) and Value', *Theory of History at Work* (10 June 2025) at [https://doi.org/10.58079/142v1].
Stop Waste Colonialism at [https://stopwastecolonialism.org].
UK Government at [https://www.gov.uk].
Wellcome Collection at [https://wellcomecollection.org/].

Secondary Literature

Abubakar, Mohammed, Joseph Oluyemi, Raji Abdulateef, Atolagbe Emmanuel, Joseph Adejoke, and Taiwo M. Williams, 'Imperialism and the Loss of Identity in Second Hand Clothes: The Nigerian Okrika Experience', *Journal of Language, Technology & Entrepreneurship in Africa*, 9/1 (2018), 151–72.
Acquave, Richard, Raphael K. Seidu, Benjamin Eghan, and George K. Fobiri, 'Consumer Attitude and Disposal Behaviour to Second-Hand Clothing in Ghana', *Scientific African*, 21 (2023) at [https://doi.org/10.1016/j.sciaf.2023.e01887].
Anderson, David and Neil Carrier, 'Khat in Colonial Kenya: A History of Prohibition and Control', *Journal of African History*, 50 (2009), 377–97.
Aplern, Stanley B., 'What Africans Got for Their Slaves: A Master List of European Trade Goods', *History in Africa*, 22 (1995), 4–43.
Appadurai, Arjun, 'Introduction: Commodities and the Politics of Value', in Arjun Appadurai (ed.), *The Social Life of Things: Commodities in Cultural Perspective* (Cambridge: Cambridge University Press, 1986), 3–63.
Appadurai, Arjun (ed.), *The Social Life of Things: Commodities in Cultural Perspective* (Cambridge: Cambridge University Press, 1986).
Appadurai, Arjun, 'Grassroots Globalization and the Research Imagination', *Public Culture*, 12/1 (2000), 1–19.
Appadurai, Arjun, 'The Capacity to Aspire: Culture and the Terms of Recognition', in Vijayendra Rao and Michael Walton (eds.), *Culture and Public Action* (Stanford: Stanford University Press, 2004), 59–84.
Arnold, David, *Colonizing the Body: State Medicine and Epidemic Disease in Nineteenth-Century India* (Berkeley, Los Angeles, London: University of California Press, 1993).
Aspers, Patrick and Jens Beckert, 'Value in Markets', in Patrick Aspers and Jens Beckert (eds.), *The Worth of Goods: Valuation and Pricing in the Economy* (Oxford, New York: Oxford University Press, 2011), 3–38.
Assael, Brenda, *The Circus and Victorian Society* (Charlottesville, London: University of Virginia Press, 2005).
Atkins, Keletso E., *The Moon is Dead! Give Us Our Money! The Cultural Origins of an African Work Ethic, Natal, South Africa, 1843–1900* (Portsmouth, London: Heinemann; James Currey, 1993).

Ayorkor Manieson, Lydia and Tiziana Ferrero-Regis, 'Castoff from the West, Pearls in Kantamanto? A Critique of the Second-hand Clothes Trade', *Journal of Industrial Ecology*, (2022), 1–11.

Bair, Jennifer, 'Global Capitalism and Commodity Chains: Looking Back, Going Forward', *Competition & Change*, 9/2 (2005), 153–80.

Bair, Jennifer, 'Constructing Scarcity, Creating Value: Marketing the *Mundo Maya*', in Nina Bandelji and Frederick F. Wherry (eds.), *The Cultural Wealth of Nations* (Stanford: Stanford University Press, 2011), 177–96.

Bair, Jennifer and Marion Werner, 'Commodity Chains and the Uneven Geographies of Global Capitalism: A Disarticulations Perspective', *Environment and Planning A*, 43 (2011), 988–97.

Baldwin, Peter C., *Contagion and the State in Europe, 1830–1930* (Cambridge, New York, Melbourne: Cambridge University Press, 1999).

Baldwin, Peter C., 'How Night Air Became Good Air, 1776–1930', *Environmental History*, 8/3 (2003), 412–29.

Barnes, David S., 'Confronting Sensory Crisis in the Great Stinks of London and Paris', in William A. Cohen (ed.), *Filth: Dirt, Disgust, and Modern Life* (Minneapolis: University of Minnesota Press, 2005), 103–32.

Baston, Kim, '"New" Hippodrama, or "Old" Circus?: Legacy and Innovation in Contemporary Equestrian Drama', *Popular Entertainment Studies*, 7/1–2 (2016), 21–38.

Beckett, Ian F., 'Buller and the Politics of Command', in John Gooch (ed.), *The Boer War: Direction, Experience, Image* (London, Portland: Frank Cass, 2000), 41–55.

Beckert, Sven, Ulbe Bosma, Mindi Schneider, and Eric Vanhaute, 'Commodity Frontiers and the Transformation of the Global Countryside: A Research Agenda', *Journal of Global History*, 16/3 (2021), 435–50.

Beinart, William, 'European Traders and the Mpondo Paramountcy, 1878–1886', *Journal of African History*, 20/4 (1979), 471–86.

Beinart, William, 'Production, Labour Migrancy and the Chieftaincy: Aspects of the Political Economy of Pondoland' (unpubl. PhD diss.: University of London, 1979).

Beinart, William, *The Political Economy of Pondoland 1860–1930*, African Studies Series 33 (Cambridge, New York, Melbourne, Madrid, Cape Town, Singapore, São Paulo, Delhi: Cambridge University Press, 1982).

Bender, Steffen, *Der Burenkrieg in der deutschsprachigen Presse: Wahrnehmung und Deutung zwischen Bureneuhporie and Anglophobie, 1899–1902*, Krieg in der Geschichte 52 (Paderborn: Schöningh, 2009).

Berger, Iris, *Threads of Solidarity: Women in South African Industry, 1900–1980* (Bloomington, Indianapolis, London: Indiana University Press; James Currey, 1992).

Berghoff, Hartmut and Jakob Vogel, 'Wirtschaftsgeschichte als Kulturgeschichte: Ansätze zur Bergung transdisziplinärer Synergiepotentiale', in Hartmut Berghoff and Jakob Vogel (eds.), *Wirtschaftsgeschichte als Kulturgeschichte: Dimensionen eines Perspektivenwechsels* (Frankfurt a. M., New York: Campus, 2004), 9–41.

Bhana, Surenda and Joy B. Brain, *Setting Down Roots: Indian Migrants in South Africa, 1860–1911* (Johannesburg: Witwatersrand University Press, 1990).
Blackburn, Sheila, '"Between the Devil of Cheap Labour Competition and the Deep Sea of Family Poverty?": Sweated Labour in Time and Space, 1840–1914', *Labour History Review*, 71/2 (2006), 99–121.
Blackburn, Sheila, *A Fair Day's Wage for a Fair Day's Work?: Sweated Labour and the Origins of Minimum Wage Legislation* (London: Routledge, 2007).
Brahm, Felix, *Merchandise of Power: Der Waffenhandel zwischen Europa und Ostafrika (1850–1919)*, Globalgeschichte (Frankfurt a. M., New York: Campus, 2022).
Bramwell, William, 'Loyalties and the Politics of Incorporation in South Africa: The Case of Pondoland, c.1870–1913' (unpubl. PhD diss.: University of Warwick, 2015).
Brauner, Christina, *Kompanien, Könige und caboceers: Interkulturelle Diplomatie an Gold- und Sklavenküste im 17. und 18. Jahrhundert*, Externa 8 (Cologne: Böhlau, 2015).
Brooks, Andrew, 'Riches from Rags or Persistent Poverty? The Working Lives of Secondhand Clothing Vendors in Maputo, Mozambique', *Textile*, 10/2 (2012), 222–37.
Brooks, Andrew, 'The International Second-Hand Clothing Trade: Contributions to Sustainability and the Circular Economy', *Sustainability*, 17 (2025), 1–14.
Brooks, Andrew and David Simon, 'Unravelling the Relationship between Used-Clothing Imports and the Decline of African Clothing Industries', *Development and Change*, 43/6 (2012), 1265–90.
Brown, Karen, *Mad Dogs and Meerkats: A History of Resurgent Rabies in Southern Africa* (Athens: Ohio University Press, 2011).
Bulloch, William, 'Emmanuel Klein: 1844–1925', *The Journal of Pathology and Bacteriology*, 28/4 (1925), 684–91.
Burke, Timothy, *Lifebuoy Men, Lux Women: Commodification, Consumption, and Cleanliness in Modern Zimbabwe* (Durham: Duke University Press, 1996).
Butler, Judith, *Notes towards a Performative Theory of Assembly* (Cambridge: Harvard University Press, 2016).
Calisto Friant, Martin, Walter J. V. Vermeulen, and Roberta Salomone, 'A Typology of Circular Economy Discourses: Navigating the Diverse Visions of a Contested Paradigm', *Resources, Conservation and Recycling*, 161/104917 (2020), 1–19.
Callaway, Helen, 'Dressing for Dinner in the Bush: Rituals of Self-Definition and British Imperial Authority', in Ruth Barnes and Joanne B. Eicher (eds.), *Dress and Gender: Making and Meaning*, Cross-Cultural Perspectives on Women (New York, Oxford: Berg, 1992), 232–47.
Carradice, Phil, *Nautical Training Ships: An Illustrated History* (Stroud: Amberley, 2009).
Charpy, Manuel, 'The Spoils of War: Use and Transformation of Secondhand Uniforms during the First World War in France', in Manuel Bass-Krueger, Haley Edwards-Dujardin, and Sopie Kurkdijan (eds.), *Fashion, Society, and the First World War: International Perspectives* (London et al.: Bloomsbury, 2021), 208–28.
Church, Roy, 'Advertising Consumer Goods in Nineteenth-Century Britain: Reinterpretations', *The Economic History Review: New Series* 53/4 (2000), 621–45.

Colesky, Theo, 'A Comparative Study on Customs Tariff Classification' (unpubl. LLD diss.: University of Pretoria, 2014).

Comaroff, Jean, 'The Empire's Old Clothes: Fashioning the Colonial Subject', in David Howes (ed.), *Cross-Cultural Consumption: Global Markets, Local Realities* (London: Routledge, 1996), 19–38.

Comaroff, Jean and John L. Comaroff, *Of Revelation and Revolution: The Dialectics of Modernity on a South African Frontier* (Chicago, London: The University of Chicago Press, 1997).

Cooper, Frederick, 'What is the Concept of Globalization Good for? An African Historian's Perspective', *African Affairs*, 100 (2001), 189–213.

Cooper, Frederick, 'Postcolonial Studies and the Study of History', in Ania Loomba, Suvir Kaul, Matti Bunzl, Antoinette Burton, and Jed Esty (eds.), *Postcolonial Studies and Beyond* (Durham, London: Duke University Press, 2005), 401–22.

Coplan, David B., 'The Emergence of an African Working-Class Culture', in Shula Marks and Richard Rathbone (eds.), *Industrialisation and Change in South Africa: African Class Formation, Culture and Consciousness 1870–1930* (New York, London: Longman, 1982), 358–75.

Corvellec, Hervé, Alice F. Stowell, and Nils Johansson, 'Critiques of the Circular Economy', *Journal of Industrial Ecology*, 26 (2022), 421–32.

Craik, Jennifer, *The Face of Fashion: Cultural Studies in Fashion* (London, New York: Routledge, 1994).

Craik, Jennifer, 'The Cultural Politics of the Uniform', *Fashion Theory*, 7/2 (2003), 127–47.

Craik, Jennifer, *Uniforms Exposed: From Conformity to Transgression* (Oxford, New York: Berg, 2005).

Cronin, Anne M., *Advertising Myths: The Strange Half-Lives of Images and Commodities* (London, New York: Routledge, 2004).

Day, Nicola, *The Demographic Imagination and the Nineteenth-Century City: Paris, London, New York*, Cambridge Studies in Nineteenth-Century Literature and Culture 97 (Cambridge: Cambridge University Press, 2015).

Deacon, Harriet, 'Racial Segregation and Medical Discourse in Nineteenth-Century Cape Town', *Journal of Southern African Studies*, 22/2 (1996), 287–308.

Decker, Stephanie, *Postcolonial Transition and Global Business History: British Multinational Companies in Ghana and Nigeria* (New York: Routledge, 2023).

DeLacy, Margaret, *The Germ of an Idea: Contagionism, Religion, and Society in Britain, 1660–1730* (Basingstoke, New York: Palgrave Macmillan, 2016).

Desai, Ashwin, 'Indian South Africans and the Black Consciousness Movement under Apartheid', *Diaspora Studies*, 8/1 (2015), 37–50.

Dimier, Véronique and Sarah Stockwell (eds.), *The Business of Development in Post-Colonial Africa*, Cambridge Imperial and Post-Colonial Studies (Cham: Palgrave Macmillan, 2020).

Donaldson, Bruce C., *A Grammar of Afrikaans*, Mouton Grammar Library 8 (Berlin, New York: Mouton de Gruyter, 1993).

Du Bois, Duncan L., 'Smallpox and Vaccination in Colonial Natal, 1850–1894', *Natalia*, 51 (2021), 37–52.
Dubow, Saul, *Scientific Racism in Modern South Africa* (Cambridge, New York, Melbourne: Cambridge University Press, 1995).
Dubow, Saul, 'How British was the British World?: The Case of South Africa', *Journal of Imperial and Commonwealth History*, 37/1 (2009), 1–27.
Dunaway, Wilma A. (ed.), *Gendered Commodity Chains: Seeing Women's Work and Households in Global Production* (Stanford: Stanford University Press, 2014).
Epple, Angelika, 'Jenseits globaler Warenketten: Commodityscapes, Verflechtungen, Relationierungen und die Rückkehr der Akteure', in Christiane Berth, Dorothee Wierling, and Volker Wünderlich (eds.), *Kaffeewelten: Historische Perspektiven auf eine globale Ware im 20. Jahrhundert* (Göttingen: V & R unipress, 2015), 274–80.
Epprecht, Marc, 'The Native Village Debate in Pietermaritzburg, 1848–1925: Revisiting the "Sanitation Syndrome"', *Journal of African History*, 58/2 (2017), 259–83.
Etherington, Norman, *Preachers, Peasants and Politics in South-East Africa, 1835–80: African Christian Communities in Natal, Pondoland and Zululand*, Studies in History Series 12 (London: Royal Historical Society, 1978).
Feinstein, Charles H., *An Economic History of South Africa: Conquest, Discrimination and Development* (Cambridge: Cambridge University Press, 2005).
Ferguson, Christine, 'Footnotes on *Trilby*: The Human Foot as Evolutionary Icon in Late Victorian Culture', *Nineteenth-Century Cultures*, 28/2 (2006), 127–44.
Fleetwood Wilson, Guy D. A., *Letters to Somebody: A Retrospect* (London, New York, Toronto, Melbourne: Cassell and Company, Ltd., 1922).
Fontaine, Laurence (ed.), *Alternative Exchanges: Second-Hand Circulations from the Sixteenth Century to the Present*, International Studies in Social History 10 (New York: Berghahn Books, 2008).
Forth, Aiden, *Barbed-Wire Imperialism: Britain's Empire of Camps, 1876–1903*, Berkeley Series in British Studies (Oakland: University of California Press, 2017).
Foster, Robert J., 'Tracking Globalization: Commodities and Value in Motion', in Chris Tilley, Webb Keane, Susanne Küchler, Mike Rowlands, and Particia Spyer (eds.), *Handbook of Material Culture* (London, Thousand Oaks, New Delhi: Sage Publications, 2006), 285–302.
Foutch, Ellery E., 'Moving Pictures: Magic Lanterns, Portable Projection, and Urban Advertising in the Nineteenth Century', *Modernism/modernity*, 23/3 (2016), 733–69.
Frazer, Garth, 'Used-Clothing Donations and Apparel Production in Africa', *The Economic Journal*, 118/523 (2008), 1764–84.
French, David, *Military Identities: The Regimental System, the British Army, and the British People c.1870–2000* (New York: Oxford University Press, 2005).
Freund, Bill, 'Labour Studies and Labour History in South Africa: Perspectives from the Apartheid Era and After', *International Review of Social History*, 58/3 (2013), 493–519.
Gänger, Stefanie, 'Circulation: Reflections on Circularity, Entity, and Liquidity in the Language of Global History', *Journal of Global History*, 12 (2017), 303–18.

Geary, Christraud M., 'Political Dress: German-Style Military Attire and Colonial Politics in Bamum', in Ian Fowler and David Zeitlyn (eds.), *African Crossroads: Intersections between History and Anthropology in Cameroon*, Cameroon Studies 2 (Providence, Oxford: Berghahn Books, 1996), 165–92.

Gereffi, Gary, John Humphrey, Raphael Kaplinsky, and Timothy J. Sturgeon, 'Introduction: Globalisation, Value Chains and Development', *Institute of Development Studies Bulletin*, 32/3 (2001), 1–8.

Gereffi, Gary, John Humphrey, and Timothy J. Sturgeon, 'The Governance of Global Value Chains', *Review of International Political Economy*, 12/1 (2005), 78–104.

Gereffi, Gary, Miguel Korzeniewicz, and Roberto P. Korzeniewicz, 'Introduction: Global Commodity Chains', in Gary Gereffi and Miguel Korzeniewicz (eds.), *Commodity Chains and Global Capitalism* (Westport, London: Greenwood, 1994), 1–14.

Giddins, Robert, 'Delusive Seduction: Pride, Pomp, Circumstance and Military Music', in John MacKenzie (ed.), *Popular Imperialism and the Military: 1850–1950*, Studies in Imperialism (Manchester, New York: Manchester University Press, 1992), 25–49.

Ginsberg, Madeleine, 'Rags to Riches: The Second-Hand Clothes Trade 1700–1978', *Costume*, 14 (1980), 121–35.

Giuntini, Andrea, 'ITU, Submarine Cables and African Colonies, 1850s–1900s', in Gabriele Balbi and Andreas Fickers (eds.), *History of the International Telecommunication Union (ITU): Transnational Techno-Diplomacy from the Telegraph to the Internet*, Innovation and Diplomacy in Europe 1 (Berlin, Boston: De Gruyter, 2020), 37–54.

Gosling, Edward P., 'Tommy Atkins, War Office Reform and the Social and Cultural Presence of the Late-Victorian Army in Britain, *c.*1868–1899' (unpubl. PhD diss.: Plymouth University, 2016).

Gregson, Nicky, *The Waste of the World: Consumption, Economies and the Making of the Global Waste Problem* (Bristol: Bristol University Press, 2023).

Gregson, Sarah and Michael Quinlan, 'Subcontracting and Low Pay Kill: Lessons from the Health and Safety Consequences of Sweated Labour in the Garment Industry, 1880–1920', *Labor History*, 61/5–6 (2020), 534–50.

Grewe, Bernd-Stefan, 'Wie verortet man eine globale Verflechtungsgeschichte? Global Commodity Chains und die Verkettung lokaler Kontexte', in Borsi Barth, Stefanie Gänger, and Niels P. Petersson (eds.), *Globalgeschichten: Bestandsaufnahme und Perspektiven*, Globalgeschichte 17 (Frankfurt a. M., New York: Campus, 2014), 41–74.

Grewe, Bernd-Stefan, 'Global Commodities and Commodity Chains', in Giorgio Riello and Roy Tirthankar (eds.), *Global Economic History* (London, New York: Bloomsbury Academic, 2019), 215–28.

Hahn, Hans-Peter, 'Consumption, Identities, and Agency in Africa: An Overview', in Hartmut Berghoff and Uwe Spiekermann (eds.), *Decoding Modern Consumer Societies*, Worlds of Consumption (New York: Palgrave Macmillan, 2012), 69–88.

Hahn, Hans-Peter, 'Cultural Appropriation: Power, Transformation, and Tradition', in Christian Huck and Stefan Bauernschmidt (eds.), *Travelling Goods, Travelling Moods:*

Varieties of Cultural Appropriation (1850–1950) (Frankfurt a. M., New York: Campus, 2012), 15–35.

Hahn, Hans-Peter, *Materielle Kultur: Eine Einführung*, Ethnologische Paperbacks (Berlin: Reimer, 2014).

Hahn, Hans-Peter, 'Notizen zur Umwertung der Werte: Perspektiven auf ökonomische Konzepte im interdisziplinären Diskurs', in Inga Klein and Sonja Windmüller (eds.), *Kultur der Ökonomie: Zur Materialität und Performanz des Wirtschaftens*, Edition Kulturwissenschaft 25 (Bielefeld: transcript, 2014), 17–36.

Hamilton, Carolyn, 'Backstory, Biography, and the Life of the James Stuart Archive', *History in Africa*, 38 (2011), 319–41.

Hamilton, Shane, 'Analyzing Commodity Chains: Linkeages or Restraints?', in Warren Belasco and Roger Horowitz (eds.), *Food Chains: From Farmyard to Shopping Cart*, Hagley Perspectives on Business and Culture (Philadelphia: University of Pennsylvania Press, 2009), 16–25.

Hamlin, Christopher, *Public Health and Social Justice in the Age of Chadwick: Britain, 1800–1854*, Cambridge History of Medicine (Cambridge, New York, Melbourne: Cambridge University Press, 1998).

Hardy, Anne, *The Endemic Streets: Infectious Diseases and the Rise of Preventive Medicine, 1856–1900* (Oxford: Clarendon Press, 1993).

Harries, Patrick, *Work, Culture, and Identity: Migrant Laborers in Mozambique and South Africa, c.1860–1910* (London: James Currey, 1994).

Hay, Margaret J., 'Changes in Clothing and Struggles over Identity in Colonial Western Kenya', in Jean Allman (ed.), *Fashioning Africa: Power and the Politics of Dress* (Bloomington, Indianapolis: Indiana University Press, 2004), 67–83.

Headrick, Daniel R., *The Tools of Empire: Technology and European Imperialism in the Nineteenth Century* (New York, Oxford: Oxford University Press, 1981).

Hendrickson, Hildi, 'Bodies and Flags: The Representation of Herero Identity in Colonial Namibia', in Hildi Hendrickson (ed.), *Clothing and Difference: Embodied Identities in Colonial and Post-Colonial Africa*, Body, Commodity, Text (Durham, London: Duke University Press, 1996), 213–44.

Hesse, Jan-Ottmar and Patrick Neveling, 'Global Value Chains', in Teresa Da Silva Lopes, Christina Lubinski, and Heidi J. S. Tworek (eds.), *The Routledge Companion to the Makers of Global Business*, Routledge Companions in Business, Management and Accounting (Abington, New York: Routledge, 2019), 279–93.

Hiralal, Kalpana, 'The Economic Role of the Indian Commercial Class in Colonial Natal', *Alternation*, 7/2 (2000), 135–47.

Hiralal, Kalpana, 'Indian Family Businesses in Natal, 1870–1950', *Natalia*, 38 (2008), 27–37.

Hofmeyr, Isabel, *Dockside Reading: Hydrocolonialism and the Customs House* (Durham, London: Duke University Press, 2022).

Honeyman, Katrina, *Well Suited: A History of the Leeds Clothing Industry 1850–1990*, Pesold Studies in Textile History 11 (Oxford: Oxford University Press, 2000).

Hopkins, Terence K. and Immanuel Wallerstein, 'Patterns of Development of the Modern World-System', *Review: A Journal of the Fernand Braudel Center for the Study of Economies, Historical Systems and Civilizations* 1/2 (1977), 111–45.

Howe, Anthony, *Free Trade and Liberal England, 1846–1946* (Oxford, New York: Oxford University Press, 1998).

Iqani, Mehita and Bridget Kenny, 'Editorial: Critical Consumption Studies in South Africa: Roots and Routes', *Critical Arts*, 29/2 (2015), 95–106.

Isla, Veronica L., 'Investigating Second-Hand Fashion Trade and Consumption in the Philippines: Expanding Existing Discourses', *Journal of Consumer Culture*, 13/3 (2013), 221–40.

Jackson, Peter, Neil Ward, and Polly Russel, 'Mobilising the Commodity Chain Concept in the Politics of Food and Farming', *Journal of Rural Studies*, 22 (2006), 129–41.

Johnstone, Frederick A., *Class, Race and Gold: A Study of Class Relations and Racial Discrimination in South Africa* (London: Routledge & Kegan Paul, 1976).

Joseph, G. W., 'Some Remarks on Second-Hand Clothing and the Spread of Infectious Disease', *Public Health*, 28/4–12 (1915), 267–70.

Keegan, Timothy, 'Trade, Accumulation and Impoverishment: Mercantile Capital and the Economic Transformation of Lesotho and the Conquered Territory, 1870–1920', *Journal of Southern African Studies*, 12/2 (1986), 196–216.

Kenny, Bridget, 'Servicing a Racial Regime: Gender, Race, and the Public Space of Department Stores in Baltimore, Maryland, and Johannesburg, South Africa, 1940–1970', in Mia Bay and Ann Fabian (eds.), *Race and Retail: Consumption across the Color Line* (New Brunswick: Rutgers University Press, 2015), 99–119.

Kepe, Thembela and Lungisile Ntsebeza, 'Introduction', in Thembela Kepe and Lungisile Ntsebeza (eds.), *Rural Resistance in South Africa: The Mpondo Revolts after Fifty Years*, Afrika-Studiecentrum Series 22 (Leiden, Boston: Brill, 2011), 1–20.

Klopper, Sandra, 'Gentlemen at Leisure: Riding Breeches in the Photographic Portrait Images of Black South African Men', in Tim Barringer, Geoff Quilley, and Douglas Fordham (eds.), *Art and the British Empire* (Manchester, New York: Manchester University Press, 2007), 327–36.

Kopytoff, Igor, 'The Cultural Biography of Things: Commoditization as Process', in Arjun Appadurai (ed.), *The Social Life of Things: Commodities in Cultural Perspective* (Cambridge: Cambridge University Press, 1986), 64–91.

Köster, Roman, *Müll: Eine schmutzige Geschichte der Menschheit* (Munich: C. H. Beck, 2023).

Laband, John, 'African Military History: A Perspective', *Journal of African Military History* 1 (2017), 24–40.

Laden, Sonja, '"Making the Paper Speak Well", or, the Pace of Change in Consumer Magazines for Black South Africans', in Louise Bethlehem, Leon de Kock, and Sonja Laden (eds.), *South Africa in the Global Imaginary*, Imagined South Africa 4 (Leiden, Boston: Brill, 2004), 248–77.

Langkjær, Michael A., '"Then How Do You Explain Sgt. Pompous and the Fancy Pants Club Band?": Utilization of Military Uniforms and Other Paraphernalia by Pop Groups and the Youth Counterculture in the 1960s and Subsequent Periods', *Textile History*, 41/Supplement 1 (2010), 182–213.

Lemire, Beverly, *Dress, Culture, Commerce: The English Clothing Trade before the Factory, 1660–1880* (London: Palgrave Macmillan, 1997).

Lemire, Beverly, 'The Secondhand Clothing Trade in Europe and Beyond: Stages of Development and Enterprise in a Changing Material World, c.1600–1850', *Textile*, 10/2 (2012), 144–63.

Lemire, Beverly, *Global Trade and the Transformation of Consumer Cultures: The Material World Remade, c.1500–1820*, New Approaches to Economic and Social History (Cambridge: Cambridge University Press, 2018).

Levitt, Sarah, 'Bristol Clothing Trades and Exports in the Georgian Period', in Fabio Tongiorgi (ed.), *Per una storia della moda pronta: Problemi e ricerche* (Florence: Edifir, 1991), 29–42.

Liboiron, Max and Josh Lewapsky, *Discard Studies: Wasting, Systems, and Power* (Cambridge, London: The MIT Press, 2022).

Lloyd's Greater Britain Publishing Company, *Twentieth Century Impressions of Natal: Its People, Commerce, Industries, and Resources* (Durban: Lloyd's Greater Britain Publishing Company, 1906).

Long, Norman and Magdalena Villarreal, 'Small Products, Big Issues: Value Contestations and Cultural Identities in Cross-Border Commodity Networks', *Development and Change*, 29 (1998), 725–50.

Lowenhaupt Tsing, Anna, *Friction: An Ethnography of Global Connection* (Princeton, Oxford: Princeton University Press, 2005).

MacDonald, Janet W., *Supplying the British Army in the First World War* (Barnsley: Pen & Sword, 2019).

Madida, Ngqabutho, 'A History of the Colonial Bacteriological Institute 1891–1905' (unpubl. master's thesis: University of Cape Town, 2003).

Magee, Gary B., *Productivity and Performance in the Paper Industry: Labour, Capital, and Technology in Britain and America, 1860–1914* (Cambridge, New York, Melbourne: Cambridge University Press, 1997).

Magee, Gary B. and Andrew S. Thompson, *Empire and Globalisation: Networks of People, Goods and Capital in the British World, c.1850–1914* (New York: Cambridge University Press, 2010).

Mager, Anne K., *Beer, Sociability, and Masculinity in South Africa*, African Systems of Thought (Bloomington: Indiana University Press, 2010).

Magubane, Zine, 'Mines, Minstrels, and Masculinity: Race, Class, Gender, and the Formation of the South African Working Class, 1870–1900', *The Journal of Men's Studies*, 10/3 (2002), 271–89.

Marichal, Carlos, Steven C. Topik, and Zephyr Frank, 'Conclusion: Commodity Chains and Globalization in Historical Perspective', in Zephyr Frank, Gilbert M. Joseph, Carlos

Marichal, Emily S. Rosenberg, and Steven C. Topik (eds.), *From Silver to Cocaine: Latin American Commodity Chains and the Building of the World Economy, 1500–2000* (Durham: Duke University Press, 2006), 352–60.

Martin, Richard and Harold Koda (eds.), *Swords into Ploughshares: Military Dress and Civilian Wardrobe* (New York: The Metropolitan Museum of Art, 1995).

Martin, William G., 'The Making of an Industrial South Africa: Trade and Tariffs in the Interwar Period', *The International Journal of African Historical Studies*, 23/1 (1990), 59–85.

Mattfeld, Monica, '"I See Them Galloping!": War, Affect, and Performing Horses in Matthew Lewi's *Timour the Tartar*', in Monica Mattfeld and Karen Raber (eds.), *Performing Animals: History, Agency, Theater*, Animalibus: Of Animals and Cultures 11 (Pennsylvania: The Pennsylvania State University Press, 2017), 41–7.

Maynard, Margaret, *Fashioned from Penury: Dress as Cultural Practice in Colonial Australia* (Cambridge: Cambridge University Press, 1994).

Mbem, Nobungcwele H., 'Rethinking Railway Histories of the Transvaal: Examining the Relationship between Infrastructure, Modernities and People, 1860s–1960s' (unpubl. master's thesis: University of Pretoria, 2018).

Mendelsohn, Adam, *The Rag Race: How Jews Sewed Their Way to Success in America and the British Empire* (New York: New York University Press, 2015).

Mertens, Jeremy, 'A Transnational History of Immigration Restriction: Natal and New South Wales 1896–97', *The Journal of Imperial and Commonwealth History*, 34/3 (2006), 323–44.

Milgram, Lynne B., 'Refashioning Commodities: Women and the Sourcing of Secondhand Clothing in the Philippines', *Anthropologica*, 46/2 (2004), 189–202.

Miller, Monica L., *Slaves to Fashion: Black Dandyism and the Styling of Black Diasporic Identity* (Durham: Duke University Press, 2009).

Miller, Stephen M., 'Redvers Buller', in Steven J. Corvi and Ian F. Beckett (eds.), *Victoria's Generals* (Barnsley: Pen & Sword, 2009), 51–73.

Mills, Stephen, 'The Origins, Development, Decline and Reuse of Cloth Mills of the Stroud Valleys of Gloucestershire: A Study in Industrial Archaeology' (unpubl. PhD diss.: University of Leicester, 1997).

Mintz, Sydney, *Sweetness and Power: The Place of Sugar in Modern History* (New York: Viking Penguin, 1985).

Mkhize, Sibongile S., 'Exploring the Second Hand Clothes Trade: The Case of Durban, South Africa' (unpubl. master's thesis: University of KwaZulu-Natal, 2003).

Mlambo, Alois S., 'From Dirt Tracks to Modern Highways: Towards a History of Roads and Road Transportation in Colonial Zimbabwe, 1890 to World War II', *Zambezia*, 11/2 (1994), 147–66.

Mnisi, Jabulani G. and Mthobeli Ngcongo, 'Looking Back to Look Forward: Re-Humanization through Conspicuous Consumption in Four African Masculine Sartorial Subcultures—from Diamond Field's Dandies to Izikhothane', *African Identities*, 21/2 (2023), 341–54.

Mokoena, Hlonipha, 'The Rickshaw Puller and the Zulu Policeman: Zulu Men, Work, and Clothing in Colonial Natal', *Critical Arts*, 31/3 (2017), 123–41.

Mooney, Graham, *Intrusive Interventions: Public Health, Domestic Space, and Infectious Disease Surveillance in England, 1840–1914*, Rochester Studies in Medical History (Rochester: Rochester University Press; Boydell & Brewer, 2015).

Morgan, Kenneth O., 'The Boer War and the Media (1899–1902)', *Twentieth Century British History*, 13/1 (2002), 1–16.

Mukarji, Projit B., 'Cat and Mouse: Animal Technologies, Trans-Imperial Networks and Public Health from Below, British India, *c.*1907–1918', *Social History of Medicine*, 31/3 (2017), 510–32.

Müller, André, 'Black and Coloured Entrepreneurship in Historical Perspective', *South African Journal of Economic History*, 5/2 (1990), 1–15.

Müller, Simone M., *The Toxic Ship: The Voyage of the Khian Sea and the Global Waste Trade*, Weyerhaeuser Environmental Book (Seattle: University of Washington Press, 2023).

Münch, Ole, *Cutler Street Market: Interkultureller Austausch im Londoner East End, 1780–1850*, Moderne Zeit: Neue Forschungen zur Gesellschafts- und Kulturgeschichte des 19. und 20. Jahrhunderts 33 (Göttingen: Wallstein Verlag, 2022).

Murillo, Bianca, *Market Encounters: Consumer Cultures in Twentieth-Century Ghana*, New African Histories (Athens: Ohio University Press, 2017).

Myerly, Scott, *British Military Spectacle: From the Napoleonic Wars through the Crimea* (Cambridge: Harvard University Press, 2014).

Na'amneh, Mahmoud M. and Abdel H. Al Husban, 'Identity in Old Clothes: The Socio-Cultural Dynamics of Second-Hand Clothing in Irbid, Jordan', *Social Identities*, 18/5 (2012), 609–21.

Nicol, Martin, 'A History of Garment and Tailoring Workers in Cape Town: 1900–1939' (unpubl. PhD diss.: University of Cape Town, 1984).

Norris, Lucy, *Recycling Indian Clothing: Global Contexts of Reuse and Value* (Bloomington, Indianapolis: Indiana University Press, 2010).

Norris, Lucy, 'The Limits of Ethicality in International Markets: Imported Second-Hand Clothing in India', *Geoforum*, 67 (2015), 183–93.

Nutton, Vivian, 'The Reception of Fracastoro's Theory of Contagion: The Seed that Fell among Thorns?', *Osiris*, 6 (1990), 196–234.

O'Rourke, Kevin H. and Jeffrey G. Williamson, *Globalization and History: The Evolution of a Nineteenth-Century Atlantic Economy* (Cambridge, London: The MIT Press, 1999).

Omissi, David and Andrew S. Thompson, 'Introduction: Investigating the Impact of the War', in David Omissi and Andrew S. Thompson (eds.), *The Impact of the South African War* (Basingstoke, New York: Palgrave Macmillan, 2002), 1–20.

Padayachee, Vishnu and Robert Morrell, 'Indian Merchants and *Dukawallahs* in the Natal Economy, *c.*1875–1914', *Journal of Southern African Studies*, 17/1 (1991), 71–102.

Parkes, Louis C., 'Enteric Fever and Infected Blankets', *The Practitioner*, 71 (1903), 297.

Pearce, Spencer, 'Fracastoro on Syphilis: Science and Poetry in Theory and Practice', in Pierpaolo Antonello and Simon A. Gilson (eds.), *Science and Literature in Italian Culture from Dante to Calvino: A Festschrift for Patrick Boyde*, European Humanities Research Centre (Oxford: Legenda, 2004), 115–35.

Peoples, Sharon, 'Embodying the Military: Uniforms', *Critical Studies in Men's Fashion*, 1/1 (2014), 7–21.

Perrot, Philippe, *Fashioning the Bourgeoisie: A History of Clothing in the Nineteenth Century* (Princeton: Princeton University Press, 1997).

Pierie, Gordon H., 'Slaughter by Steam: Railway Subjunction of Ox-Wagon Transport in the Eastern Cape and Transkei, 1886–1910', *The International Journal of African Historical Studies*, 26/2 (1993), 319–43.

Posel, Deborah, 'Races to Consume: Revisiting South Africa's History of Race, Consumption, and the Struggle for Freedom', *Ethnic and Racial Studies*, 33/2 (2010), 157–75.

Pratt, Mary L., *Imperial Eyes: Travel Writing and Transculturation* (New York: Routledge, 2008).

Prestholdt, Jeremy, *Domesticating the World: African Consumerism and the Genealogies of Globalization*, California World History Library 6 (Berkeley: University of California Press, 2008).

Prestholdt, Jeremy, 'Africa and the Global Lives of Things', in Frank Trentmann (ed.), *The Oxford Handbook of the History of Consumption* (Oxford, New York: Oxford University Press, 2012), 85–108.

Radin, Margaret J., *Contested Commodities: The Trouble with Trade in Sex, Children, Body Parts, and Other Things* (Cambridge, London: Harvard University Press, 1996).

Radin, Margaret J., 'Contested Commodities', in Martha E. Ertman and Joan C. Williams (eds.), *Rethinking Commodification: Cases and Readings in Law and Culture* (New York, London: New York University Press, 2005), 81–95.

Rawlinson-Mills, Elizabeth, '"That Far-off Southern Tomb": Visions and Versions of South Africa in British Newspaper Poetry of the 1899–1902 South African War', in Barbara Franchi and Elvan Mutlu (eds.), *Crossing Borders in Victorian Travel: Spaces, Nations, and Empires* (Newcastle upon Tyne: Cambridge Scholars Publishing, 2018), 106–31.

Reid, Darren, 'The Aborigines' Protection Society as an Anticolonial Network: Rethinking the APS "from the Bottom up" through Letters Written by Black South Africans, 1883–87', *Journal of Colonialism and Colonial History*, 22/2 (2021).

Ribeiro Lins, Gustavo, 'Economic Globalization from Below', *etnográfica*, 10/2 (2006), 233–49.

Richards, Thomas, *The Commodity Culture of Victorian England: Advertising and Spectacle, 1851–1914* (Stanford: Stanford University Press, 1990).

Richardson, David, 'West African Consumption Patterns and Their Influence on the Eighteenth-Century English Slave Trade', in Henry A. Gemery and Jan S. Hogendorn (eds.), *The Uncommon Market: Essays in the Economic History of the Atlantic Slave*

Trade, Studies in Social Discontinuity (New York, San Francisco, London: Academic Press, 1979), 303–30.

Richardson, Peter, 'The Recruiting of Chinese Indentured Labour for the South African Gold-Mines, 1903–1908', *Journal of African History*, 18/1 (1977), 85–108.

Riedi, Eliza, 'Assisting Mrs Tommy Atkins: Gender, Class, Philanthropy, and the Domestic Impact of the South African War, 1899–1902', *The Historical Journal*, 60/3 (2017), 745–69.

Rief, Silvia, 'Jenseits der Trennung von Produktion und Konsum: Begriffliche Konzepte zur Analyse der gesellschaftlichen Institutionaliserung von Versorgungsweisen und Versorgungsprozessen', *Österreichische Zeitschrift für Geschichtswissenschaft*, 30/1 (2019), 20–51.

Rischbieter, Julia L., *Mikro-Ökonomie der Globalisierung: Kaffee, Kaufleute und Konsumenten im Kaiserreich 1870–1914*, Industrielle Welt 80 (Cologne: Böhlau Verlag, 2011).

Roche, Antony, 'The Infected Blankets', *The Lancet*, 161/4162 (1903), 1615.

Roche, Daniel, *The Culture of Clothing: Dress and Fashion in the 'Ancien Régime'*, Past & Present Publication Series (Cambridge: Cambridge University Press, 1994).

Roque, Ricardo and Kim A. Wagner, 'Introduction: Engaging Colonial Knowledge', in Ricardo Roque and Kim A. Wagner (eds.), *Engaging Colonial Knowledge: Reading European Archives in World History*, Cambridge Imperial and Post-Colonial Studies (Basingstoke, New York: Palgrave Macmillan, 2012), 1–34.

Ross, Robert, 'The Top-Hat in South African History: The Changing Significance of an Article of Material Culture', *Social Dynamics*, 16/1 (1990), 90–100.

Ross, Robert, *Clothing: A Global History, or, The Imperialists' New Clothes* (Cambridge, Malden: Polity Press, 2008).

Ross, Robert, Marja Hinfelaar, and Iva Peša, 'Introduction: Material Culture and Consumption Patterns: A Southern African Revolution', in Robert Ross, Marja Hinfelaar, and Iva Peša (eds.), *The Objects of Life in Central Africa: The History of Consumption and Social Change, 1840–1980* (Leiden, Boston: Brill, 2013), 1–13.

Ross, Robert, Marja Hinfelaar, and Iva Peša (eds.), *The Objects of Life in Central Africa: The History of Consumption and Social Change, 1840–1980* (Leiden, Boston: Brill, 2013).

Rovine, Victoria L., *African Fashion, Global Style: Histories, Innovations, and Ideas You Can Wear*, African Expressive Cultures (Bloomington: Indiana University Press, 2014).

Rudolph, Mona, 'Das *global commodity*-Narrativ: Deskriptive und analytische Potenziale und Fallstricke', in Gabriele Lingelbach (ed.), *Narrative und Darstellungsweisen der Globalgeschichte*, Schriften des Historischen Kollegs 108 (Munich: De Gruyter, 2022), 129–42.

Ruether, Kirsten, 'Heated Debates Over Crinolines: European Clothing on Nineteenth-Century Lutheran Mission Stations in the Transvaal', *Journal of Southern African Studies*, 28/2 (2002), 359–78.

Ruether, Kirsten, 'Asking Appropriate Questions, Reconsidering Research Agendas: Moving between London and Lusaka, In- and Outside the Archive', *Administory*, 4/1 (2019), 110–24.

Russel, David, '"We Carved Our Way to Glory": The British Soldier in Music Hall Song and Sketch, *c.*1880–1914', in John MacKenzie (ed.), *Popular Imperialism and the Military: 1850–1950*, Studies in Imperialism (Manchester, New York: Manchester University Press, 1992), 50–79.

Sanger, George, *Seventy Years as a Showman* (London, Toronto: J. M. Dent & Sons, Ltd., 1927).

Schendel, Willem van and Itty Abraham (eds.), *Illicit Flows and Criminal Things: States, Border, and the Other Side of Globalization*, Tracking Globalization (Bloomington, Indianapolis: Indiana University Press, 2005).

Scheper-Hughes, Nancy, 'Parts Unknown: Undercover Ethnography of the Organs-Trafficking Underworld', *Ethnography*, 5/1 (2004), 29–73.

Scheper-Hughes, Nancy and Loïc Wacquant (eds.), *Commodifying Bodies*, Body & Society (London, Thousand Oaks, New Delhi: Sage Publications, 2002).

Searle, Geoffrey R., *The Quest for National Efficiency: A Study in British Politics and Political Thought, 1899–1902* (Berkeley, Los Angeles: University of California Press, 1971).

Searle, Geoffrey R., '"National Efficiency" and the "Lessons" of the War', in David Omissi and Andrew S. Thompson (eds.), *The Impact of the South African War* (Basingstoke, New York: Palgrave Macmillan, 2002), 194–211.

Seekings, Jeremy, '"Not a Single White Person Should be Allowed to Go Under": *Swartgevaar* and the Origins of South Africa's Welfare State, 1924–1929', *Journal of African History*, 48 (2007), 375–94.

Shell, Hanna R., *Shoddy: From Devil's Dust to the Renaissance of Rags* (Chicago, London: The University of Chicago Press, 2020).

Skelley, Andrew R., *The Victorian Army at Home: The Recruitment and Terms and Conditions of the British Regular, 1859–1899* (Montreal: McGill-Queen's University Press, 1977).

Smith, Charles W., *Auctions: The Social Construction of Value* (Berkeley, Los Angeles: University of California Press, 1990).

Smith, Iain R., 'Capitalism and War', in David Omissi and Andrew S. Thompson (eds.), *The Impact of the South African War* (Basingstoke, New York: Palgrave Macmillan, 2002), 56–75.

Smith, William, *Advertise: How? When? Where?* (London: Routledge, Warne, and Routledge, 1863).

Solomon, Vivian, 'Early Commonwealth Action against Shipping Conferences: The Case of South Africa', *Journal of Imperial and Commonwealth History*, 9/3 (1981), 308–17.

Solomon, Vivian, *The South African Shipping Question, 1886–1914*, Historical Publication Society 3 (Cape Town: Historical Publication Society, 1982).

Stark, David, *The Sense of Dissonance: Accounts of Worth in Economic Life* (Princeton: Princeton University Press, 2011).

Stearn, Roger, '"To Rid the Army of a Scandal": The Uniforms Act of 1894', *Journal of the Society for Army Historical Research*, 71/288 (1993), 226–31.

Steere-Williams, Jacob, '"Coolie" Control: State Surveillance and Labour of Disinfection across the Late Victorian British Empire', in Robert Heynen and Emily van der Meulen (eds.), *Making Surveillance States: Transnational Histories* (Toronto, Buffalo, London: University of Toronto Press, 2019), 35–57.

Steere-Williams, Jacob, *The Filth Disease: Typhoid Fever and the Practices of Epidemiology in Victorian England*, Rochester Studies in Medical History (Rochester: Rochester University Press, 2020).

Stimson, A. M., 'The Longevity of B. Typhosus Outside of the Human Body', *Hygienic Laboratory Bulletin*, 35 (1907), 177–91.

Stoler, Laura A., *Along the Archival Grain: Epistemic Anxieties and Colonial Common Sense* (Princeton: Princeton University Press, 2010).

Strachan, Hew, 'The Boer War and Its Impact on the British Army, 1902–14', in Peter B. Boyden, Alan J. Guy, and Marion Harding (eds.), *'Ashes and Blood': The British Army in South Africa 1795–1914* (London: NAM, 1999), 85–98.

Sunderland, David, 'General Introduction', in David Sunderland (ed.), *Communications in Africa, 1880–1939* (London: Routledge, 2012), pp. ix–lxiv.

Swanson, Maynard, 'The Sanitation Syndrome: Bubonic Plague and Urban Native Policy in the Cape Colony, 1900–1909', *Journal of African History*, 18/3 (1977), 387–410.

Tallie, Tyrone H., *Queering Colonial Natal: Indigeneity and the Violence of Belonging in Southern Africa* (Minneapolis, London: University of Minnesota Press, 2019).

Thomas, Lynn M., 'The Modern Girl and Racial Respectability in 1930s South Africa', in Alys E. Weinbaum, Lynn M. Thomas, Priti Ramamurthy, Ute G. Poiger, Madeleine Yue Dong, and Toni E. Barlow (eds.), *The Modern Girl Around the World: Consumption, Modernity, and Globalization*, New Directions in Women's Studies (Durham, London: Duke University Press, 2008), 96–119.

Thomas, Nicholas, *Entangled Objects: Exchange, Material Culture, and Colonialism in the Pacific* (Cambridge: Harvard University Press, 1991).

Thompson, Andrew S., 'Tariff Reform: An Imperial Strategy, 1903–1913', *The Historical Journal*, 40/4 (1997), 1033–54.

Thompson, Andrew S., *Imperial Britain: The Empire in British Politics, c.1880–1932* (Harlow, New York: Longman, 2000).

Thompson, Andrew S., 'Publicity, Philanthropy and Commemoration: British Society and the War', in David Omissi and Andrew S. Thompson (eds.), *The Impact of the South African War* (Basingstoke, New York: Palgrave Macmillan, 2002), 99–123.

Thorsheim, Peter, *Inventing Pollution: Coal, Smoke, and Culture in Britain since 1800*, Ohio University Press Series in Ecology and History (Athens: Ohio University Press, 2018).

Todzi, Kim, 'Colonial Business in Postcolonial Germany: The Imperial Afterlives of C. Woermann, 1919–1945', *Contemporary European History*, 34/4 (2025), 1295–308.

Tomlinson, Jim, 'Thrice Denied: "Declinism" as a Recurrent Theme in British History in the Long Twentieth Century', *Twentieth Century British History*, 20/2 (2009), 227–51.

Topik, Steven C., 'Historicizing Commodity Chains: Five Hundred Years of the Global Coffee Commodity Chain', in Jennifer Bair (ed.), *Frontiers of Commodity Chain Research* (Stanford: Stanford University Press, 2009), 37–62.

Topik, Steven C., 'Produktbiographien, Warenketten und Kaffeegeschichten', in Christiane Berth, Dorothee Wierling, and Volker Wünderlich (eds.), *Kaffeewelten: Historische Perspektiven auf eine globale Ware im 20. Jahrhundert* (Göttingen: V & R unipress, 2015), 21–33.

Tranberg-Hansen, Karen, *Sulaula: The World of Secondhand Clothing and Zambia* (Chicago: University of Chicago Press, 2000).

Trentmann, Frank, 'Materiality in the Future of History: Things, Practices, and Politics', *Journal of British Studies*, 48/2 (2009), 283–307.

Treuherz, Julian (ed.), *Hard Times: Social Realism in Victorian Art* (London: Manchester City Art Galleries, 1987).

Tynan, Jane, *British Army Uniform and the First World War: Men in Khaki* (Basingstoke: Palgrave Macmillan, 2013).

Ugolini, Laura, 'The Illicit Consumption of Military Uniforms in Britain, 1914–1918', *Journal of Design History*, 24/2 (2011), 125–38.

United Nations Economic Commission (UNECE) and Economic Commission for Latin America and the Caribbean (ECLAC), *Reversing Direction in the Used Clothing Crisis: Global, European and Chilean Perspectives* (Geneva: United Nations, 2024).

Velia, Myriam, Imraan Valodia, and Baruti Amisi, *Trade Dynamics in Used Clothing: The Case of Durban, South Africa*, SDS Research Report 71 (Durban: University of KwaZulu-Natal, 2006).

Vries, Jan de, *The Industrious Revolution: Consumer Behavior and the Household Economy, 1650 to the Present* (Cambridge, New York, Melbourne, Madrid, Cape Town, Singapore, São Paulo: Cambridge University Press, 2008).

Warwick, Peter, *Black People and the South African War 1899–1902*, African Studies Series 40 (Cambridge: Cambridge University Press, 1983).

Weber, Heike and Melanie Jaeger-Erben, 'Circular Economy: Die Wende hin zu "geschlossenen Kreisläufen" als stete Fiktion', in Heike Weber (ed.), *Technikwenden: Historische Perspektiven auf soziotechnische Um- und Aufbrüche*, Technikgeschichte: Special Issue (Baden-Baden: Nomos, 2023), 169–97.

Wehrle, Maren, 'Bodily Performativity: Enacting Norms', in Lucilla Guidi and Thomas Rentsch (eds.), *Phenomenology as Performative Exercise*, Studies in Contemporary Phenomenology 19 (Leiden, Boston: Brill, 2020), 120–39.

Welskopp, Thomas, *Amerikas große Ernüchterung: Eine Kulturgeschichte der Prohibition* (Paderborn: Brill; Schöningh, 2011).

Wenzelhuemer, Roland, *Connecting the Nineteenth-Century World: The Telegraph and Globalization* (Cambridge: Cambridge University Press, 2013).

Wenzelhuemer, Roland, Tom Menger, Valeska Huber, Heidi J. S. Tworek, Sujit Sivasundaram, Simone M. Müller, Callie Wilkinson, Madeleine Herren, and Martin Dusinberre, 'Forum *Global Dis:connections*', *Journal of Modern European History*, 21/1 (2023), 2–33.

Werner, Wolfgang, '"Playing Soldiers": The Truppenspieler Movement among the Herero of Namibia, 1915 to ca. 1945', *Journal of Southern African Studies*, 16/3 (1990), 476–502.

Westgarth, Mark, 'The Auction Ring', in Mark Westgarth (ed.), *SOLD! The Great British Antiques Story* (Leeds: Archipelago, 2019), 36–8.

Westgarth, Mark, *The Emergence of the Antique and Curiosity Dealer in Britain, 1815–c.1850: The Commodification of Historical Objects*, The History of Material Culture and Collecting, 1700–1950 (London, New York: Routledge, 2020).

Whythe, Rebecca, 'Disinfection in the Laboratory: Theory and Practice in Disinfection Policy in Late C19th and Early C20th England', *Endeavour*, 39/1 (2015), 35–43.

Whythe, Rebecca, 'Public Health and Public Safety: Disinfection, Carbolic, and the Plurality of Risk, 1870–1914', in Tom Crook and Mike Esbester (eds.), *Governing Risks in Modern Britain: Danger, Safety and Accidents, c.1800–2000* (London: Palgrave Macmillan, 2016), 127–48.

Wilhelm, Janine, *Environment and Pollution in Colonial India: Sewerage Technologies along the Sacred Ganges*, Routledge Studies in South Asian History 15 (London, New York: Routledge, 2016).

Wilson, Francis, *Labour in the South African Gold Mines: 1911–1969* (Cambridge: Cambridge University Press, 1972).

Winseck, Dwayne R. and Robert M. Pike, *Communication and Empire: Media, Markets, and Globalization, 1860–1930*, American Encounters/Global Interactions (Durham, London: Duke University Press, 2007).

Winton, Graham, *Theirs Not to Reason Why: Horsing the British Army 1875–1925* (Solihull: Helion, 2013).

Wohl, Anthony S., *Endangered Lives: Public Health in Victorian Britain* (London: Metheun, 1984).

Worboys, Michael, *Spreading Germs: Disease Theories and Medical Practice in Britain, 1865–1900* (Cambridge, New York, Melbourne, Madrid: Cambridge University Press, 2000).

Wright, John B., 'Making the James Stuart Archives', *History in Africa*, 23 (1996), 333–50.

Yogev, Gedalia, *Diamonds and Coral: Anglo-Dutch Jews and the Eighteenth-Century Trade* (Leicester: Leicester University Press; Holmes & Meier Publishers, 1978).

Zelizer, Viviana A., *Morals and Markets: The Development of Life Insurance in the United States* (New York: Columbia University Press, 1979).

Index

A. Belikoff & Co., Ltd. 157–8, 162, 170–1
African Clothing Co., Ltd. 161
Andrew Dickie & Co. 125–9
Barker, Mary A. 1–2, 4
Barry, Henry D. 32, 36
Bouverie, William 62, 66–7
Bouverie, Josiah P. 62, 65–9, 72, 76–7
Brown, William G. 163
Buller, Redvers H. 21, 36–8, 86, 95n
Cardigan Clothing Co., Ltd. 147
Cardwell, Edward 20, 25–6
Chadwick, Edwin 103, 106–7
Chamberlain, Joseph 135–6
Childers, Hugh C. E. 20, 27
Cholmeley, Montague 19
Davis, William 35
Finnemore, Robert I. 77, 84–5, 115
Fleetwood Wilson, Guy D. A. 23, 39–40
Fracastoro, Girolamo 104, 106
Fraser, George 109
Furst, Herbert E. A. 31
Gallagher, Brian 61–2, 78n, 89
Gladstone, Herbert J. 31
Hanbury, Robert W. 35, 45–6
Hely-Hutchinson, Walter 123–4
Hime, Albert H. 145
J. Catzel & Sons 158
'John Africa', Josiah 79–81
John Stevenson & Sons, Ltd. 57
kaMangaliso, Lugubu 78–9
kaMbengwana, Ndukwana 79
Klein, Emmanuel A. 100–1, 110–11, 113
Lind, James 104–6, 107n
Linder & Co. 157–8
Lowry, Henry T. 90
Lunz & Herman 126, 151–2
Mabaso, Solomon 70n, 79–81, 98
MacNicholas, Hamilton 69, 72n
Mahama, John 2–3
Mallett, Porter & Dowd, Ltd. 46–9, 53–8, 63–5, 77, 98, 150, 153–5, 163–5
Mhlangaso 69, 74
Milner, Alfred 144
Möschke, H. 56, 64
Moor, Frederick R. 90
Mqikela 69, 71
Nepean, Ethan C. 22, 40–6
O'Donnell, Michael H. 16, 62–70, 72–5, 76–7, 89–90
Potts, Norman 47–8
Ramsay, George D. 25–7, 29, 39
Randles, Bros. & Hudson 64–8, 70, 74, 77, 98, 164
Renouard, C. Paul 33–4
Rethman, John F. 62, 68
S. Morris & Co., Ltd. 157, 159
Sanger, George 36–7, 46
Samuel Moses & Sons, Ltd. 46–7, 57n, 142n, 163
Shepstone, Theophilus 86
Sigcau 69, 74
Smith, William 32–3
Snow, John 107
Somerville-Large, Brisbane W. 115–17
Southwood-Smith, Thomas 107
Stephany, Morris 49–51
Strachan & Co. 62, 74, 91
Strachan, Donald 91
Stranach, Glew, & Co. 129
Stuart, James 16, 78–81
Stumm, Wilhelm von 31
Sutton, George 146, 148
The Barnett Clothing Co. 153
Trotter, Thomas 104–6, 107n
Tweedie, Alexander 105–6, 107n
W. Bolus & Sons, Ltd. 57
Whitham, S. W. 83, 93–4, 96–7
Wolseley, Viscount 25, 30
Wood, Walter 30–1

 | HTTPS://DOI.ORG/10.1515/9783112256503-010